SKY of STONE

HOMER HICKAM

A DELL BOOK

Published by
Dell Publishing
a division of
Random House, Inc.
1540 Broadway
New York, New York 10036

Library of Congress Catalog Card Number: 2001032475

ISBN: 978-0-440-24092-1

Reprinted by arrangement with Delacorte Press

Manufactured in the United States of America

Published simultaneously in Canada

November 2002

PRAISE FOR
HOMER HICKAM'S AWARD-WINNING MEMOIRS

SKY OF STONE

"The prose of [Hickam's] third book is as vivid and alive
as that of the first, and the bond with the people of
Coalwood just as intense and complex. . . . Hickam has
made [Coalwood] live again in his writing."
—*The New York Times Book Review*

"[A] cleverly constructed, richly detailed mystery . . . This
pleasing book only reinforces his oeuvre."
—*Publishers Weekly*

"Related in such an engaging way that many readers will
forget *Sky of Stone* is nonfiction instead of an elegantly
crafted novel . . . *Rocket Boys* [aka *October Sky*] was a
National Book Critics Circle nominee, and
The Coalwood Way should have been. It will be no
surprise if *Sky of Stone* wins that, along with a few
other major literary awards." —*The Fort Worth Star-Telegram*

THE COALWOOD WAY

"Another classic coming-of-age tale . . . the rocket boy
soars again." —*People*

"Irresistible . . . as compelling and rousing as a NASA
liftoff." —*The Atlanta Journal-Constitution*

"[A] sparkling memoir." —*Chicago Sun-Times*

"Recalling a lost era, [Hickam] brings his American
hometown to life with vivid images, appealing characters
and considerable literary magic." —*Publishers Weekly*

Please turn the page for more extraordinary acclaim. . . .

OCTOBER SKY

"A thoroughly charming memoir . . . [An] eloquent
evocation of a lost time and place . . . Mr. Hickam builds
a story of overcoming obstacles worthy of Frank Capra,
especially in its sweetness and honest sentimentality."
—*The New York Times*

"Unforgettable . . . Unlike so many memoirs, this book
brings to life more than one man's experiences. It brings
to life the lost town of Coalwood, W.Va."
—*USA Today*

"A stirring tale that offers something unusual these days . . .
a message of hope in an age of cynicism."
—*The San Diego Union-Tribune*

"A great read . . . One closes the book with an immense
feeling of satisfaction."
—*The Atlanta Journal-Constitution*

"Hickam has a great story to tell. . . . [His] recollections
of small-town America in the last years of small-town
America are so cinematic that even those of us who
didn't grow up there might imagine we did."
—*The Philadelphia Inquirer*

"[Hickam] is a very adept storyteller. . . . It's a good bet
this is the story as he told it to himself. It is a lovely
one, and in the career of Homer H. Hickam, Jr., who
prevailed over the facts of his life to become a NASA
engineer training astronauts for space walks, that made
all the difference." —*The New York Times Book Review*

ALSO BY HOMER HICKAM

Torpedo Junction
Rocket Boys (aka October Sky)
Back to the Moon
The Coalwood Way

"A refreshingly hopeful book about personal triumph and achieving one's dreams."
—*San Antonio Express News*

"Great memoirs must balance the universal and the particular. Too much of the former makes it overly familiar; too much of the latter makes readers ask what the story has to do with them. In his debut, Hickam walks that line beautifully. No matter how jaded readers have become by the onslaught of memoirs, none will want to miss the fantastic voyage of BCMA, *Auk* and Coalwood."
—*Publishers Weekly* (starred review)

"Compelling." —*Chicago Tribune*

"Thoroughly captivating." —*The Christian Science Monitor*

"*Rocket Boys,* while a true story, reads like a well-written novel. It deals with a wide range of issues, including the bittersweet experience of coming of age. It also provides an intimate look at a dying town where people still allowed kids to dream and helped them make those dreams become reality."
—*Rocky Mountain News*

"[A] nostalgic and entertaining memoir." —*People*

To Johnny Basso, Bobby Likens, and fellow coal miners everywhere.

THIS STORY is based on actual events that occurred in the summer of 1961 in my hometown of Coalwood, West Virginia. Names have been changed and events rearranged and compressed to clarify for the reader what happened, and to protect certain individuals, mostly including myself.

ACKNOWLEDGMENTS

THIS MEMOIR, the third in the series of what I call my Coalwood books, required the assistance of many people, including some real coal miners to keep me straight. My uncle, Harry Ken Lavender, a man much like my father who rose from basic miner to a high management position with a coal company, read an initial draft and made several helpful suggestions. Mr. Early Smith, who worked for my father during the time period I cover in this book, was also very helpful. Mr. Martin Valeri, the last general superintendent of the Coalwood and Caretta mines, added some expert advice. Dr. Robert Likens, my fellow college boy coal miner, reviewed the manuscript when it was nearly completed and reminded me of several important events. Team leader Johnny Basso's sister, Mary, was very gracious with her time, providing me with many details concerning her late brother. Linda Hickam, my wife and first reader, saw the book from its first incarnation and made it much better, especially by keeping me on track and not off in the creative weeds. Emily Sue Buckberry, my high school buddy and forever friend, also got a look at a draft and made some great suggestions, as did David Groff, my touchstone on these books. My brother, Jim, reminded me of a great story about one of our dogs. My mother, of course, got her two cents in (make that three), as she always does. A special nod goes to Mrs. Betty McClamrock for helping Queen Elsie go back to the mountains from time to time.

Of course, I always like to mention my agents, Frank Weimann and Mickey Freiberg, who also happen to be my friends. I wouldn't get very far without them.

Continuing to inspire me are the people of Coalwood, especially those folks of the Cape Coalwood Restoration Association. All of them work so hard for the community, the county, and the state. Special accolades should go to Peggy Blevins for her great organizational skills in putting on Coalwood's annual festivals. Red Carroll, the father of Rocket Boy O'Dell and the unofficial tour guide of Coalwood, continues to be his remarkable self and a great source of wisdom to me and all who know him. His wife, Ivy, is also a most remarkable woman, as is nearly every West Virginia woman I've ever known. In fact, should Beth Rashbaum, the editor of this book, ever decide to move to the Mountain State, she would fit right in.

CONTENTS

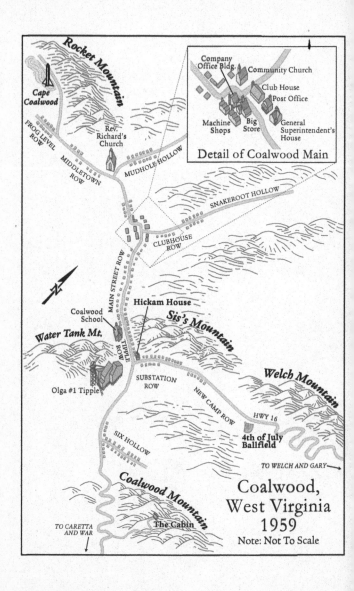

Rocket Mountain

Cape Coalwood

Frog Level Row

Middletown Row

Rev. Richard's Church

Mudhole Hollow

Snakeroot Hollow

Clubhouse Row

Main Street Row

Coalwood School

Hickam House

Sis's Mountain

Water Tank Mt.

Tipple Row

TIPPLE

Olga #1 Tipple

Substation Row

New Camp Row

Welch Mountain

HWY 16

4th of July Ballfield

Six Hollow

TO WELCH AND GARY

Coalwood Mountain

The Cabin

TO CARETTA AND WAR

Coalwood, West Virginia 1959

Note: Not To Scale

Detail of Coalwood Main

Company Office Bldg.

Community Church

Club House

Post Office

Machine Shops

Big Store

General Superintendent's House

SKY *of*
STONE

To motivate your coworkers, you must be thoroughly motivated yourself. Remember the credo of the medieval horsemen: Throw your heart across the ditch, and your horse will follow!

—Dr. Wernher von Braun,
rocket scientist

Don't be afraid to tell a man he's no good. A man can't get good if he doesn't know he's bad.

—Homer Hadley Hickam Sr.,
mine superintendent

Boys, there are only two things that are going to keep you alive in this coal mine. Me, and the tolerance of God.

—Johnny Basso, coal miner

THE COALWOOD PROPOSITION

WHEN ONCE the president of the United States called his nation to greatness, and told the world we were going to the moon, Coalwood, West Virginia, remained what it had always been, a town that mined coal. When President Kennedy also said Americans were going to do many grand and wonderful things, not because they were easy but because they were hard, Coalwood's men continued to walk out of fog-shrouded hollows and descend beneath their mountains to grub out the coal by the millions of tons to send to the blast furnaces of Ohio and Pennsylvania so as to make steel. For if coal failed, the people of Coalwood believed, steel failed. And if steel failed, so did the country, no matter what else might happen, even with a young president's dream of glory on the moon.

I was born in 1943 and raised a Coalwood boy, the second son of Homer Hickam, a mine foreman who loved the town more than his life, and Elsie Lavender, a woman who could not love Coalwood no matter how hard she tried. Although my given name was the same as my father's, my mother tagged me early on with "Sunny"—the light of her life. Believing it was more important for me to know who I was rather than what my mother hoped I might be, my first-grade teacher at the Coalwood School changed the spelling to "Sonny"—the son of Homer. Although she didn't like it, my mom chose not to argue. In Coalwood, the teachers were considered the final social arbiters.

During my childhood, I came to understand that Coalwood was more than houses, roads, and company facilities. It was also a proposition. This proposition held that if a man was willing to come to Coalwood and offer his complete and utter loyalty to the coal company, he would receive in return a sensible paycheck, a sturdy house resistant to the weather, the services of a doctor and a dentist at little or no cost, and a preacher who could be counted on to give a reasonably uncomplicated sermon. Mr. George Lafayette Carter, the man who founded Coalwood and built its mine, also opened his wallet to the local schools. He did so, according to a letter he wrote to his men in 1912, "so that any of Coalwood's children, be they sons and daughters of foremen or common miners, might aspire to greatness."

In 1926, a newspaper reporter from the *Washington Post*, having heard of Mr. Carter's proposition, visited Coalwood and filed this copy:

> *Mr. Carter owns lock, stock and barrel the model coal town of Coalwood—houses, stores, churches, police, clergy, and medical services—all that makes up the life of a miner. It is a town of remarkable contrast to the surrounding villages where squalor and poverty are their world. With houses painted and surrounded by flower gardens and lawns, Coalwood looks more like an Alpine Village than the begrimed coal towns of most of America.*

The proposition depended on everybody following Mr. Carter's rules. They were few, unwritten, and unbreakable. One of them had to do with what happened to a miner's family when he was killed. I first observed it in practice when I was six years old and in the second grade of the Coalwood School.

We were reading from a book titled *The Wind in the Willows,* a tale of a toad who could drive an automobile. I liked the book, mostly because the toad was smart and used a lot of big words. I think all of my fellow classmates wished we might also grow up and be as smart as that toad, even though he kept wrecking his car. Mr. Toad was just about to wreck it again, when Mr. Likens, the school principal, came to collect one of my classmates, a boy named Lonnie Huddle. Lonnie didn't want to go with Mr. Likens. I think he could see in the principal's face that something awful had happened. Lonnie started to cry, and pretty soon nearly every girl in class joined him. I watched Lonnie go, certain that because he had cried, he was going to get knocked around by the other boys at recess for being a sister. But the day ended without Lonnie's return.

That evening, as my family gathered around the kitchen table for supper, Dad announced that Lonnie's father had been killed in the mine. After giving my mother a furtive eye rewarded by a subtle nod of her head, he explained to me and my brother, Jim, that the company gave a widow of a deceased miner two weeks to make arrangements to get her husband buried and her family out of town. Her children, however, were not allowed back into the Coalwood School. These were the rules, he added, and that was all there was to it.

"Lonnie won't come back?" I asked. I couldn't imagine recess without him.

"Lonnie won't come back," Dad said, and went back to cutting up the ham Mom had slapped on his plate. Our conversation, such as it was, was over.

Before I went to bed that night, my mother suggested that I make up a prayer for Lonnie and his mother and his brother and two sisters. "He's gone, Sonny," she said after I said how much I liked playing tag with Lonnie and what a good reader he was in class. "It's the way of this place. Get used to it. God knows I have."

"But he's just down the street! I could go see him, tell him how sorry I am about his daddy."

"It isn't allowed," she said coldly. "He's cut off. You know about being cut off, don't you?"

I did. I had grown up hearing that being cut off was the worst thing that could happen to anybody. It meant you could no longer use the company store, or go to the company doctor and dentist, or live in a company house.

"Go ahead," she said. "Say your prayers."

I did as I was told, finishing with "God bless Lonnie and tell him I miss him."

"That's good," she said. "You've done what you can for him." She climbed up the ladder that leaned against the bunk bed and tucked my blankets so tightly around my shoulders I could barely breathe. Then she ran a rough hand over my forehead and then climbed back down. "Are you all right, Jim?" she asked.

"Yes, ma'am," Jim said.

"Did you say your prayers?"

"Yes, ma'am."

"Good boy."

Mom turned out the light and closed the door behind her. Below me, Jim said, "Sister, if you start crying, I'll get up and smack you myself."

I muttered defiance but felt the tears coming despite myself. I fought them back, except for a few that escaped and trickled down my cheek. For a long time, I lay awake, wondering what might happen to us if Dad got killed. We'd be cut off, ordered out of Coalwood. I couldn't imagine anything worse.

A few days later, when I next walked down Main Street to the company store, which was known as the Big Store, I ventured past Lonnie's house. Another miner and his family had already moved in. Little kids I didn't know were playing on the front porch. I never saw or heard from Lonnie again.

WHEN I was growing up in Coalwood, I liked the times after supper the best, because that was when my mother would pour herself a cup of coffee and my father would fix his dessert of corn bread and milk in a glass and they would sit at the kitchen table and tell stories, often about a Coalwood I didn't know, of a town filled with young men who worked the coal and of their teenage brides who kept their homes and bore their children. Jim always left the table, but I stayed behind, quietly leaning on the table with my elbows and soaking in a world that had once existed right where I was.

Mom and Dad spoke of a younger Coalwood where weekends saw raucous gatherings and miners boasted of their prowess underground and their wives bragged of the life they were building in Coalwood, and of the fine houses Mr. Carter had given them and how they kept them spotless even with the daily assault of coal dust and smoke from the endless chuffing coal trains that passed within a few yards of their front doors. My mother would laugh into her coffee cup to recall when she had hit a cow with my dad's new car, and how the cow was unfazed but the car was a shambles, and how she'd walked to the mine and waited to tell Dad when he got off the man-lift before anybody else could do it. I especially liked it when my father filled in with his side of the story, how he'd heard my mother out and then taken her into his arms, right there in front of God and everybody, and told her she could wreck all his cars she wanted, he didn't care, as long as it made her happy. In all my growing-up years, I had never seen my parents hug each other, and it was fun to imagine what it must have been like, them young and happy. For her part, my mom always frowned at Dad's version and said she never did get that coal dirt off her dress, that it was ruined even though she still had it and kept it in her cedar chest and every so often got it out and looked at it. That my mom would keep such an artifact always seemed to make Dad's eyes shine with pride.

A favorite story was about Mom's pet alligator. During the first weeks of their marriage, someone had mailed one to her from Florida as a wedding gift and she had named it Albert.

They had their dialogue down pat. "It was a tee-niny thing," she would say. "No bigger than my little finger, I swan."

"It had big teeth," Dad would growl.

And Mom would say, "No, it didn't. They were just like little needles."

"I believe it," he'd say. "I still have a scar on my finger, right here," and then he'd show off the index finger on his left hand, which was so rough and discolored by coal dirt I never could see anything, although I always pretended I could.

Mom would go on, telling how the alligator had grown larger until it filled up the bathtub. "I changed its water every day," Mom would proudly relate.

"When it climbed out of that tub and chased me down the steps, I told you it was him or me," Dad would say. "You took your own sweet time deciding which one of us it would be."

"It was a close-run thing, Homer," she'd reply, her lips perched on her coffee cup and her hazel eyes twinkling,

Then Dad would look at her and shake his head and then tell how he had loaded her and Albert into his old

Ford and drove night and day from West Virginia to the first river he could find past the Florida border, the only place Mom said she could possibly let her pet reptile go.

Then they would laugh, the story told. In later years, whenever there was a report of an alligator eating a poodle or chomping on a golfer, Dad would look up from his newspaper and say, "News of Albert, Elsie," and she would smile.

It was a good story.

The story Dad seemed to like to tell the best over the kitchen table was how he came to Coalwood. He told it with the same enthusiasm other men might display in recounting their personal experiences as a soldier in a famous battle, or as a player in a great championship game. His chance at a job with Mr. Carter's coal mine, he said, came in 1934 when the country was deep inside the Great Depression and he was only twenty-two years old. He had come out of nearby Gary, one of the toughest, meanest coal camps in all of McDowell County. Gary, he liked to say, was three mountains and a social philosophy away from Coalwood. After filling in the necessary papers, Dad said he had decided to begin a vigil outside the Coalwood mine superintendent's office. Why he'd done such a thing, he still didn't know, but Mom always interrupted his story at this point to say she knew why very well. If he hadn't gotten the job, all that remained for him was to leave West Virginia and ride the rails with thousands of other unemployed men across the country. I piped up one time and said that riding the rails sounded like fun. Mom hushed me, saying there was nothing fun about being desperate, even aboard a train. I stayed hushed, but it didn't change my opinion.

Coalwood's mine superintendent at the time was William "Captain" Laird, a graduate of Stanford University, a World War I hero, and a big-footed, flap-eared giant of a man who went around with a six-shooter strapped to his waist just in case he happened upon a union organizer. Every time the Captain (as everybody in Coalwood called him) came out of his office, he was greeted by the forlorn sight of a scrawny youth in canvas pants and flannel shirt. When the Captain returned to his command post, the thin-as-a-sapling lad was still there.

In the 1930s, union organizers had worked hard to gain a foothold in Coalwood, but had failed because of Mr. Carter's proposition. Still, every so often they'd send in an agitator hoping to spark some trouble. Suspecting a union trick, the Captain stopped long enough to give the boy a penetrating glare and, with his hand on the handle of his pistol, ask him what the Sam Hill did he think he was do-ing, standing outside his office like some kind of damned hoodoo scaring his men?

Dad said he had his speech all prepared. "There are no better miners than the Hickams of Gary and I'm one of them. Take me on and you'll never be sorry." It was a dan-gerous speech because it contained within it a boast, some-thing not done lightly in McDowell County. It was common wisdom that a man prone to boasting was not someone who could be trusted.

The Captain challenged the boy. "What makes you any different from all the rest of the fellows who want to get on around here?"

The young Homer Hickam had then made a simple and fateful reply. "Captain, you tell me to do something, it'll be done, don't matter what it is, and to the second."

The Captain had apparently heard such pledges before. "How do I know you'll really do that?" he demanded.

Dad nodded toward the pistol. "I'll write out a paper saying it's all right for you to shoot me if I don't."

Captain Laird absorbed the answer, perhaps admired it more than a little, and then asked, almost gently, "Where do you stay at night?"

The young man jerked his head back toward the rhododendron that grew up behind the mine. "Up there."

"What do you eat?"

Dad shrugged and said nothing, which was also the answer. He had drunk from the creek that ran past the mine. What did it matter about eating when there was a job at stake?

"You like chicken and dumplings?" the Captain asked.

"I'd like a job more," Dad answered.

Captain Laird bent at the knees and reared back to let out a hoot and a holler. "Well, son, how about both? Come on down to the house tonight, we'll get you squared away."

My dad would never forget his promise to the Captain, even after the Captain had retired upstate to the lovely little farm village of Elkins and Dad had taken his job. Growing up, I would hear some people say my father had become all that was good in Coalwood. Others said he had become all that was bad. But whatever side they took in their opinion of him, no one doubted he believed in Coalwood and loved it as naturally as breathing, and because I had heard his story I knew very well why.

Mom's fox story was one of her best. I loved to hear it, except its ending. She got her fox in 1947 when I was four years old and Jim was six. We were living at the time on Substation Row, a line of company houses that ran down Wolfpen Hollow. The pup came from a passing hunter who'd unearthed a litter after killing the mother fox. When my father came home that evening, he went into the basement to find Mom on the concrete floor cuddling her new "puppy" in her arms. "Funny-looking little dog," he said, only able to see its tiny face and big ears. Mom did not reply; she just kept holding her new pet.

Dad got into the basement shower and started the daily thirty minutes of hard scrubbing it took to get off the coal dirt. When he came out, he took a longer, closer look at the little creature now scuttling around on the basement floor. Whatever it was, he decided it was no dog. "Elsie," he asked, as calmly as ever he could, "is that, by any chance, a wolf?"

"It is not," my mom replied. "It is but a fox."

Dad was staggered. "You have brought a *fox* into our house?" Foxes were known as killers of chickens and cats and anything else they could catch. They were not meant to snuggle on your lap while you listened to Jack Benny on the radio.

The little fox sat down and cocked its head, coolly appraising my father. "Look how cute he sits," Mom said. "I'm going to call him Parkyacarcass, like the funny man on the radio."

Dad argued with her, but Mom would not listen. She would have her fox.

At this point in the story, Mom and Dad would say some things as surely as the snow came in the winter. "I told your mom a fox should be free," Dad would say.

"And I told your dad," she would say, "so should a person."

"Who's not free?" Dad would demand.

"You," she'd say, and then, "Me."

Dad would start to say something else, then seem to subside. "Well, that's the end of the story," he'd say.

"No, it isn't," Mom would reply, and while Dad mopped in his corn bread and milk, she'd go on with it.

Mom said Parky grew quickly into exactly what he was supposed to be, a red fox with a big bushy tail, pointy ears, long snout, razor-sharp teeth, and a subtle mind. Though he was in nearly all things a typical fox, his tail was distinctive. Most West Virginia red foxes had a little silvery tip at the end of their tails, but Parky looked as if somebody had dipped his tail in a can of silver paint. It went nearly a third of the tail's length. It made him all the more beautiful and glorious, at least in a foxy way.

I always laughed when Mom said Parky never walked on the floor but hopped around the house from chair to table to the top of my dad's head. I could just imagine Dad flailing his arms as he tried to get a fox off his head. Sometimes, I would laugh so hard my stomach hurt, the way Mom told it. Dad always stayed silent.

For a while, Mom said, Parky contented himself with jumping around the house and patrolling the backyard even though it was dominated by a mother cat named Sis. When Sis arched her back and hissed like a snake, Parky would tuck his tail between his legs and slink. Nothing on this planet could slink like a fox, Mom said, except maybe a politician in a beer joint.

It didn't take long before Parky took note of a little wooden shack up on the hill across the creek. It belonged to a neighbor and housed a few plump laying hens and the odd rooster. My mom's first inkling of Parky's interest in the chicken house came when she saw him racing low to the ground down the hill with a bundle of feathers over his shoulder and a hound dog baying at his hind feet. Parky, his tail straight out behind him like a red and silver flag in a stiff breeze, scampered across the plank that bridged the creek, then flew over the back fence and swished down the basement steps, leaving the hound dog moaning and pacing in frustration outside. When Mom ventured into the basement, she entered a snowstorm of feathers. Giving up on rescue, she sought out the owner of the chicken, confessed everything, and paid him a two-dollar bill for his trouble. That afternoon, Parky, with a feather still on his snout, sought Mom out and curled up on her lap for a quiet snooze. She said she forgave him instantly. He was, after all, but a fox.

Mom continued her story over the kitchen table, her coffee cup empty and Dad digging for the last crumb of milk-sodden corn bread in his glass.

"Parky lived free," Mom would say proudly. "Even though he came back to me, I loved most of all his free spirit. If it cost me a few dollars for a chicken now and again, I loved that he came and went as he pleased, did as he wanted. How glorious it must be to be truly free!"

"You're free, Elsie," Dad would invariably retort.

Why he would say anything, I never knew, because it always gave Mom the opening for a little speech she practiced. "Homer, as long as we're in this town, I'll never be free. You have your work, but what do I have but to wait every day to see if you're still alive? I want an end to it."

And he would say, "It's my job."

And she would reply, "Yes, but it's not mine."

Their repartee changed a bit after X rays revealed smears of coal dust on Dad's lungs. After that, she always added: "Your job is killing you, Homer, one spot on your lung at a time. I swan I won't let it kill me."

And then Dad would purse his lips thoughtfully and Mom would continue her story, getting to the part I didn't like. I could tell Dad wanted to leave, but for some reason he never did.

As time went by, she said, Parky scrambled into the basement with his chicken dinner with ever more dogs after him. The chicken house owner had staffed up on canines. He could afford them because Mom kept paying out her two dollars per hen. Then one day, Mom looked out in the yard and didn't see Parky and sensed that something was wrong. All day, there was no Parky. Mom suspected the worst, but the dogs at the chicken house were all lolling around, some of them on their backs to expose their pink plump bellies to the sun, too calm by far to have been finally successful against their little foe. At her intense questioning, the chicken house owner denied that he had done anything to Parky. In fact, he allowed he liked the little creature because Mom's payments represented the only profit he'd ever made on his enterprise.

And then Mom would lean over the table on her elbows and give my father a significant look and say, "Homer, tell me the truth. You carried him off somewhere, didn't you?"

And Dad would slowly shake his head and say, "No, Elsie. I'm sure Parky just went off the way wild animals do. He's free, like you like to think."

"I always know when you're lying," she'd say. "I can see it in your face."

The strange thing about the windup of the Park-yacarcass story was that I could see the same thing Mom saw. I guess my father didn't have a face much good for lying. After a while, I started to believe with Mom that Dad had carried the fox off, too. Maybe he'd even killed him, although I couldn't imagine it to be so. Dad was never a hunter, odd for a Coalwood man.

For long periods, Mom wouldn't tell her fox story and I would nearly forget about it. But then it would come back, related over the kitchen table with my parents rehearsing their practiced lines yet again, straight to the ambiguous conclusion. The mystery of what had happened to her fox was one of the sorest things between my mother and my father, and one that even the salve of time didn't ever seem to heal.

Sometimes, when neither seemed to have a story they wanted to tell, Dad would wait until Mom got a fresh cup of coffee, and then haul out his well-thumbed book of American poetry and read to her. It seemed to calm her and, for some reason, also gave him solace. I could see his face relax, all the lines of care dissolving as he read. The poem he most liked to read was one written by a man with the grand name of Angelo De Ponciano. To me, as much as he loved it, the poem seemed kind of sad:

> *Have you ever sat by the railroad track*
> *and watched the emptys cuming back?*
> *lumbering along with a groan and a whine—*

smoke strung out in a long gray line
belched from the panting injun's stack
—just emptys cuming back.

I have—and to me the emptys seem
like dreams I sometimes dream—
of a girl—or munney—or maybe fame—
my dreams have all returned the same,
swinging along the homebound track
—just emptys cuming back.

As a Coalwood boy, I had come to understand that God had determined that there was no joy greater than hard work, and that He made no water holier than the sweat off one's brow; and I also understood that love is God's gift to us that we might share it, and also the ache in our soul if it might be lost. But, like Dad's simple poem, and Mom's story of her fox, there was much I didn't understand that had nothing to do with God and everything to do with Coalwood. There were secrets there, altogether as vast and mysterious as the black hole that sits at the center of our galaxy and as glorious as the light that it captures. To understand them, I would have to go away and come back again.

And so I did, in the summer of 1961, when once a president called a nation to greatness, and a town I had forsaken called me home.

2

THE CALL

IN THE fall of 1960, when I was seventeen years old, I left Coalwood and crossed the West Virginia state line to attend the Virginia Polytechnic Institute in Blacksburg, Virginia. My brother was already there on a football scholarship, but the reason I'd picked VPI was that it had one of the toughest engineering schools in the country. It was my intention to become as fine an engineer as ever existed upon this planet so that Dr. Wernher von Braun, the famous rocket scientist, would hire me the day I graduated. I had already gotten a head start in that direction in high school. When *Sputnik,* the world's first earth satellite, had been launched in October 1957, five other Big Creek High School boys and I had decided to join the space race between the United States and Russia and build our own rockets. We launched them from an old slack dump we called Cape Coalwood and had done so well we'd even gone to the 1960 National Science Fair and returned to Coalwood with a gold and silver medal for propulsion. We were, for a little while, as famous as any boys from McDowell County were ever likely to be.

Upon my arrival in Blacksburg, I was a bit surprised to learn VPI had a military cadet corps in which I was required to serve. Jim, being a football player, had escaped the corps, but I found myself not only trying to cope with classroom work but also the regimen required of a "rat" freshman. Fortunately, the mysterious regulations and ancient military traditions of the corps intrigued me enough that I set out to master them. The most desirable quality for a cadet turned out to be standing up straight, which I could do, and knowing how to march, which I could learn, and polishing brass and spit-shining shoes, which I could tolerate. By the time my freshman year was done, I had even managed to get myself promoted to private first class.

VPI academics, however, proved to be more difficult, especially chemistry and mathematics. Without the incentive of building my rockets, I had trouble paying attention in those classes. Sometimes I'd fall asleep, but most of the time my mind simply wandered off on its own. No matter how hard I tried, I just couldn't focus on those blackboards filled with dull equations and tedious formulae. Where was the glory in it? Where was the adventure? Where were the rockets? I missed them and I missed the boys and I missed Miss Riley, the high school teacher who'd kept me on the straight and narrow during my years as a rocket boy. If it hadn't been for English class, I might have even gone on academic probation. My shoddy work did not go unnoticed. After the winter quarter, Dr. Johnston, the dean of Applied Science and Business Administration, under whose auspices English was taught to engineers, called me into his office. He retrieved one of my themes from a pile on his desk. "Read this for me, Mr. Hickam," he said.

I read where he pointed his finger: *The rocket was steaming like a teakettle.*

"What is that?"

I sorted through my possible answers. "A simile?" I guessed.

"Yes!" He put my theme back on the stack and patted it. "Did you know, Mr. Hickam, that I'd warrant there is not a single other engineering student in this whole school who would know a simile if it jumped out of a bush and bit him? Or could invent one?"

I didn't know that and said so.

"You have a rare talent for writing," Dr. Johnston continued. "You ought to do something with it."

"Thank you, sir," I said, still not fully comprehending what he was getting at.

He picked up another paper and turned it in my direction. "Do you know what this is?"

I recognized it quite well, although it was nothing I cared to study. "My grade transcript," I said.

"Indeed it is," he answered, "and based on it, I fear you are wasting your time here at VPI. Perhaps you should leave us and go to another college, one stronger in the liberal arts, for instance, where your writing talents might be better honed."

Now I knew why I was sitting in front of the dean's desk. "But I can't leave, sir," I said, coming close to whining. "I have to be an engineer."

"Do tell," he said, leaning back in his chair with a doubtful expression on his face. "And why is that?"

Since he'd asked me, I urgently explained to Dr. Johnston that I had to study engineering because I needed to go help Wernher von Braun. The great man had even sent me an autographed picture, I said. I owed him for that, and I also owed my high school teachers, especially Miss Riley. She had fought for me, for all the rocket boys, so we could build our rockets, and she had done that even though she had cancer, which kept her terribly weak. I also told him about the people in Coalwood who'd gone way out on a limb for me and the other boys. "You see, sir," I concluded, "that's why I *have* to stay here until I become an engineer!"

"It's an interesting story," Dr. Johnston said, "but the odds are still against you."

Often when I found myself intellectually cornered, I tried to remember to quote somebody who was intelligent. "In the queer mass of human destiny, the determining factor has always been luck," I said, quoting Mr. Turner, Big Creek's principal.

"If that's your belief, I predict you will also have trouble with statistics," Dr. Johnston answered dryly.

The good dean dismissed me with the admonition to take my grade transcript and go instantly to see Dr. Byrne, the assistant dean of engineering. I did as I was ordered, finding this dean in his office working diligently behind a huge metal adding machine on his desk. He waved me into a chair, pecked in a few numbers, and then pulled the handle. Out flew a coil of paper, which he inspected, crumpled up, and tossed into a wastepaper can. "Someday," he said, patting the huge steel contraption, "these things will be no bigger than a shoebox."

"Yes, sir," I said, handing over my grades and silently doubting the accuracy of his prediction.

Dr. Byrne reflected on my sorry document for a moment, then said, "Not everyone is cut out to be an engineer, Mr. Hickam. Perhaps you should save us the trouble of flunking you and leave voluntarily."

I once again explained why I couldn't quit. "I suspect Wernher von Braun will get along fine without you," Dr. Byrne observed with some confidence. He eyed a stack of college catalogs on the corner of his desk. "Why don't you just thumb through these catalogs, eh? You might find a nice little liberal arts college that would suit you just fine."

I was cornered. "There's another reason I have to be an engineer," I said desperately.

"Let's hear it." The assistant dean yawned. He acted as if he'd heard everything to come out of a student's mouth, which he probably had, except what I said next.

"The moon program," I said.

"What about it?"

"I think I might be responsible for it."

"This I really must hear," Dr. Byrne said, and leaned forward, his arms folded on top of the adding machine.

So I told my tale. It had happened back in the spring of 1960, when then-senator John F. Kennedy was fighting for his political survival in the West Virginia presidential primary. I had come upon him standing forlornly on top of a Cadillac automobile over in Welch, the county seat, and it was my opinion he was in trouble. For one thing, his back seemed to be hurting him. He kept rubbing the small of it with his fist, and when he did, his eyes would squint in pain. He wasn't doing very well with his speech, either. The miners standing around listening to him were pretty listless. Being a boy of the hills, I immediately recognized what his problem was, at least as far as his speech. The senator's audience wanted a little entertainment. Why else would they come to hear a politician after a hard day's work in the mines?

At the time, I was wearing a suit I'd just purchased to wear to the National Science Fair, and despite the fact that pride was the number one West Virginia sin, I was completely and utterly full of myself. I thought, as my mom would say, that I was the cat's meow. The suit I had picked was a bright orange, all the better, I figured, to stand out at the fair. I decided to shake things up by asking a question. For some reason, as soon as I raised my hand, the senator took note of me. My high school pal Emily Sue Buckberry was with me and I heard her moan, "Oh, God, you're going to embarrass the whole county!"

I did better than that. I embarrassed pretty much the whole state! "What do you think the United States ought to do in space?" I asked a man who'd just talked himself hoarse about unemployment and welfare and food stamps and the raw deal that coal mining was in general.

Kennedy stopped rubbing his back long enough to eye me for what seemed about a century. Then he turned my question back on me. From his lofty perch, he demanded, "What do *you* think we should do in space?"

So I told him, not because I had given it a lot of thought, but because I'd been looking at the moon a lot through a telescope a junior engineer named Jake Mosby had set up for us boys on top of the Coalwood Club House roof. It just popped out of me. *"We should go to the moon!"* I said with such vigor that I got applause and cheers from everybody still standing around. There was some laughter, too, but it was good-natured, since the entertainment value of the senator's entire enterprise had gone up a notch.

The clapping and cheering and laughing seemed to surprise Senator Kennedy. He straightened a little, surveyed the crowd and their grinning faces, and then, as if he had a sudden inspiration, he said maybe I was right, that what we needed to do was get the country moving again, and if going to the moon could help that, maybe it was just the thing. Then he'd asked me what we should do on the moon when we got there, and I said we should find out what it was made of and go ahead and mine the blamed thing. That idea, too, had just popped into my head. Our audience responded with more whoops and hollers and cries that West Virginians could go and "mine that old moon good!" I got a benevolent smile from the senator before Emily Sue dragged me off to Belcher and Mooney's men's store to exchange my beautiful orange suit for something drab and awful.

After that, I'd gone on to win the gold and silver medal for propulsion in the National Science Fair, and Senator

Kennedy had gone on to win his elections in West Virginia and the entire country, too. He'd done it by proposing to get the nation moving again, not only around the world but in space, too. To make good on his promise, he'd recently stood up before Congress and announced: *I believe this nation should commit itself, before this decade is out, to landing a man on the moon and returning him safely to the earth.*

"You can see now, sir, why I have to be an engineer, can't you?" I asked. "This is all my fault."

Dr. Byrne perused my grade transcript a little longer, then rolled his eyes. "Well, I'll tell you what, boy," he said, reaching across the adding machine to take my hand and give it a good shake, "I still don't think you're going to get through my engineering school, but if half of what you say is true, which I sincerely doubt, then I can certainly see why you've got to try. Good luck to you. I think you'll need it."

I quoted my uncle Robert. "Luck's a chance but trouble's sure; I'd be rich if I wasn't poor."

Dr. Byrne laughed out loud. "Get out of my office, Hickam," he said by way of summarizing our interview.

I got out and, since I knew the deans were watching, got to studying. I even stayed awake during chemistry class, at least a significant percentage of the time. During spring quarter, my grades climbed until I was a solidly average engineering student, not bad for a tough place like VPI, I thought.

On a Saturday in early May, I was told to go to the squadron lounge, that a visitor was waiting there for me. It turned out to be my mom, which was quite a surprise. "Sonny boy," she said, smiling from her seat on the couch. "How nice you look in your uniform."

Her hair had turned a bit grayer during the past year and her pretty, heart-shaped face looked a bit more drawn and there were a few more wrinkles on her forehead, but otherwise she was the same Mom. I sat beside her. "What are you doing here?" I asked anxiously. It had to be something terrible for her to have made the trip all the way to Blacks-burg, uncountable mountains away from Coalwood.

"I'm on my way to Myrtle Beach," she said. "I finally found a house down there that I can afford. I had to act fast to get it and I did. It just needs a little fixing up, and that's what I'm heading down there to do."

Mom had always said a house in Myrtle Beach was what she wanted more than anything in the world, and she'd kept on about it for years. Myrtle Beach, a coastal resort city in South Carolina, was the vacation destination of half the coal miners and their families in West Virginia every summer, in-cluding us, and Mom had fallen in love with the place. Still, she'd surprised me by actually following through with her dream, especially since Dad was still some years away from retirement. "Where's Dad?" I asked.

"He went over to the football practice field to see Jim," she said. "He's going to drive me to the beach and then go back to Coalwood."

That news didn't surprise me. Somebody had once asked Mom what it would take to get my dad out of Coalwood, and she had replied, "Dynamite."

I had a sudden idea. Usually, my best ones seemed to come without much thought, don't ask me why. "Mom, could I come down this summer and help you fix the place up?" I was already thinking about making a run on the girls down at the beach, too, which I failed to mention.

Mom looked me over. "Maybe," she said. "We'll see."

"We'd be a great team," I said eagerly. I tried to recall the words Dad had used when he'd tried to convince the Captain to take him on. "You tell me what to do, don't matter what it is, and I'll do it."

Mom gave me a wan smile. "Can I shoot you if you don't?"

"You sure can."

She nodded, then said, "Sonny, here's the thing. It

wasn't just the house at Myrtle Beach I came by to tell you about. Tuck Dillon's been killed in the mine."

I let her message sink in. Tuck Dillon was one of Dad's best foremen. He'd been Coalwood's scoutmaster for a while, too. I'd risen all the way to the proud rank of Scout Second Class under his tutelage. I was instantly and naturally sad that he'd gotten killed, but I was wondering why she'd felt it necessary to drive fifty miles out of her way to let me know about it.

"Your dad's taking it pretty hard," she said.

"Why?" My question just jumped out of my mouth. I didn't mean to be disrespectful, but I could never remember Dad being particularly bothered by mine accidents. He did everything he could to keep them from happening, of that I was certain considering the hours he spent there, but when they happened, they happened and that was that.

Mom answered, "It's complicated," and I knew better than to follow up with another question. I could always tell when she was through talking about something. My survival over the years had honed this particular talent.

I walked Mom across the campus to the football practice field, all the while describing the school buildings and the drill field and the memorials and how I'd learned to march and all the funny things they made us do as cadets. Mom stayed silent the entire time, which was a bit worrisome. A quiet Mom usually spelled trouble. I suspected I hadn't yet found out her complete purpose in coming to Blacksburg. She could have written me a letter about her Myrtle Beach house, and about Mr. Dillon, too. What was she up to? My whole life, my mom had always been up to something even when I thought she wasn't.

We found Dad at the practice field, his fingers clawed into the wire fence, watching the team go through their spring drills. "He's the best player out there," Dad said of brother Jim as we walked up.

Mom looked at Dad and then at me. "Here's Sonny," she said. "Doesn't he look good in his uniform?"

"Hello, little man," Dad said, glancing in my direction. Then, after putting on his old snap-brim hat, "You ready to go, Elsie?"

"I thought maybe you and Sonny could have a little talk," she said.

"What about?" Dad wondered.

I'm sure I didn't know, either, but it always amazed me when Dad didn't pick up on what Mom was after. It was clear as rainwater she wanted us to have a father-son moment, whether we wanted one or not. To save us both, I gave Dad a quick rundown of everything I could think of. "Engineering drawing's my favorite subject this quarter," I rattled on, "and I get to stop wearing the rat belt in another couple of weeks, and I've been asked to write a column in the school newspaper."

Dad blinked thoughtfully while I made all my points. When it was probable that I had finished, he asked, "Are you going to write for the paper?"

"I think so."

"You were always a good speller," he allowed. Then he looked at Mom and asked, "*Now* are you ready to go, Elsie?"

Mom gave me a terse hug and climbed into the Buick. I noticed what appeared to be a small wooden and wire cage in the backseat. I looked closer and saw Chipper, Mom's pet squirrel. I opened the car door and put my hand on the cage, and he threw himself against it, trying to bite me through the screen. "You're taking Chipper to Myrtle Beach?" I couldn't believe it. Chipper had never been outside Coalwood.

"I am," Mom said, and once again I knew she was done with the subject.

Dad settled in behind the huge steering wheel and drummed his fingers on it. "Come on, Elsie," he said. "Miles to go."

"Love you, Sonny," Mom said, giving me her hand. I grasped it and then let it slip away when Dad pushed the Buick's accelerator, spinning wheels in the gravel. Off they went, man, woman, and squirrel, heading south.

I watched until they had disappeared around a curve, and then I walked back to my dormitory and went to my room and sat down at my desk and thought about all that had just happened. After a while, I hit on what I believed to be the real reason for Mom's visit, and it came as a shock. She had come to tell me that not only was she going to Myrtle Beach, she planned on staying there. That's why she'd taken Chipper with her. She might leave Dad behind in Coalwood, but she wasn't going to abandon her beloved squirrel.

I went out that night and stood in the dim lights of the World War II Memorial, where I could worry in peace. I had known only one boy the whole time I grew up in McDowell County whose parents were divorced, and he was a sorry soul. Now, though I doubted they were going to go through the formality of it, my mother and father were getting a divorce, too, at least geographically. I worried about that for a while, came to no conclusion, then said a prayer for Tuck Dillon. I had really liked Mr. Dillon. He had been a good man and hadn't deserved to die. Mom's comment about Dad taking his death hard was still a mystery, though. What had that meant? At the practice field, he'd looked like the same old Dad.

A letter came from Mom the following week. She was having a wonderful time already, she wrote, and was getting the workers going on her house. In my letter back, I begged her to let me come to Myrtle Beach. Where else, after all, could I go? *Myrtle Beach, Myrtle Beach* became my new song. If Mom would agree to it, I was going to have a summer of fun in the sun like none I'd ever experienced. Then, to my joy, she wrote and said: *If you want to come down here, I guess I can't stop you.* At the time I credited myself with the capability of being able to read between Mom's lines. As far as I was concerned, she could hardly wait to see my bright, shining face beaming up at her from the sands of Myrtle Beach.

After the final parade at the end of the school year, the cadets of my squadron boxed up their uniforms, tidied up their rooms, and took off for wherever their summers led them. I said good-bye to everyone, including my roommate, George Fox, whose parents had come to pick him up. My plan was to spend one more night in the dormitory, then hitchhike down to Myrtle Beach the next day. In my room, I crawled on top of my bunk, pulled out a tattered paperback, and quickly became engrossed in *Starship Troopers*. It was at least the fifth time I'd read it. I loved everything Robert Heinlein wrote. Next to John Steinbeck, he was my favorite author. I liked the way he made me want to turn the page even when I knew what was going to happen.

I heard the phone ringing in the booth down the hall, and it kept ringing until somebody picked it up. I subsided back into my book until there came a knock at my door. It was Butch Harper, a fellow cadet who was still waiting for his father to pick him up. "Telephone, Sonny," he said.

I had never received a telephone call during my entire time at VPI, so I was mildly astonished. Who could be calling me? It had to be bad news, that's all I knew. I walked like a condemned man down the hall and crawled inside the booth. When I nervously answered, I heard Mom's voice. "I was afraid you'd already started down here," she said.

"I'm sticking my thumb out first thing in the morning," I told her.

She was silent, as if she was chewing something over in

her mind. "No," she said finally. "You have to go home, to Coalwood."

Her words didn't entirely register. For one thing, I'd stopped thinking of Coalwood as my home. I'd put that old place behind me, just as she had. And as far as going to it now, why ever would I want to do that? *Myrtle Beach, Myrtle Beach!* I started to tell her my opinion, but she interrupted me before I could get a word out of my mouth. "It's the Tuck Dillon accident," she said. "They're blaming your father."

I struggled to understand. Somebody was blaming Dad for a mine accident? I couldn't recall anybody ever getting blamed for somebody getting killed in the mine. If you got killed, it was because you didn't follow the rules, or because God had booby-trapped the place with too much methane or loose slate or some-such a million years ago. Nobody could do much about that, not even my dad.

"There's going to be a big investigation," she continued, breaking through my thoughts, "and who knows what's going to come out? Your dad's alone. Somebody in the family needs to be with him."

Her meaning eluded me. When had Dad ever needed anybody other than his foremen when it came to things at the mine? And why would he need me, of all people? Why couldn't Jim go to Coalwood? He was the first son and Dad's favorite, anyway. It was true Jim was going to summer school, but it hadn't started yet. I took a breath, preparing my defense, but before I got a word out, she said, "Sonny, don't argue with me. Just go."

I realized that I wasn't in a debate but in the midst of a typical Elsie Hickam discussion, which meant she was telling me whatever she wanted to tell me and then I was supposed to do exactly what she said. I fumbled for a response but only managed a feeble question. "How's

Chipper?" I asked. It was the best I could do while I tried to think of some way out of her box.

"My little boy? He loves it down here. I've got a big cage for him on the back porch so he can look at the bay."

"Has he bit anybody yet?"

"Nobody important."

Chipper was the meanest squirrel who ever drew breath. Even so, I liked him, mainly because he usually took great care to bite my brother before he got around to me. "How's the beach?" I asked, still flailing.

"Beautiful. Sun's out, water's blue, the house is going to be great once I get it fixed up."

I decided to try for a simple reduction of my sentence. "How about I go to Coalwood for two weeks?"

"One more thing," she said.

I braced myself.

"There's something wrong with Nate Dooley."

"The secret man?"

"Don't call him that!" she snapped. "Just go see Mrs. Dooley and find out what you can. You owe Nate that much."

"I owe him?"

"If it hadn't been for him, you'd be dead."

And with that, perhaps thinking of the money she was spending on the long-distance call, she hung up. I sat in the booth for a while, the receiver still in my hand. When I looked up, I found Butch watching me with a worried expression. "Trouble?" he asked.

"The worst kind," I confirmed.

"What is it?"

"I have to go . . ." I started to say "home" but caught myself in time. "To West Virginia," I said instead.

"What's there?" he wondered.

A fragment of Dad's poem popped into my mind:

my dreams have all returned the same,
swinging along the homebound track
—just emptys cuming back.

"What's there?" Butch asked again.
"Coalwood," I said, and to me that said it all.

3

THE SECRET MAN

A LOT of people in Coalwood said I was lucky to be alive, considering the close calls I had growing up. I liked to act out scenes in every book I read, and sometimes I suppose I carried my little productions to the extreme. After I finished reading *All Quiet on the Western Front,* I started digging shallow trenches on the side of Sis's Mountain and Roy Lee Cooke and I and a couple of other boys in my grade challenged the older boys to a fight. They complied, dug their trenches, and then we started throwing corn stobs at each other. One of the stobs, thrown by my brother, managed to knock me all the way down the hill. I had blood running into my eyes, but I climbed back up to our trench line and kept fighting until finally Mom declared an armistice. I had a bump on my head for a week, but I was still alive.

I came my nearest to dying back in 1948 when President Harry Truman decided to show Mr. Carter he was in charge of everything, even Coalwood. After John L. Lewis and his United Mine Workers had battered every other coal operation in southern West Virginia into submission, they had turned their attention to our little town like a salivating dog spying a bloody bone. Union agitators were dispatched to Coalwood in droves and, very soon, wildcat strikes were hitting the mine every day. On top of that, President Truman and John L. were allies, and Mr. Carter the younger—his father having passed away in 1936—never stood a chance. The postwar economy was booming and the nation needed steel and steel needed coal. On the pretext of keeping the coalfields calm, President Truman called out federal troops to go in and occupy Coalwood. For a reason nobody could ever quite figure, he sent in the navy. I was five years old at the time. Just as the sailors began to roll into town in their gray trucks, I came down with something that made me feel like I was going to catch on fire and go up in smoke. I was just running along, trying to chase down Teresa Annello to convince her to be my Maid Marian (I'd just read *Robin Hood*), and all of a sudden, it was like somebody had knocked me up the side of my head with a poleax. I fell down like a half-empty sack of potatoes. Jim carted me home and dumped me on the porch, complaining to Mom that I'd embarrassed him all over Substation Row.

Even though it had the navy to worry over, Coalwood's gossip fence quickly spread the story of my ailment. Most people predicted I was going to die. Coal camp youngsters with high fevers usually did, after all. Prayers started going up to heaven, propelled from both the white and colored churches, but they were mostly for my soul, since it was figured I was pretty much a goner. If I didn't have the consumption, a known killer, it was probably scarlet fever, a true murderer.

Coalwood was in between company doctors at the time. My mom decided that since the navy had upset everything in town, their doctor was fair game. The morning after the arrival of the sailors, she appeared at the hastily established navy dispensary that had been set up in the Club House. The doctor, a young lieutenant junior grade, heard my mom out and then, his hands forming a little steeple, coolly advised her that he was there to tend to his sailors, not coal camp children. She could, however, take it up with his commanding officer, who would be in his office in, oh, maybe a few hours. Mom thanked him kindly and went outside, caught the morning shift going to work, and told the miners about the kindly doctor within and his generous attitude toward Coalwood's children. The men stared at her until one of them, a man by the name of Nate Dooley, stepped up to her. "I'll help you, Elsie," he said. And he did, by accidentally kicking in the doctor's door in his haste to welcome him to town.

The navy doctor, firmly escorted by Mom and Mr. Dooley, arrived at our house and sat on the chair opposite the couch in the living room, where Mom had encamped me. I was too sick to care. Every bone in my body felt like it was broken, and my brain swam in a molten lake of fire.

While Mr. Dooley sat on the stairs with his arms folded on his knees, the doctor felt my brow and stuck a thermometer under my tongue and frowned at me. He had straw-blond hair and a wisp of a mustache that didn't look like it would ever amount to much. Mom sat on the chair across from the couch while he pondered what he was about to say. After he inspected the thermometer and made me say "ah" about a dozen times, and felt around my throat, he said, "The boy's got scarlet fever, Mrs. Hickam."

The intake of my mother's breath was like a nearly missed note on a flute. It was quick, and half air. "Whooping cough, I thought maybe," she said in a voice as quiet as I'd ever heard it. "Or strep throat at its worst."

"No. Scarlet fever. Classic case," the doctor said, fastidiously wiping off the thermometer with alcohol and placing it back into his big black navy medicine bag. "If it doesn't kill your son outright, it'll probably turn into rheumatic fever and attack his heart."

"What about penicillin?" Mom asked, having heard of the new wonder drug from her brothers, who were veterans of World War II. She glanced at Mr. Dooley, who nodded encouragement.

The navy doctor released a great sigh. "May I point out to you that I was 'persuaded' to come here? I have made a diagnosis but I can't just give out medicine. Any penicillin I may have is federal property. Besides that, I'm not licensed to practice in this state except on federal employees."

Mom leaned forward, her nose just a few inches from that of the doctor-sailor. "Let me get this straight," she said. "You have penicillin in that bag of yours which might cure my son?"

The doctor blinked. "Mrs. Hickam, I just said—"

Mom moved her nose an inch closer, her hands turned into fists. *"And you won't give it to him?"*

The doctor grabbed his bag to his chest and scrambled to his feet. "Mrs. Hickam, I have my orders to not treat civilians!"

Mr. Dooley had heard enough. He stood up and very gently eased Mom aside and grabbed the doctor by the lapels of his navy suit, lifted him right off the ground, his polished brown shoes swinging. Sick as I was, I still admired it. "You'll be giving the boy all the medicine he needs, won't you?"

The doctor nodded eagerly. "Of course!"

And so, after he got let down, the doctor gave me my shot, the first of many he would give me over the course of the next few weeks. I would get well, but Mr. Dooley was another case.

After he left our house, Mr. Dooley went to work. Too late to catch the regular man-trip, he went down on the man-lift and started to walk into his section along the main line. He hadn't gone far before a line of coal cars came rocketing around a turn so fast he couldn't get out of the way. The first car hit him and flung him headfirst against a crib support. Although he woke up some days later, he was never again the same. His mind was pretty much gone.

When it was determined that Mr. Dooley wasn't going to get any better, everybody up and down Coalwood's fence line said it was a shame, but it was also a problem. Mr. Dooley fell between Coalwood's rules. As far as his usefulness to the mine was concerned, he might as well have been dead. By all rights, he and his wife should have been cut off.

The company, still dealing with the naval occupation, ignored Mr. Dooley and let him lie in his house with his missus tending him. While Dad was inside the mine one day, Mom went to the Captain's office and barged inside. Nate Dooley, she said, had saved her son and he wasn't going to be cut off, not now, not ever, not if the Captain wanted to ever see her face in Coalwood again. She'd also do everything she could, she said, to take her husband with her.

When Dad came home from work that night and heard from Mom what she had done, he was mortified at her brashness, but it was too late to do anything about it. The Captain had agreed to Mom's demands, one of the very few times he'd given in on anything. Mr. Dooley had been assigned the job of bathhouse attendant for the rest of his days. He was kept on full pay, just as if he worked the hardest, dirtiest, meanest job in the mine. When Mr. Carter gave in to President Truman and sold out, and the Ohio steel company that bought the mine took over, Mr. Dooley stayed right where he was, even though nobody bothered to tell the men from Ohio about it.

It could be rightfully said that because of me, Nate Dooley had become the town's secret man. By the time I grew up and went off to college, he still was.

4

HOMEBOUND

I STOOD at my favorite hitchhike site in Blacksburg, just past Doc Roberts's Shell Service Station, and stuck out my thumb in the opposite direction from where I wanted to go. It was the morning after I'd received the phone call from my mom ordering me to go back to Coalwood to be with my father. I was resigned to do what she'd told me, but there was also a plan percolating in the back of my brain. I didn't know its particulars, not yet, but in general it consisted of getting in and out of Coalwood in a hurry.

After only a few minutes, a beat-up Chrysler came along. Its driver was a milling machine salesman who proceeded to talk my ear off, something to do with a legend about an Indian boy named Falling Rocks who'd gotten lost somewhere along the New River. "Do you see that sign?" he asked as we crossed a mountain. I did. It said LOOK OUT FOR FALLING ROCKS. "They're still looking for him!" the salesman said, and then slapped his knee and laughed heartily.

I joined him with a chuckle, that being the polite thing

to do and also because the car was going too fast for me to jump out.

"Where you headed, son?" the salesman asked after his guffaws petered away.

"Coalwood, West Virginia."

He frowned thoughtfully. "Seems like I sold a milling machine there one time. Who's the boss of the machine shop?"

"Bill Bolt."

"Big guy, tough as a rock?"

"That would be him."

"Small world."

I agreed and said so out loud. If conversation was what it took to get my ride, I was paying full price.

We cruised along until we reached the town of Narrows, where the salesman had a client. I stuck my thumb out again, and soon an eighteen-wheel tractor-trailer driver picked me up and carried me across the West Virginia state line. There was no sign announcing I was back in the Mountain State, but I didn't need one. On the Virginia side were smooth, meadowed ridges, green dimpled valleys, healthy fields of corn, and contented herds of plump cattle. On the West Virginia side were hump-backed, rock-strewn hills furrowed by hollows choked with tangled masses of rhododendron. My nose picked up the drifting pungent odor of a nearby coke oven, too. Such ovens were built back into the sides of mountains and used to bake raw coal into the hard, dry stuff—coke—that was needed to make steel. I'd been away from them long enough that now they seemed to stink to high heaven.

Thankfully, the driver of the truck was quiet as we bumped along, my mind gradually turning dark with uncharitable thoughts about my spoiled summer plans. To add to my dour mood, it began to rain. The road we were on paralleled a set of curving railroad tracks filled with endless lines of coal cars, the heavy locomotives chuffing past, straining to pull their heavy loads. The air was filled with black soot, mixing with the rain to form a gray scum on the windshield, which the wipers only smeared. On the sides of the surrounding mountains were dingy little wood and tar-paper houses, some of them hardly more than shacks, their wet tin roofs glittering in the wan light. The people sitting on the porches looked thin and poor and ill clothed. West Virginia politicians liked to say we mountaineers might be poor but we were proud. Hearing that, my mother liked to say that if there was anything more pitiful than a proud poor person, she didn't know what it was. Since she'd grown up about as poor as anybody could get, I guess she had the right to her opinion.

The truck wound its way into Bluefield, a city in the hills where railroad tracks converged from all around the southern end of the state. Bluefield was a prosperous town, its downtown of narrow, winding streets lined by busy shops and majestic banks.

The driver finally spoke. "Where you heading, boy?"

"Coalwood, sir."

"Where's that?"

"McDowell County."

"That's a rough place."

"I grew up there," I said.

He looked me over. "You don't look like somebody who'd come out of a hellhole like that."

I didn't know whether to thank him or take offense, so I did neither. I just said, "I'm a college boy now."

"I'll be letting you off just a piece more down the road," he said.

"Thank you, sir."

We turned southerly onto Highway 52 and drove over a high bridge that spanned a dozen railroad tracks clogged with coal cars as far as could be seen. The economy was picking up, or so I'd read in the newspapers, and that meant more people were buying automobiles, which meant more steel was being made and, to make the steel, more coal was being dug. I had the sudden thought that maybe Tuck's death was connected to the improving economy. As a Coalwood boy, I knew very well that the busier the mine got, the more dangerous it got, too.

Outside Bluefield, the grade increased rapidly and my driver fought the gears until he found the right one. As we trundled past the campus of Bluefield State College, I studied its low brick buildings. Bluefield State was where we rocket boys had won the Southern West Virginia Science Fair. It seemed to me now like it was something that had happened a century ago, not just the year before. The man was right who said if you take your eye off time, it'll jump down a hole like a scared rabbit.

The truck driver let me off in Bluewell, a small community just past Bluefield. The rain was coming down faster and there was no traffic, so I started hiking. By the time I reached a small punch mine—one dug into the mountainside to get at a shallow vein—I was dripping wet. I ducked inside a tin shed in front of the mine, stripped off my shirt, and wrung it out. As it happened, one of the miners just off from work took pity on me and offered me a ride all the way to Welch. We talked a little, exchanging names until we found one in common. He knew Jack Burnette, one of Dad's engineers. Mr. Burnette was also another one of our scoutmasters. Coalwood men competed for the honor of being our scoutmaster—all of them, that is, except my dad. He didn't like going into the woods very much. Maybe if the Boy Scouts could have held camp-outs inside the mine, he might have taken the position.

In Welch, I walked around the county seat's tilted streets looking for a Coalwood citizen who might give me a ride the rest of the way to my fair hometown. I found, instead, and to my great delight, Miss Freida Riley, my most wonderful teacher of chemistry, physics, and rockets at dear old

Big Creek High. She was just coming out of the Flat Iron
Drug Store. "Is it really you, Sonny?" she asked, her eyes
lighting up.

"Yes, ma'am, it is," I said, grinning. Miss Riley was as
gloriously beautiful as ever except she was thinner,
probably because of her Hodgkin's disease cancer. She'd
let her glossy black hair grow out a bit, too. I felt like hug-
ging her, but I held back, such familiarity not being the
West Virginia way.

"How'd you get so wet?" she wanted to know.

"I've been hitchhiking in the rain," I told her. "I'm just
in from college."

"Tell me everything!"

We went inside the Flat Iron and sat down at a tiny
wrought-iron table and ordered chocolate milk shakes.
Even when she'd been my teacher, I could always talk easily to Miss Riley, so I told her in some detail about the
deans who thought I might be less than pure engineering
material, and about my mom going off to Myrtle Beach,
and about my dad's situation, at least as best I knew it. She
heard my stories and then said, "Sonny, when I was your
teacher, I used to worry about you all the time. When your
dad got hurt in the mine, and your friend Mr. Bykovski got
killed, I was certain that you were going to stop your rockets and just give up. I gave you some advice then. Do you
remember what it was?"

Mr. Bykovski, a machinist by trade, had been the first
man to help the Big Creek Missile Agency. Dad had exiled
him to work inside the mine for his unauthorized rocket
building, and there, one awful night, he'd been killed. After
that, I'd sworn off building rockets, and Miss Riley had
gotten after me because of it.

"You said," I recalled, "if I had a job to do, I was supposed to do it whether I liked it or not."

She narrowed her eyes. "To be precise, I said when you

don't like a job, you *especially* give it everything you've got. I also said you'd regret it for the rest of your life if you stopped building your rockets."

"I remember now," I said. "It was good advice."

"Afterward, you went all the way to the National Science Fair and I haven't worried about you since. You're going to get through everything life has to throw at you, Sonny. You'll get through VPI just fine and then you'll go to NASA and show them how to do things. I'll just watch from the sidelines and applaud."

"I'll keep doing my best," I promised.

"Do better," she said, summing up her philosophy in two words.

"And you, Miss Riley?" I asked. "How are you?"

"My cancer is in remission, but it's probably only temporary," she said straight out. "I'm off to West Virginia University this summer for education classes to help me teach better. I'm going to fight this disease as long as I can. They'll have to carry me out of my classroom!"

"You're the best teacher I ever had," I said. "If it hadn't been for you, the rocket boys would have never gotten anywhere."

Her smile lit up the whole room. "I'll carry those words with me forever."

Miss Riley had to go down to Woolworth's to meet her sister, Iva Gray, so we finished our shakes, which she paid for, and I escorted her back outside. She waved good-bye, and I sadly watched her go.

I went back to wandering the Welch streets seeking someone from Coalwood who'd give me a ride. In front of the municipal parking building, where once I'd questioned the future president of the United States, I found Mr. Maynard Fleming, one of Dad's foremen who lived on Coalwood's Substation Row. He said he'd be glad to give me a lift. He retrieved his car out of the parking building, and soon we were motoring our way on the high road out of Welch that followed the winding Tug River. "I hear you're getting bad grades down there at VPI," he said.

It didn't surprise me that Mr. Fleming would know my business. The gossip fence in Coalwood was an active one. "I made A's in English," I said.

"Does that mean you can at least *spell* engineer?" he asked with a chuckle.

"I can not only spell it," I said. "I can conjugate it. I engineer today, I engineered yesterday, I have engineered many times before."

"That's a good one," he replied, although I didn't notice him laughing.

We drove on in silence until, just as we topped Welch Mountain, Mr. Fleming said, "Bad business about Tuck Dillon, Sonny. I guess you heard all about it."

Mr. Fleming was the first Coalwoodian I'd come across, and already we were talking about Tuck. That meant everybody in Coalwood was talking about him, too. "All I know is what my mom told me, which wasn't much. What happened?"

Mr. Fleming, in the Coalwood style, considered his answer carefully. "There was a lot of rain that night," he said. "Ten times what it is now. Lightning and thunder like I never seen before. It was like a bunch of atom bombs going off. All the fans got knocked out and your dad pulled the men on the hoot-owl shift out of the mine. But Tuck somehow ended up down in his section on a motor. He ran into a patch of fire damp and got blowed up. That's all I know."

I considered his account. The fans were the huge blowers on the surface that ventilated the mine. A motor was what Coalwood miners called the electric trams that traveled on the rails that went into every working section of the mine. *Fire damp* was the colloquial term for methane, an explosive gas that seeped naturally out of exposed coal. The purpose of the fans was to keep the methane from building up. Coalwood was a notoriously gassy mine. If the fans went down for just a short time, dangerous concentrations of methane could collect in a hurry. It wouldn't take much—perhaps no more than an electric spark from a motor—to cause an explosion.

"That doesn't sound like anything an experienced man would do," I observed.

"It sure as hell doesn't sound like Tuck Dillon," Mr. Fleming huffed. "He was always real careful, always doing safety checks for this or that on his section. The bosses got onto him all the time for going too slow. It was because he was always checking."

The "bosses" Mr. Fleming was referring to probably included my dad. I decided to ask another question. "What's wrong with Nate Dooley?"

He shot me a look. "Nate? What makes you think anything's wrong with him?"

"Just something I heard."

Mr. Fleming gripped the steering wheel. "You know we don't talk about him, not to . . ." He stopped, as if he was searching his mind for the right word.

I found it for him. "An outsider?" It gave me an odd sense of satisfaction to realize he considered me exactly that.

Mr. Fleming didn't reply. He just kept turning the steering wheel back and forth, back and forth, taking the twists in the road. Then we hit a little straight stretch, and through the rain-streaked windshield I could see the tips of the roofs of New Camp Row. A bit farther and the headlights illuminated a familiar white sign with black letters. It said COALWOOD and beneath it, UNINCORPORATED.

I was back.

5

THE CAPTAIN'S HOUSE

AFTER MR. FLEMING let me out, I stood, oblivious to the rain, and just stared at our old house, dimly lit by the streetlight on the corner. When Dad had taken the mine superintendent's job in 1954, we moved into the big white house on the corner of Substation and Tipple Rows, which everybody in town called the Captain's house. Until we Hickams moved in, Captain Laird and his wife, my third-grade teacher, had been its only tenants.

The windows in the house were dark. Dad had either already gone to bed or, more likely, was still at the mine. I contemplated the old crab-apple tree by the garage. Daisy Mae, my cat and confidante for so many years, lay buried beneath it. She had been hit by a car driven by one of my father's many enemies. I had once come to terms with who I was and what I was going to do with my life beneath that tree just before I'd gone off to the National Science Fair. Then I thought: *What in God's good name am I doing here?* I felt like a ghost somehow blown out of shining heaven back to dull earth.

I took a deep breath and tasted the sharp, acrid odor of coal. Less than a hundred yards away sat the mine, its buildings almost lost in the swirling wet darkness. I heard the ringing sound of a hammer on steel coming from the little tipple machine shop. It made me think of Mr. Bykovski. Four years ago, my visit to him in that shop had sealed his fate—and mine.

I opened the back gate and went into the yard. A scramble of paws at the basement steps announced the imminent appearance of our dogs. Poteet appeared first, followed by Dandy, our pure-bred golden cocker spaniel. Poteet was a thin black mongrel who had been taken in by my mom, primarily to keep Dandy company. She trotted up to me, her tongue lolling, and gave me a perfunctory sniff, and then whined in recognition. I stroked her head, then did the same for Dandy and felt the ancient dog shudder as if afraid. Poteet nuzzled Dandy's neck. It looked like she was consoling him. Mom had written to me some months back that Dandy was just about blind. Then he licked my hand and I knew he'd finally remembered me, at least by smell.

Satisfied with the overall situation, Poteet led Dandy out of the rain and back down into the basement. I climbed the steps to the back porch. There were two covered pans in front of the door and a note. It said *Supper,* and was signed *Rosemary.* I figured it was from Rosemary Sharitz, our next-door neighbor. Cecil Sharitz, her husband, was one of Dad's most trusted foremen. In Mom's absence, I supposed the Sharitzes were looking after Dad as best they could.

I picked up the pans, took them inside, and switched on the light with my elbow. The first thing I saw was Mom's mural of Myrtle Beach painted on the kitchen wall. She had worked on it for years and had finally finished it just before I'd graduated from high school. It showed a beach, a rolling surf, some shells, seagulls, blue skies, a few puffy clouds, palm trees, a house, and a woman standing alone atop a sand dune. The woman, I believed, was Mom. There was no one else in the picture, not Dad or me, or my brother, Jim, either.

Then I looked closer. Mom had apparently worked on her painting recently. There was what appeared to be a small dog sitting beside her. It was red, had pointy ears, a long snout, and a bushy, half-silver tail wrapped around its legs. It was her fox, Parkyacarcass.

I studied the painting for a long time. Mom was gone, but the sad story of her fox continued right where Dad would see it every day. "What happened to you, Parky?" I asked the little fox in the mural. "Where did you go?"

The electric stove sat bare and cold. I opened the bread and snack drawers but found them empty. The refrigerator had some milk in it and some old lunch meat, both past their prime. In Mrs. Sharitz's pans, I found a stew in one and green beans in the other. There was plenty, more than enough for two people, so I turned on the stove and set the pans on it, stirring them a bit.

While the food heated, I decided to go down into the basement and have a look around my old rocket laboratory. The other rocket boys and I had spent hours there, building our rockets, loading them with various chemical concoctions, and, until we'd blown it up, testing our propellants in the coal-fired hot water heater. Mom had gotten herself a new electric hot water heater out of that deal, so she'd never yelled at us about it too much.

I opened the door and went down the wooden steps, hoping to see old Lucifer, our tomcat, asleep at the bottom of the steps on a rug. The rug was still there but he wasn't. I ducked my head beneath the big furnace pipes and went to the back of the basement, where I found the sinks and shelves that were all that was left of our lab. Someone, Dad probably, had pitched out all our chemicals. The bare shelves looked as lonely and forlorn as I felt.

Sherman Siers had been the rocket boy who'd helped

me most often mix up our compositions. I imagined him standing there, dressed in his heavy coat, rubber gloves, and the ridiculous ball cap with a piece of clear plastic taped to its bill that was supposed to protect his eyes. Some people said we were lucky we hadn't blown the house, and ourselves, up. I figured we just knew what we were doing, not counting the hot water heater incident. That had been all my fault, anyway, when I'd gotten too cocky and full of myself. I had to watch that tendency the whole time I was a rocket boy.

Where was Sherman now? Was he coming back to Coalwood for the summer? He'd gone to West Virginia Tech up in Montgomery, working his way through. Likely he'd stay there, I supposed, to keep working to help pay the tuition. O'Dell Carroll and Billy Rose were in the air force. Roy Lee was married and attending Concord College. Quentin Wilson, the "brains" of the Big Creek Missile Agency, had hitched a ride to Huntington and just showed up at Marshall College. There, he'd gone to the registrar's office, introduced himself, reminded them that he was, after all, the cowinner of a National Science Fair medal, and informed them he was willing to give their school a try. The Marshall officials had been so astonished by his brass that they'd signed him up and given him a little scholarship and odd jobs to pay for his tuition. Now I didn't know where he was. I wondered if I'd ever see any of the boys again.

I had absorbed all the old memories I could stand in the basement and went back upstairs and finished heating the stew and beans. I ate my share, put the rest in the refrigerator, taped Rosemary's note to the refrigerator door, then carried my little duffel bag upstairs. When I opened my bedroom door, I caught the familiar whiff of model airplane glue and old books. There was my desk, marred by paste and paint, and my dresser with charred steel rocket nozzles and splintered nose cones arranged atop it. The shelves on the wall were choked with my books. A wedge on the top shelf featured the complete set of Hardy Boys mysteries. In another place was a row of science fiction—Heinlein, of course, along with Verne and Asimov and others. John Steinbeck's books were there, too. *My room, my wonderful room.* Yet it wasn't exactly mine. I wasn't that boy who used to live in it, not anymore. I wasn't exactly certain who I was, but I knew I wasn't him.

I sat on my bed beneath the window that faced the coal mine. How often had I lain in that bed, Daisy Mae asleep by my leg, and looked up at the ceiling, dappled by the lights from the tipple, and wondered where my future would take me? Surely I would go to Cape Canaveral or someplace where I could work on the space program. Roy Lee had called us the "designated refugees" of Coalwood, propelled by our parents and all the townspeople to leave to find a new life—propelled by all, that is, except for my father. He'd wanted me to leave, all right, but he'd also wanted me to return as a mining engineer to help him run the mine. It was the only time he'd ever asked me to do anything important for him, and I had turned him down. I doubted that he'd yet forgiven me for it, or ever would.

It was past midnight when I awoke to the sound of footsteps on the stairs. Every step had a distinctive creak, and I remembered each one. Dad was in from the mine. He walked past my bedroom door without pausing, and then I heard his bedroom door click shut. For some reason, it gave me a sense of peace just knowing he was home, and I went right back to sleep.

MORNING BROUGHT a dull gray light announcing there had been a sunrise somewhere behind Substation Mountain. The clouds had been blown away, but it would still take some time before the sun could struggle high enough to top

Coalwood's mountains and penetrate its narrow valleys. Dad's bedroom door was standing open, his bed roughly made. The kitchen revealed no sign of his being there. An investigation of Mrs. Sharitz's pots showed that he hadn't opened them. There was no note from him or evidence that he'd eaten breakfast. Dad had come and gone, like a shadow. I wasn't even sure he knew I was back.

I contemplated going up to the mine to say hello to him, maybe even nose out what kind of trouble he was in, or see if he would tell me what was wrong with Nate Dooley. But it was nearly nine o'clock, and I realized Dad was probably already inside the mine. He wouldn't be out until sometime later in the afternoon. I cast around for something to do in the meantime and decided to go down to the machine shop. Coalwood's machinists had once been my rocket builders. I wanted to let them get a look at me, to see how far I'd come as a college man. Maybe I'd also swing by Ginger Dantzler's house. Ginger was the daughter of Mr. Devotee Dantzler, the company store manager. She and I had been almost boyfriend-girlfriend there for a while, but one thing or another had kept us from it. Maybe Ginger would know something about Tuck or Nate, too, and maybe, I thought hopefully, we could even fire up our friendship, if just a little.

I checked on the dogs in the basement. They had plenty of food and water and seemed reasonably content. Then I looked around for Lucifer, but there was still no sign of him. The old tom had been known to spend a few days at a time in the mountains, so I wasn't unduly worried.

I sorted through the keys hanging on a nail in the basement until I found one for the Buick. I didn't figure Dad would care if I took his old car out for a spin, so I drove it down Main Street, through Coalwood Main, and then over the railroad tracks to the machine shop. As soon as I walked through the door, I smelled the deliciously pungent mixture of hot oil and burning oxyacetylene. How I loved that smell! To me, it meant progress, work done, and satisfaction. The machines wound down and the torches spat off, and men came up to me, pushing their goggles up on their foreheads. "Sonny, the rocket boy!" somebody said, and I saw big grins. Responding to their rapid-fire questions, I told them I was doing the best I could in college and hadn't flunked out, not yet, no matter what they'd heard. Their eyes told me they were pleased at the news.

Clinton Caton, the machinist who'd done most of the lathe work on the Big Creek Missile Agency's rocket nozzles, grasped my hand. "Got a rocket drawing?" he asked eagerly. "I'll get right on it if you do!"

I didn't and said so. Mr. Caton's creased face lost its smile. The other men looked grim. I hated to disappoint them. They'd always liked being rocket builders more than working on Dad's mine machinery.

"Sonny boy!" The hearty voice that boomed behind me belonged to Bill Bolt, the machine shop supervisor. Leaning back in his chair, he waved to me from his office. "Come have a word!"

Mr. Bolt offered me a chair, then closed the office door, muffling the roar of the machinery as the men outside revved up their lathes and drill presses again. He sat down at his desk and leaned back in his chair, his hands clasped behind his head. Mr. Bolt's hair was filled with silver threads I'd never noticed before, but otherwise he was the same hearty fellow I'd always known. He asked me about college, and I covered my classes and talked a bit about the cadet corps, too. "You like all that marching around?" he asked. "Never figured you for a soldier."

"Some people around here used to say the army was going to love us rocket boys," I reminded him. "They said we'd already had our combat training down at Cape Coalwood, what with our rockets blowing up and chasing us around the hollow."

Mr. Bolt laughed. "I might have been the one who said

it. You boys did dig a few craters in that old slack dump." He shook his head, smiling at the memory. Then his smile faded. "Have you talked to your dad about the Tuck Dillon mess?"

"I haven't seen him yet," I said. "He came in after I went to bed, was gone before I got up."

"Late to bed, early to rise, that's your daddy." He ran his tongue inside his lips. I knew he had something to say. "Sonny, Homer's got steel company, state, and federal inspectors all over him. They're turning the mine upside down, trying to figure out how Tuck got himself killed."

"What do you think happened, Mr. Bolt?" I asked worriedly. "Was Dad to blame?"

He squirmed a bit. "That's a good question," he finally allowed.

"Yes, sir," I replied softly. "That's why I need to hear the answer."

He considered my comment, then nodded. "I'll tell you what I know. There was a big thunderstorm that night, a hellacious storm, lightning firing all around. A big old shagbark hickory tree behind the church got hit, killed it deader'n a hammer. A lot of fans went down, you know how they do. The hoot-owl shift was told not to go inside—too dangerous, what with the fans going in and out, the methane building up down there. Tuck went inside sometime after three o'clock in the morning from what I heard, I guess to inspect his section—10 West. When he drove his motor inside it, the section blew up. It was the fire damp for sure. The blast was so big it lifted the motor completely off the track and tossed it against a row of posts. Then the roof fell down. Tuck was thrown clear. At least they were able to have an open-casket funeral. That was a bit of a comfort to his missus. Just about everybody in Coalwood showed up for it. Never seen so many flowers in my life."

I struggled to imagine the blast, which must have been like a red-hot hurricane. "Why would Tuck drive a motor into a section that wasn't ventilated?"

Mr. Bolt folded his hands on his desk. He stared at them as if he'd never seen them before. "I'm not a miner, Sonny. Might be a reason I wouldn't know." He looked up, gave me a crooked smile. "So what're you doing home?"

"I'll just be here a couple of days," I said, and left it at that.

Mr. Bolt nodded. "How does Coalwood look to a college boy?"

"Older and smaller," I replied honestly.

"I don't know if we've shrunk, but none of us are getting any younger around here, that's for sure."

"I didn't mean you, Mr. Bolt," I said, rushing to apologize.

"It's all right, Sonny. Everybody gets older. That's the one sure thing in this old world." He nodded at his machinists, back to their posts. "If you get bored while you're here, my fellows are always willing to crank you out a rocket or two."

"Thanks," I said, "but I'm out of the rocket business. Without the other boys . . ." I shrugged. "Well, what would it prove?"

Mr. Bolt eyed me. "What did it *ever* prove?"

I reflected on his question. "I guess it proved we could go to work for Wernher von Braun someday."

"Is that what you still want to do?"

"Yes, sir," I said. "I guess I have to."

"Attaboy. 'Have to' is the start of 'got done.'"

I thought of the secret man. "Mr. Bolt, what's wrong with Nate Dooley?"

He shrugged. "Nate? Nothing, far as I know."

"Mom said there was."

"Did she?" He smiled. "So how does Elsie like being

down in Myrtle Beach? Finally got where she always wanted to be."

I told him that she liked it fine. I could tell he wanted to ask me more about her, but he resisted the impulse. As we walked out of his office, he clapped me on my shoulder. "I suppose you're glad to be out of this old place and all its problems, ain't ya?"

I considered my answer and lit on honesty. "Yes, sir, pretty much."

"Don't blame you."

I shook Mr. Bolt's hand, waved at his men, and left. Outside, I found Tag Farmer, Coalwood's constable, leaning against his car, his arms crossed. When he caught sight of me, he shoved the bill of his officer's cap up with one finger. "Heard you were back, Sonny," he said. "Thought we should have a word."

Tag looked like he had put on a few pounds since I'd last seen him, but otherwise he wasn't much different. His company-provided khakis were immaculate as always, and his Sam Browne belt was polished and glistening. He wore no weapons, not even a nightstick. Coalwood had never provided many criminals that needed shooting or bashing. Tag used his fists every so often, but that was usually with outsiders from Gary, Bradshaw, or Matewan, places like that. Tag's main job was slowing down the cars on Main Street, or keeping tabs on John Eye's joint up Snakeroot Hollow on Saturday nights, or perhaps investigating what boy had plinked out a streetlight with a BB gun.

I shook Tag's offered hand, and we passed a few words back and forth. I told him about college, and when I asked, he said his mother was doing fine. "When's your mom coming home?" he asked.

I shrugged. "I don't know, Tag. She has a lot of work to do on her house."

"Why aren't you down there helping her?"

"She ordered me here to be with Dad during this Tuck

Dillon thing, said it wasn't good for him to be alone right now. What's your opinion on Tuck, Tag?"

Tag mulled over my question. "Never been a mine that couldn't kill you," he finally allowed.

I recalled that Tag had tried to work in the mine when he'd come home from the Korean War but had froze on the man-lift at the bottom of the shaft. He'd told his foreman he'd rather face a million screaming Chinese troops than take another step. The Captain had hired him as the town constable right after that, and he had never, to my knowledge, tried to go down in the mine again.

"What happens now?" I wondered.

Tag hooked a thumb in his belt. "Inspectors have been in here for a week now," he said. "After they finish, there'll be a hearing to try to figure out what went wrong and who's at fault."

I went to the heart of it. "You mean, to see if my dad's at fault," I said. "Who'll run the hearing?"

"First testimony will be by the steel company. Then, if the state don't like the results, it'll hold its own testimonies. Then, if the feds don't like either one, they'll hold another set. They'll keep going until they get the answer they want."

The way Tag had put it, it sounded as if at least three outfits were soon going to be after my father like starving dogs. "Is that what usually happens?" I worried.

"Naw. It usually stops with the mine owners. They don't want the state or the feds in their knickers, so they're pretty tough in finding out what happened. Somebody'll be down here from Ohio pretty soon to get the testimonies going, I expect."

"Is Dad going to get blamed?"

Tag nodded. "That's the talk."

"That would be rough on him."

"It would kill him, Sonny," Tag said succinctly. He got out a big red bandanna and blew his nose. "Damn allergies this time of the year. That's another reason I never worked the mine—too much dust. That and being scared to death of that low roof. I need to see the sky above me, not a hanging slab of rock."

I remembered Mom's admonition about Coalwood's secret man. "Tag, what's wrong with Nate Dooley?"

Tag looked up in surprise. "Nate? He broke his wrist. About all I know."

I thought to myself—*ah ha!* That must have been what Mom had heard. "Is his wrist okay now?"

Tag shrugged. "He's got a cast on it. I guess it's fine."

It was clear that Tag was done with me, said what he had to say, heard from me all he'd wanted to hear. He climbed back in his car and headed on down toward Frog Level. I drove Dad's Buick back through Coalwood Main and spotted Mrs. Dantzler at the post office, so I got out and said hello. Mrs. Dantzler was a woman who always looked like she was dressed for a dinner dance at the White House. She was also Ginger's mom. When I asked her about her youngest daughter, she laughed. "Ginger's going to about every camp there is this summer, Sonny—majorette camp, cheerleader camp, she's even going to tennis camp. In between, she's visiting relatives in Mississippi and Kentucky. Doesn't look like she'll be here much the next couple of months."

Her answer disappointed me but was no surprise. Ginger was a girl with big dreams. It figured that she'd be off improving herself in every way she could this summer, unlike me, who was so far stuck in Coalwood. I thanked Mrs. Dantzler and headed on up to the mine, hoping to see Dad.

I put the car back in the garage, then walked to the path that led up to the tipple grounds. Off-shift miners lounging around the gas station across from our house gave me a wave. One of them shouted out a question on my grades at VPI.

"I haven't flunked out yet!" I called in reply.

"Attaboy!" came back a chorus. I figured it would take maybe an entire minute before the news had flashed up to New Camp and down to Frog Level.

Dad's office was a low brick building grimy with years of caked-on coal dirt. I trudged up its nasty black wooden steps and peeked inside. Wally Barnes, Dad's clerk, looked up from his desk. "Well, look who the cat drug in," the tiny man said. "The rocket boy hisself."

Even though he never went inside the mine, Wally was wearing a miner's helmet with safety stickers plastered all over it. I guess he just liked to look the part. I glanced at Dad's office door, firmly closed. "Dubonnet's in there," Wally said, spitting tobacco juice into a paper cup. "They're fighting."

That news didn't surprise me. In 1946, after battling the Germans during World War II, John Dubonnet had come to Coalwood looking for work. Mom and Dad and Mr. Dubonnet had all been in the same class at Gary High School. They were friends then. In fact, Mom had even dated Mr. Dubonnet for a while. At Dad's recommendation, Captain Laird had taken him on. Later, it turned out that Mr. Dubonnet was actually an undercover union organizer. Dad had never forgiven him for the duplicity. About the time Dad got the Captain's job, Mr. Dubonnet, who never married, took over Coalwood's local and moved into the Union Hall. The two former Gary boys had been tangling over one thing or another ever since.

"Can I go in?" I asked Wally.

Wally shrugged. "I guess so, if you don't mind hearing a little yelling. They've been at it for over an hour."

"What's it about this time?"

"The usual," Wally replied, spitting again into his cup. "Dubonnet wants more money for less work."

"I guess that's his job," I said.

Wally scowled as if he didn't like the idea of any Hickam, even me, taking up for a union man. "You gonna build any rockets while you're here?" he demanded.

"I'm out of the rocket-building business," I said.

"Well, what *are* you going to do?"

"Maybe if I can ever talk to my dad," I replied, "I can figure it out."

"Give it a shot," he said, nodding toward the door.

I knocked and, even though I didn't hear a response, went on in. Dad was at the huge oak desk he'd inherited from the Captain. He had his head down, writing a note in what I recognized as his daily journal. Woody Marshall, one of his top foremen, sat at a nearby table. Mr. Dubonnet was sitting on a folding chair, bent over with his elbows on his knees. I glanced around at the walls. Nothing had changed, the same mine maps, the same photograph of Captain Laird. There was at least a new 1961 calendar provided by the Joy Mining Machine Company. A pert blonde in a skimpy bathing suit graced it.

Mr. Dubonnet stared at me for a moment, and then recognition spread across his thin face. He had been a star halfback in high school, and I thought he always looked like he was ready to put on a football helmet and step out onto the field for some heroics. "Well, I'll be—" he said. "Sonny Hickam home from college!"

Dad looked up but didn't seem to share Mr. Dubonnet's enthusiasm for my sudden presence. "We're trying to have a meeting here, Sonny," he said.

I came close to being sharp-tongued by replying *Nice to see you, too, Dad.* But I didn't. I knew better. So I said, "Just wanted to say hello."

It seemed every time Dad looked at me, it was as if he were looking at me for the first time. He cocked an eyebrow and scrutinized me carefully. After he'd finished his study of my features, he asked, "What are you doing in Coalwood?"

"Mom said I needed to keep you company."

Dad closed his damaged eye and pondered me with his good one. It was like looking down the barrel of a gun. His eye had been nearly put out the same night Mr. Bykovski had been killed. During the rescue attempt, a cable had snapped and slashed Dad across the face.

"Company, huh?" I thought I detected a hint of a smile for just a moment, but then it disappeared. "For how long?"

"Until she says I've done it enough, I guess."

"Well, you've done it enough," he said. "Go to Myrtle Beach and help your mom."

That was the first good thing I'd heard since I'd been back in Coalwood. "Yes, sir!" I said quickly, before he could change his mind. "I'll hitch out in the morning."

"Take the Buick," Dad said. "Your mom could use a chauffeur. I've got the company truck to get around here."

This was getting better and better! I couldn't believe my luck! With the Buick as bait, I could cut a vast swath through the available females at the beach. "I'll call Mom, tell her the plan," I said, even allowing a grin to appear on my face before I could stop it.

Dad frowned a warning. "Don't tell your mother anything! Just go."

He was absolutely correct. The best thing to do with Mom was to just show up down there, make it a done deal. I could tell her that Dad was fine and so was Nate Dooley, not counting his broken wrist. I nodded to Mr. Marshall and Mr. Dubonnet and started to make my escape, but then I thought to ask a question. I hung by the door. "Dad, where's Lucifer?"

The frown on Dad's face faltered, temporarily replaced by a look I had trouble figuring out. He worked on it for a moment and got the frown back. "Dead, most likely. Every morning, he walked across the road to Substation

Mountain to hunt. About three months ago, your mom said she saw him go but he never came back."

"He was a real old cat, wasn't he, Homer?" Mr. Dubonnet asked.

"Nearly as old as Sonny."

"Cats do that," Mr. Marshall said severely. "Go away to die."

"Dogs, too," Mr. Dubonnet said, and the two men nodded to one another, acknowledging their joint knowledge of feline and canine expiration.

Lucifer, dead and gone. Our old cat. "Why didn't Mom write me, let me know?" I asked, feeling a big lump forming in my throat.

Dad leaned back in his chair, studying me. "What was Lucifer to you?"

"He was part of the family."

Dad kept his study of me, and all of a sudden I felt as if it were just the two of us in the room. I guess Dad felt the same way or else he would have never said what he did. "Sonny," he said carefully, and tiredly, "in case you haven't noticed, we don't have a family anymore."

6

SAD TIMES

EVEN THOUGH I was going to get everything I wanted, I felt peculiarly restless, as if I'd done something wrong. I went home and was drawn to the basement to look at Lucifer's thin gray rug at the base of the steps. Mom had placed it there just for him after the harsh West Virginia winters had started to chase his old bones inside. When I knelt and picked up the rug, I could still see some of his black fur entwined in its fabric. He had been a tough old tom, but sometimes I would look into his yellow eyes and sense there was more going on inside him than I could possibly know. Once, I'd been in the mountains with Sherman and we'd seen a sick fawn and stayed with it until it died. Afterward, when I came home, I swear Lucifer just seemed to know what I'd seen. Wisdom seemed to radiate out of his eyes, wisdom that said dying is the destination of us all— deer, cat, or human, it didn't matter. Somehow, he'd made me feel better about the whole thing. "Good ol' cat," I whispered, fingering his tattered, grimy rug. "Fine fellow."

Still uneasy, I went upstairs and sat at my desk,

skimming *Cannery Row*, trying to lose myself inside the written word. It didn't work and I shelved it. I hoped Dad would come home and maybe we'd talk, about what I wasn't certain, but it didn't matter because he never did. Shortly after dark, the telephone rang. It was Mrs. Sharitz. "Your dad not home yet? You're welcome to come over here for supper."

I thanked her but said I was fine. I explained that I was going to be in Coalwood for just one more night and after that I was heading for Myrtle Beach. "Tell Elsie we miss her," Mrs. Sharitz said. "I'm feeding the dogs and keeping an eye on the place."

"Yes, ma'am," I said. "Thank you for that."

"Sonny?"

I suspected the real reason Mrs. Sharitz had called was about to be told. "Ma'am?"

"I don't think your dad should be alone," she said. "Cecil is worried about him. I guess we all are—since Tuck."

I "yes ma'amed" her and left it at that because I thought she was wrong. My dad didn't need anyone, and never had, as far as I knew. I hung up, feeling ever more doleful, and thought briefly about leaving for Myrtle Beach immediately but decided the smart thing to do was to wait for morning. The way that old Buick guzzled gasoline, I'd run out of it before I'd gotten much farther than Bluefield. It wasn't like gas stations stayed open all night.

The night wore on and I cast around for something to do. I remembered the Dugout, the teenage dance hall over in the town of War, two mountains and eight miles away. It was a Saturday night, and, after all, girls didn't come much prettier than McDowell County girls. I could get in some dance practice for Myrtle Beach and maybe even meet somebody new. My enthusiasm for life went up several notches at the thought.

I poked into my closet and found some khaki pants and a short-sleeved shirt that didn't have too many wrinkles. They were all I needed for the Dugout. My brother was the one who'd been the fancy dresser. He had almost single-handedly kept open Belcher and Mooney's men's store in Welch during his high school years. Mom had tried to hand me down some of his things, but, besides being too large, they were always a bit too fine for me. I was always just a khaki cotton pants kind of boy.

As I drove the Buick through the night, every curve in the mountain road came back to me. When I reached War, I parked by Big Creek High School and walked across the bridge to the Owl's Nest Restaurant. The Dugout was in its basement and my excitement rose as I got nearer, but I discovered, to my vast disappointment, that it was dark and dead. I went inside the restaurant and talked to the counter maid. "Ed's gone off to Florida for the summer," she said of the Dugout's disc jockey. "Be back in the fall, I expect. Maybe not, though. I heard he's cleaning swimming pools down there. There's good money in that. Say, ain't you Sonny Hickam? Good on you for winning that science fair medal. Wanta cheeseburger?"

"On the house?" I asked hopefully. My stomach was growling.

She raised her eyebrows. "Sure, plus thirty-five cents."

"How much do they cost otherwise?"

"Thirty-five cents."

I was starved so I took her up on her offer, poor as it was, and then trudged back to the Buick and drove to Coalwood, contemplating the taste of fresh West Virginia onions and life in general. I dawdled the Buick along. I was in no hurry to get anywhere because I had nowhere to go. "Sad times," I said to myself, remembering the phrase Roy Lee had often used on me when I was down in the mouth about something.

When I got back to Coalwood, I slowed at the mine and eased my way down Main Street. I figured Tag Farmer was around somewhere. Although there was no official speed limit in town, it was pretty much what Tag thought it ought to be, and there was no use getting pulled over.

At Coalwood Main, I drifted past the Club House, the big three-storied neo-Georgian mansion that the elder Mr. Carter had built for his son and his new bride. The bride, a New Yorker, had taken one look at Coalwood and headed back to Yankeeland, so it had never been used for its original purpose. During the 1920s, it had been converted into a boardinghouse for single miners, but it had since been remodeled several times. Although the Club House still housed visitors and a few permanent guests such as Dr. Hale, Coalwood's dentist, it was also used for holiday parties, retirement banquets, wedding receptions, and just about every important social occasion.

I had the sudden urge to visit Cape Coalwood. I knew I wouldn't see much, not in the dark, but it just didn't seem right to be in town and not see the place where once the other boys and I had found a certain measure of glory. When I reached Frog Level Row and bumped up on the dirt road that led to the cape, I floored the Buick, just for the fun of it. *Finally, some excitement!* I roared around a curve and saw, too late, a good-sized boulder sitting in the middle of the road. I hit the brakes, but the Buick rode up on the big rock and I heard the shrieking of agonized steel. Every idiot light the Detroit engineers had decided to stick onto the instrument panel went bright red, and then the engine died.

It took a while for my heart to stop trying to beat its way out of my chest. When I climbed out, I heard something liquid pattering into the dust beneath the car. I was no auto mechanic, but I suspected that probably wasn't a good thing.

I walked around the Buick, kicked one of its tires in frustration, and then began trudging toward home, oblivious to the merry stars twinkling brightly in the narrow swath of black sky between the mountains. Once, when I had lived in Coalwood, I had seen those same stars as evidence of the glorious future I was going to have in space. Now I hardly saw them at all. My head was down, my hands jammed in my pockets, my immediate future an unknowable mystery except for one sure thing: I wasn't going to Myrtle Beach in the morning.

7

MR. DUBONNET'S OFFER

THE ANNOYING ring of the home telephone downstairs woke me up the next morning, and even though I put a pillow over my head, the blamed thing wouldn't stop. There was only one person I knew who could be so persistent, so I threw on my shirt and pants and went to answer it. "So how's life?" Mom asked in as sweet a tone of voice as she ever used on me. I was instantly on guard. It was a question loaded for bear, and I knew I was the bear.

I sorted through possible answers and landed on a considerably condensed version of the truth. "Dad's fine, Nate Dooley's fine although he has a broken wrist, and I wrecked the Buick last night."

She didn't seem surprised at any of my news, which told me she already knew it. "Are you hurt?" she asked.

"No, but the Buick is." When she didn't answer for an entire second, I improvised a plea for sympathy. "Mom, can I come to Myrtle Beach now? Dad doesn't want me here."

"Did he tell you that?"

"Pretty much."

"How bad's the Buick?"

I allowed a mild groan, still looking for some motherly compassion. "I ran into a rock. It must have rolled down off the mountain. Something got busted up underneath."

"Where did it happen?"

"I was going down to Cape Coalwood. I just wanted to see it."

"What did your dad say about that?"

"Nothing yet. I haven't seen him this morning."

"Then you'd better talk to him," she said.

"Then can I leave Coalwood?"

"No, you can't leave Coalwood. I told you your daddy needs your company while all this mess about Tuck Dillon gets sorted out. Sometimes I think you never listen to a word I say!"

"He doesn't act like he needs my company," I said. "He told me to take the Buick and head for Myrtle Beach."

Her chuckle filled my ear. "Well, you kind of messed yourself up on that score, didn't you?"

"Yes, ma'am. I guess I kind of did. But how long do I have to stay?"

"Until I say you can leave."

"When will that be?"

"I'll let you know," she replied. "I'm hanging up now. I've got roofers in today. Talk to you later."

"But—" I began, but it was too late. She'd already hung up. I looked at the receiver, then slammed it down. The bell inside the phone protested with a single surprised chime.

I jumped when I heard Dad say, "You break that telephone, young man, you'll be paying for it, too!"

I waited for him to yell at me about the Buick, but he was leaning over the dining-room table digging into a pile of letters and bills, and it seemed he had other things on his mind. "Do you ever study at all down there?" he demanded, and I saw his index finger pressing against my VPI grade report. "Mediocre in math, mediocre in chemistry, mediocre in everything except English. What are you going to be? A literary engineer?"

I opened my mouth to explain and then closed it. I had no explanation except to say I was doing the best I could. Even I didn't believe that was entirely true.

His forehead, creased with deep furrows, lifted. "What the blue blazes were you doing down at Frog Level, anyway?"

"I went to see Cape Coalwood," I said.

"There's nothing to see," he said. "Your old shed is long gone—weekend carpenters got it for the lumber, I expect—and your slab of concrete is covered up with silt. There was a flood this past spring, washed a good part of that dump away. Last time I was down there, there were already saplings pushing up. We're not dumping on it anymore. Give it a few more years, it'll be a forest."

The shed he was talking about was the Big Creek Missile Agency's proud blockhouse. The slab was our launchpad. The dump was once the finest rocket range this side of Cape Canaveral. Every vestige of the old cape had been destroyed. Dad had managed to diminish in a few words a place I considered grand and glorious.

He went back to stirring the mail, my grades thankfully pitched to one side. "In case you're wondering," he said, "a tow truck hauled the car over to Welch to the dealer about an hour ago. Tag found it where you abandoned it and called me."

"Let me know how much it costs and I'll pay for the repairs," I said.

He looked up. "You? With what?"

"I'll get a job," I said. "I'll send you the money."

He fingered a letter, tossed it down unopened. "What kind of job?"

I explained my plan, which I had just made up. I was going to hitch to Myrtle Beach that very day (I didn't mention Mom's latest directive), and there I'd beg for a job aboard one of the tourist fishing boats, baiting hooks and swabbing decks. I would keep mailing money back to Dad until the Buick repairs were covered.

Dad heard me out, then shook his head. "That's your craziest plan yet," he said. "Anyway, I talked to your mom this morning, too. She doesn't want you down there. She says she has her hands full as it is without having you to worry about."

That shut me up and also told me exactly what kind of box I was in. Dad didn't want me in Coalwood and Mom didn't want me in Myrtle Beach. What was I supposed to do, live up in the woods somewhere?

"What are you thinking?" Dad asked, as if he really wanted to know.

"I was wondering what you were going to do about Tuck Dillon," I said. It wasn't the only thing I was thinking about, of course, but it was one of them. The accident just didn't make sense.

"Tuck Dillon." The way he said it, as if correcting my pronunciation, made it sound like I had no right to say Tuck's name out loud.

I stuck with it. "They say—" I began.

He interrupted me, his voice weary but tinged with defiance, as if he were doing me an extreme favor merely by replying. "Don't tell me what 'they' say. I don't care."

It was amazing that Dad could still push buttons inside me I didn't even know were there. I choked back a bitter response. "I just want to help," I said.

His good eye drilled into me. "The one thing I'm sure of in this old world, little man," he said, "is I don't need *your* help."

And with that said clearly and just as clearly heard, he walked away and out the back door while I stood in the dining room for the longest time, my face burning.

I HAD nothing to do at the house except to continue to make myself miserable. Though I was pretty good at doing that when I put my mind to it, I decided instead to go down to the Big Store for a soda pop. Maybe I could mull a few things over down there.

One thing about Coalwood hadn't changed. It was nearly impossible to walk anywhere. I hadn't taken ten steps out of the front gate before a car stopped. It was Tag Farmer, driving his company-supplied Dodge. I subsided onto its bench seat. The floor was littered with empty pop bottles. "Morning, Sonny," he said. "Did you wear your eyes out in college?" I didn't know what he meant and said so. He chuckled. "You couldn't see that rock?"

Thanks to the fence-line, the gossip circuit that went up and down every hollow and cranny of Coalwood, everybody in town was sure to have chewed over my battering of the Buick until they'd reached some consensus, most probably about my stupidity or lack of driving skills. I longed to be back at college, where I had only the occasional department dean to hold forth on my inadequacies, not an entire town. Although I knew it would probably do no good, I told Tag my side of it.

"There's already a rumor you rolled the Buick," he said. "I heard Cleo Mallett claim it was three times."

The gossip was worse than I'd feared. "Tag, you know I didn't roll the Buick! I just hit a big rock and knocked the oil pan loose or something!"

He laughed. "Remain calm, boy. That's the way it is around here. Have you forgotten so fast? Everything has to be a little bigger than the way it really happened. How else would we occupy our time, after all, if we didn't make up a few tall tales now and again?"

"I haven't forgotten. I just hoped I was exempt since I'm not a Coalwood citizen anymore."

Tag gave me a sharp look. "Who said you weren't a Coalwood citizen?"

"Me, I guess," I replied glumly.

I'd given him something else to laugh about. "Sonny, you ain't never going to be nothing else but a Coalwood boy, don't matter how far off you go or how big you get. Don't ever forget that."

I started to argue with him, then gave it up as a lost cause. For all I knew, he might have even been right.

When we got to Coalwood Main, Mr. Bledsoe, a roof bolter, came out of the post office, strolled up to the Dodge, and started complaining to Tag about his neighbor's yard. "I swan, he hasn't mowed it in two weeks. Hidy, Sonny. Back from school and already tore up your old man's Buick? Fast one for good and bad, ain't you? Rolled it over twice! You must have been flying. Lucky you didn't kill yourself. You best get those grades up, too, young man. So, Tag, what you gonna do about that long grass?"

I started to reply, then clapped my mouth shut. What good would it do? I wasn't the least bit interested in Mr. Bledsoe's problems, either, so I excused myself and headed for the Big Store.

Junior, the venerable clerk of the drugstore section, was wiping down the counter. He despised fingerprints and smudges. All the glass cabinets and aluminum soda and milk-shake dispensers were shining like mirrors.

Junior's eyes widened behind his wire-rimmed spectacles when he saw it was me. His close-cropped hair had turned gray around the edges since I'd seen him last, and deep creases had appeared on his chocolate-colored face, but he was still Junior. "Sonny Hickam! Back to Coalwood, I swan!"

"I'm just visiting," I said defensively. I put my quarter down and Junior served up a pop and then wanted to know all about my life as a college boy. "It's tolerable," I told him.

"Well, you better get those grades up," he said. "And stop rolling your daddy's car."

"Yes, sir." I sighed.

"How's your daddy? He holding up all right on this Tuck Dillon thing?"

Before I could answer, a big hand grabbed my shoulder. I nearly spit out my pop. It was Mr. John Dubonnet, the union chief.

"Sonny, good to see you, my man," he said. "Making Coalwood proud in college, are you? Your grades could be a mite better, I guess, but you'll make it. You come from good stock, at least on your mama's side. Those Lavenders never could drive. Guess that explains your accident down at Frog Level. One time, your mama hit a cow with your daddy's brand-new roadster. Didn't hurt the cow but totaled the car." He laughed, I suppose at the memory of Dad's wrecked roadster.

I took a moment to absorb his greeting, filled as it was with information, genealogy, history, gossip, and a curious kind of logic all at once. "Hello, Mr. Dubonnet," I finally replied.

He kept smiling. "When you going back to school?"

"September."

"And how are you going to pay for the Buick? I hear your daddy said he's giving you the bill."

Junior brought his chores a little closer to hear my answer. Whatever I said would be all around town in less than an hour after I said it, so I knew I'd best choose my words carefully. I worried over them a bit, then polished them up. "I don't know," I said, smooth as grease.

"Well, I have an idea," Mr. Dubonnet answered instantly. "Why don't you go to work in the mine?"

My laugh just burst out of me. I couldn't help it. I heard Junior behind me chuckle, too. I guess neither of us had ever heard anything so outrageously ridiculous.

Mr. Dubonnet ignored my response. "A couple of years ago," he said patiently, "when Mr. Van Dyke was the general superintendent, he got it in his head that Coalwood college boys ought to be able to work in the mine during the summer to help pay their tuition. I—that is to say, the union—agreed to it, even though nobody ever signed up. But I think it's still a good idea. As a matter of fact, Bobby Likens came to me a few days ago, asked for work. I said I'd make it happen if you signed on, too."

Bobby Likens was the son of the Coalwood School principal. I didn't know him very well. He was four years older than me, so he'd always run with a different pack of boys. I'd heard in one of Mom's letters that he had just graduated from Emory and Henry College. She had also written that he was on his way to medical school. I guessed that was why he needed the money. I was glad I wasn't in the same situation. My parents were paying my way through school. "No, thanks," I said to Mr. Dubonnet. But I thought to myself: *Never, not in a million years.*

Mr. Dubonnet tilted his snap-brim hat back on his head. "Give it some thought, son. You could make some good money. You'd be doing Bobby a favor, too."

"Why not just let him work by himself?"

He shook his head. "One boy makes a problem. Two boys make a crew. It's complicated."

I puzzled over his answer for a moment, then decided that even if it didn't make sense, it didn't matter. "I'm not going to work in the mine, Mr. Dubonnet."

"You'd make three dollars and fifty cents an hour," he said.

Three dollars and fifty cents an hour! A veritable fortune! Before I could stop myself, I asked, "What would I have to do?"

"All you'd have to do is join the union," he answered.

Junior whistled. It was my sentiments, exactly. There

was about as much chance of a Hickam joining the United Mine Workers of America as a Republican being elected to office in McDowell County.

Mr. Dubonnet nodded to me, then went off to the grocery section. "So what you gonna do, rocket boy?" Junior asked. He might as well have gotten out a pen and pad to write down what I was about to say.

"I'm not a rocket boy anymore," I said slowly so he'd get it down just right for the fence-line gossipers. "I'm a college boy. And I'm not going to work in the mine."

Junior responded with a sympathetic but doubtful smile. I had the sudden opinion that he knew my fate better than I did.

8

THE UMWA

WHEN I got home, the black phone—the one connected to the mine—was ringing. I answered it. "Your dad wants you up here," Wally said.

"What for?" I asked cautiously.

"The estimate for the Buick is ready."

"Estimate?"

"You did tell your dad you would pay for the repairs to his car, didn't you?"

"Yes, but I wasn't serious."

Wally laughed. "He thought you were. Looks like you managed to tear off the oil pan and knock the engine nearly off its mounts."

I gulped. "Is it going to cost a lot of money?"

"Well, those Welch mechanics aren't going to do the work for free."

Wally could really irk me. "I'm on my way," I snapped.

I found Wally at his desk. A quick glance through the open door showed that Dad wasn't in his office. "Where is he?"

Wally ignored my question and slid a sheet of yellow paper across his desk. It was the estimated bill from the Buick dealer in Welch, to the tune of $135.78, approximately $135.78 more than I had to my name. Reluctantly, I confessed that fact to Wally.

"Your dad will pay the dealer after the repairs are complete," he said, shrugging, "and then you will pay your dad. That's the deal."

I looked at the bill again. One little rock had done all that? "Tell him I'll send the money after I get work."

Wally shifted in his old chair, making it squeak. "And what work might that be? Are you going to launch rockets and charge admission? Maybe ten people would be willing to give you a buck for that." He gave me a sly grin to show me how clever he thought he was.

I considered making some sharp retort but decided Wally wasn't worthy of my wit, not that I had any. I walked down Main Street, trying to get a fix on things. I hadn't gone more than ten yards before Coalwood's garbage truck pulled up beside me. I hauled myself inside the cab. "You look like a boy who needs a ride," Red Carroll said, his big, droopy, hound-dog eyes giving me the once-over.

Red Carroll, rocket boy O'Dell's dad, was never far from a smile, and his tongue stayed in his cheek a lot, but he had the reputation of being a solid man, always ready to help somebody who needed it. He was also one of the few grown men in Coalwood I called by first name, don't ask me why. "You sticking around town for a while?" he asked after finding a gear to get us moving.

"Looks like," I muttered.

"O'Dell's doing great in the air force," he reported as he swerved around Mrs. Jack Rose, who'd stopped her car to chat with Mrs. Fleming, out for a walk with her son Zack. "As soon as he finishes electronics school, he's off to Germany. I'm real proud of him."

"So am I, Red," I said. I was envious, too. At least O'Dell knew where he was going, and was seeing some of the world while he was at it.

"Well, come see me sometime, Sonny," Red said as he let me off at Coalwood Main. "Beulah still cooks a great supper. Be proud to have you."

I thanked Red most sincerely and then walked through the center of town, my mind churning. I walked and thought down to the Community Church, turned around, and walked and thought some more past the Club House and the Big Store. Off-shift miners on the Big Store steps watched me go by, then turn around and walk back again. One of them was Hub Alger, who was about my age and had decided to make a career of the mine. "You're making us dizzy, Sonny, going back and forth," Hub said.

"I'm trying to figure something out," I replied, stopping to slouch against the wall.

He offered his pouch of Red Man. "Wanta chew?"

"No thanks."

Pick Hylton, another miner, said, "What are you trying to figure?"

"How to get some money."

He laughed, as did the others. "Sonny, you ever figure that one out," he said, "you let us know!"

I sat with Hub and Pick and the others for a while, listening to their mine gossip, mostly about what foreman was doing what to whom. I got offered pretty much every kind of chewing tobacco known to mankind while I was there—Red Man, Brown Mule, Bull Durham, Mail Pouch, and 3 Black Crows—but I had never been a chewer. When the men weren't talking, they were spitting into paper cups, given to them for free by Junior inside the drugstore. By their talk, the mine was busy, causing a lot of work to be done in a hurry, just as I had suspected. The men, I noted, studiously avoided mentioning Tuck Dillon, and I didn't bring the subject up. After a while, Hub had to go and the others broke up the knot, and I went back to walking until I found myself standing in front of the Union Hall. I looked at it for a long time. That little corner of my mind that sent me off in tangents sometimes gave me a kick in the pants by recalling something my old buddy Roy Lee had once told me when I was complaining about this or that. "If you don't want to get run over, Sonny, you need to get off the road."

Maybe, I thought, it was time I got off one road but onto another—my own.

I took a deep breath, and marched inside the Union Hall. I found Mr. Dubonnet at his desk. He looked up. A slow grin spread across his weary face at the sight of me. I signed the papers he shoved in my direction. "Come back tonight," he said. "It's the weekly meeting. We'll get you joined up."

I DIDN'T go home. I sat on the rock wall in front of the Club House and dozed in the sun a bit and then wandered up and down Club House Row until at last it was seven o'clock, the time designated for the union meeting. The Union Hall glowed with lights. It had once been the Norfolk and Western train depot before the tipple had been moved to Caretta and the tracks through Coalwood Main had been taken out. It was a single-story wooden building with the trapezoidal-shaped roof characteristic of the old stations. The place quickly filled up with men sitting in a sea of folding metal chairs. In front of the room was a table with union officials around it. Mr. Dubonnet was there along with Mr. Mallett, the union secretary. Mr. Mallett, plump and rosy-cheeked, was a nice man, although his two oldest sons were dumb brutes with a history of trying to beat me up during strikes. He also had a wife who could arm-wrestle with Rocky Marciano and win.

I found a chair in the rear of the hall. A few men took note of me and fell to whispering. I pushed my thick, horn-rimmed glasses up on my nose and crossed my arms and settled back into my chair, just as if I had made a habit of attending union meetings nearly every day.

After a short while, Mr. Dubonnet gaveled the meeting to a start. There was some old business, a droning report of the minutes by Mr. Mallett, and then the first new business came up, which was the induction of new members. Mr. Dubonnet consulted his list. It was apparently a short one.

"Sonny Hickam," Mr. Dubonnet intoned. "Come forward."

As I walked down the aisle, I could feel the eyes of every man in the hall on me. There was a low murmur among them. As I stepped up to the table, Mr. Jocko Paraganni, a retired miner, rose and whispered something in my ear. I couldn't make it out. "What?" I asked, but Mr. Paraganni just gave me a toothless grin.

In a ponderous tone, Mr. Dubonnet said, "Sonny Hickam, you have just taken the first step required to enter the brotherhood of the United Mine Workers of America. You are to keep the motto you've just been told by the sergeant at arms secret unto death."

"The secret union motto seals you to us for life," Mr. Mallett added.

"But I didn't hear—" I began, but before I could finish my protest, I was interrupted by Mr. Mallett going on to say how important it was that I never, ever reveal the secret motto. When I started to say again that I still didn't know what it was, I was drowned out by a rumble of agreement from the assembled men. I gave up, figuring maybe I could ask somebody later what it was. Of course, when I thought about it, if nobody was supposed to tell it, how would I ever find out what it was?

"Bobby Likens, please step forward," Mr. Dubonnet intoned.

Bobby came up, gave me a terse nod, then faced the congregation. He had a square-jawed, bantam-rooster look to him that, along with wire-rimmed spectacles, caused him to resemble a young Teddy Roosevelt. His sandy hair was cut short in a crew cut, and he was wearing a smart checked shirt, trim khakis, and penny loafers, as befitted a true college boy. Mr. Paraganni leaned over and whispered into his ear, and Bobby looked puzzled. I suspected he hadn't heard the secret motto any better than I. For all I knew, maybe that was what Mr. Paraganni intended.

Mr. Dubonnet had Bobby and me raise our hands and he read us the union oath. It sounded like Bobby and I were supposed to be henceforth more loyal to the union than anything else in the world, even the United States of America. Although I didn't entirely go along with it, I went ahead and swore. A lot of the men in the building had gone off to fight in World War II and Korea. Their oath to the union hadn't stopped them, and I figured it wouldn't stop me, either.

"Welcome, brother," Mr. Dubonnet said, and clasped my hand. "It's good to have a Hickam back in the fold of the working man."

"Hear, hear!" came the shout from the assembly.

"You've made a man's decision tonight, Sonny," Mr. Mallett said in a soft voice. "A very brave thing, I swan."

"Thank you, sir."

"You may call me Leo."

"We'll hear from our new brothers now," Mr. Dubonnet said, and nodded to me.

I was still slightly dazed by what I'd done. "I guess this means I won't be beat up by union boys anymore," I said weakly.

That got me a laugh, and I decided to quit while I was ahead. "I'm happy to be a member," I mumbled, and then shut my mouth. Mr. Dubonnet nodded to Bobby.

Bobby shrugged, and said, "You all know me and my

parents and my brother Jack. I grew up here, played football, basketball, and tennis, studied hard in school, and never gave anybody much trouble. Next year, I'll be going to medical school, which is going to cost way more than my parents can afford. I'm here tonight because I need a job, not because I'm in love with the union. If anybody has a problem with that, let's get it out in the open right now. Otherwise, I'll see you in the mine."

Bobby tightened his fists at his hips and waited out his audience. Nobody saw fit to argue with him. I was impressed by his willingness to stand up and say what he thought, even though I doubted the need for it. "Thank you, Bobby," Mr. Dubonnet said dryly. "We appreciate your honesty."

Bobby shook some proffered hands from miners sitting up front, and then he got around to saying something to me. "Thanks for taking the job, Sonny," he said. "They weren't going to open up the program unless they got two boys."

"Do you think we did the right thing?" I wondered.

"I know I did," he said, jutting out his jaw and pushing his spectacles up on his pug nose.

I pushed my glasses up on my nose, too, and then let out a worried breath. "My folks are going to kill me." It came out pretty much a whine.

He inspected me. "You know, Sonny," he said, "when I was a boy, I never hung around with you much, but I heard some things."

"Like what?"

"Like you could be a bit of a wimp. I hope that's not true. You and me, we've got to stick together this summer."

"I'm no wimp," I squeaked.

"In that case," he said, "you might want to stop sounding like one."

His duty done, at least by his lights, Bobby Likens strode

up the aisle and out of the hall. I watched his back with narrowed eyes. I'd heard some things about Bobby Likens, too, like he could be a real arrogant snot. At least three good retorts to his crack about me being a wimp bubbled up into my brain, worthless now that he was gone.

Mr. Dubonnet gave me the elbow. "Got you told, didn't he? Got us all told, for that matter."

My heavy glasses had sneaked down my nose and I pushed them back into place. "I don't need to be told anything," I grumped, then went back to my chair in the rear of the assembly and tried to let my brain catch up with all that I'd done.

Mr. Dubonnet surveyed the audience and announced, "Bernie, now it's your turn. Let's hear what you've got to say."

Bernie Trulock walked up the aisle between the folding chairs. Bernie had grown up in Coalwood and I knew him fairly well. He'd married one of the Campbell girls, I recalled. He was a thin, limber-looking young man. Either he'd forgotten to shave or there was a mustache trying to bloom on his upper lip, too. "Doc here?" Bernie asked as he came up front.

"I'm here, Bernie," came the reply. Doc Lassiter emerged from a corner of the room. Like everything and everybody in Coalwood, Doc looked older and smaller than I remembered. As always, he carried his black doctor's bag.

Doc came to stand in front of the assembly. "Welcome, Doc," Mr. Dubonnet said.

"We'll see how welcome I am," Doc muttered.

Bernie began a little speech wherein he declared Doc was an awful doctor, always had been, and went on and on about some money Doc had charged him for his wife being sick "with just a little old cold."

"Thank you, brother," Mr. Dubonnet said when Bernie wrapped up. During the entire verbal blistering, the doctor had listened with a passive expression on his face. In fact, he seemed downright bored by Bernie's diatribe, enough so he'd even looked at his watch once as if he had an appointment, which, considering the demands on a coal camp physician, he probably did.

Mr. Dubonnet turned to the doctor. "Now, help me out here, Dr. Lassiter. It's in the union contract that the company will provide your services to every man and family member if they pay five dollars a month per family. According to his pay stub, Bernie here has done that." He fingered another piece of paper. "But it says here you've charged the B. Trulock family forty-seven dollars and eighty-two cents since April seventh. Would you please be so kind as to explain?"

Doc Lassiter pursed his lips, rocked in his polished black leather shoes. "I have a higher oath than even your union contract," he said with just a trace of distaste for the last two words. "A doctor has a duty to his patient to keep treatment confidential."

"Well, there ain't no sense to this, Doc," Bernie maintained, his voice rising an octave. "You gave my wife a little old shot or two, that's all."

"I gave you a shot, too, Bernie," Doc said, his voice becoming a little hotter.

"Yeah, but I warn't even sick!" Bernie blared. "You're just trying to make money off me on the side, you old fool! I ought to kick your butt!"

Mr. Mallett had been writing in a notebook as hard and fast as he could go, but at Bernie's threat, he stopped and looked up sharply. Mr. Dubonnet fixed his mouth into a straight line. "Bernie, there will be no threats here. We're just trying to get to the bottom of this."

"Aw, crap, John," Bernie growled. "This old quack's trying to steal my money. That's the long and the short of it."

Doc retained his dignified posture. "My answer remains the same. I have a duty of confidentiality."

The door slammed in the back of the hall and everybody turned to look. It was Mrs. Trulock. Her skirt swished as she walked down the aisle. I noted she wore brown and white shoes—saddle shoes as they were called—probably left over from her high school days and indicating that money was in short supply in the Trulock household. She went all the way up front and then turned around and faced us. "Go on, Doc," she said. "You tell it. You got my permission. Tell it all." She glanced at Bernie. "Go on, tell our shame."

"What you talking about, woman?" Bernie growled.

Mr. Dubonnet quieted the resulting hubbub from the assembly. "If there's something to tell, Doc," he said, "I think you have Mrs. Trulock's permission."

Doc shrugged. "I am treating Mrs. Trulock for a venereal disease," he said. A low murmur shot through the hall. He waited until it ran its course. "Mrs. Trulock asked me to give Bernie a shot and tell him it was for the flu. She also told me to charge what a doctor in Welch would charge for the shots, said it wasn't right to take the company for something this wretched."

While Doc was talking, Mrs. Trulock's hands gradually crept to her face. After he was done, she sobbed in them while Bernie stood stock-still, white as a ghost. "Woman," he said.

"If you don't stay out of those damn old whorehouses in Cinder Bottom," she said from within her cupped hands, "you're going to kill us all with disease, Bernie Trulock."

"Woman," he said once more, but his hands went to his face, too.

It was so quiet in the hall that all I could hear were the choked sobs of the Trulocks. Some of the men looked particularly grim, but whether it was for the Trulocks or Doc or from fear that maybe they had picked something up in the Keystone houses, too, I couldn't say. I felt ashamed and embarrassed, as if I were listening in on a family argument.

Mr. Mallett had kept his pencil poised during all this but now slowly started writing again. Mr. Dubonnet was the first to speak. "Bernie," he said quietly. "I think you have your answer."

Bernie took his hands away from his face and made to touch his wife on her shoulder, but she twitched away and then walked back down the aisle. The door slammed behind her. Bernie pulled himself out of his slouch, stood as straight as he could. "Yeah" was all he said, and then he followed his wife.

A long silence followed, again broken by Mr. Dubonnet. "Doctor Lassiter, I'm afraid we owe you an apology," he said stiffly. "You have always been a source of great comfort to our brotherhood, willing to get out in all kinds of weather to see to our pain. On a personal note, I would trust my health to you quicker than to any doctor alive at the fanciest hospital in the world. Coalwood is lucky to have you. I promise you this union will not trouble you again."

Doc Lassiter nodded, picked up his bag, and made his way down the aisle. Before he got far, a man started clapping and then everybody joined in. Doc Lassiter did not acknowledge it. He just left the Union Hall with a straight back, his black bag swinging.

Then I thought of something and chased after Doc. I caught him at the edge of the road. He eyed me carefully. "Well, Sonny Hickam, I thought I'd seen everything until I saw what you did tonight."

"Yes, sir. Can you get me out of it?" I was half serious.

"Not at all. I think it's just the thing for you. Turn the boy into a man, eh?"

"Can I be a man after I'm dead? First, Dad's going to kill me, and Mom won't be far behind."

That made him laugh. "Nothing happens to anybody which he is not by nature fit to bear."

I hoped he was right. "Doc, I have a question for you. How did Nate Dooley break his wrist?"

His grin disappeared, replaced by a frown. "Sonny, despite what you just saw and heard, I don't discuss my patients with anyone not in their immediate family."

Although Doc sounded adamant, the fact is I sincerely doubted him, due to personal experience. I had once fallen into a hole full of scrap steel and suffered a deep cut, nearly bleeding to death in the process. Doc had sewn me up, but before I made it home, most of the town knew every detail, down to how many stitches I'd received.

"I just want to know how he broke his wrist, sir, not anything else," I said judiciously.

"I'm afraid I can't help you," the doctor said icily.

"Why?"

He cocked his head at me. "You know, boy, just because you're a member of the union doesn't give you the right to question your betters out on the road at night. I said I can't help you because if you must know, I didn't set Nate's wrist. And now, if you'll excuse me, I've got a baby due to arrive any minute up Snakeroot Hollow. It's Estelle Franklin's first and she'll need some hand-holding."

And with that, Doc marched off, leaving me scratching my head.

9

THE CLUB HOUSE

I OWED Dad the courtesy of telling him what I'd done, so I tried to stay awake until he came home. I watched the *Tonight Show* until I fell asleep on the couch. Although I was convinced that I mostly tossed and turned all night, somehow Dad came home, turned off the television set, and left again without me knowing it. Surely that meant he didn't know I'd joined the union. Otherwise, he'd have woken me up and yelled at me about it. No matter what, the yelling was going to be long and loud when it came, not only from Dad but Mom, too, and I just wanted to get it over with.

My breakfast—Wheaties soaked in sour milk—didn't help my mood, but I forced myself to eat some of it, then headed down to Coalwood Main to start the processing with the company. I felt like I was one of those buffaloes I'd seen in the cowboy movies that got started on a stampede and went right over a cliff. Just as I'd never gone to work in a mine, the buffalo had probably never jumped off a cliff, either. Who knew for certain the result? Mr. Buffalo and Mr. Sonny Hickam just went ahead and kept going.

My first stop was Olga Coal Company's administrative office beside the Big Store. I went into the door marked GENERAL SUPERINTENDENT. This was Mr. Bundini's office. Carol Todd DeHaven, Mr. Bundini's secretary and assistant, looked up from her desk as I entered. She knew exactly why I was there and immediately produced all the forms I needed. She asked if she could see my freshly inked union card. "Never thought I'd see this day," she remarked, looking the card over. "What did your daddy say?"

I told her I hadn't seen him since I'd joined the union. "Well, he knows about it," she said. At my raised eyebrows, she said, "He has to sign off on every man coming to work."

While I filled in the necessary forms, I got the chance to reflect anew on what I'd done and also wonder why Dad had let me do it. I started hoping that maybe it was all a big joke and maybe Dad and Mr. Dubonnet would suddenly step around the corner, laughing at me. Unfortunately, it didn't happen. The next thing to do, Carol said, was to go to the Big Store. She gave me a list of equipment I needed. "I have to buy all this stuff?" I asked. It was a revelation that the company didn't provide all the things a man needed to work in the mine. I'd never thought about it. "I don't have any money," I confessed. In fact, I was $135.78 in the hole, which was the reason I'd gotten into this mess in the first place.

"The store will give you credit and deduct it from your paycheck," Carol answered with a reassuring smile.

I went into the Big Store and back to the counter where the mine equipment was kept. Mrs. Anastapoulos, the clerk, gave me an uncertain look when I appeared and showed her my list. "I'll need credit," I said.

"What new miner don't?" she answered, and then sent me to the office window to get signed up.

"You want some cash money, too?" the clerk asked.

"How about one hundred and thirty-five dollars and seventy-eight cents?"

He laughed, although I wasn't sure if he knew what the joke was. He probably did, though, considering the efficiency of Coalwood gossip. He gave me twenty dollars in scrip, company money good for spending only at the company store.

Mrs. Anastapoulos had all my stuff laid out when I got back. "I already have some hard-toe boots at home," I said, hoping to save a dollar or two.

"How old are they?" When I said I didn't know, she replied, "Well, these boots just got approved by the union, so they're the kind you have to have."

I knew better than to argue, so she wrote me up for the new boots, a pair of leather gloves, a black helmet, and a cylindrical aluminum lunch bucket. She showed me how the lunch bucket worked. The top part held the food, the bottom part the water. "You'll need work clothes if you don't have any," she continued, and then dragged out two pairs of khaki pants and shirts. She seemed to know my size. She wrote up the ticket. "Take it to the clerk," she ordered.

I looked at the amount. *Sixty-two dollars.* When I came outside, a huddle of miners sitting on the store steps saw me and what I was carrying and started singing:

> *You load Sixteen Tons, whadaya get?*
> *Another day older and deeper in debt*
> *Saint Peter don't you call me 'cause I can't go*
> *I owe my soul to the company store*

"You'll be sorry," Pick and Hub and the others chorused.

"Don't I know it," I muttered under my breath.

At the house, I went upstairs, put down my purchases, and sank down on my old bed. I looked around and it felt as if the room were condensing all around me. I had the sudden opinion that I was going to go crazy if I stayed there. But where could I go? Then I thought, *I'll call my mother, beg her to come and save me!* She will fix everything! Why, she'll probably even sock John Dubonnet in the nose for getting me into this mess!

But I knew I couldn't do it and it wouldn't help, even if I tried. When Mom found out what I'd done, she would be more likely to order me murdered than take up for me. She'd probably have Dad killed while she was at it. We were both in trouble with her, that much I knew. But that would show her what kind of trouble we were capable of without her, wouldn't it? *Maybe she'd even come home!* But my next thought was in the opposite direction. I was so thoroughly messing up, she would never come back, or want me with her in Myrtle Beach, either. Was it possible for me to make things any worse? Oh, yes, indeed. That I could always do, and so I did.

I looked out the window, toward the tipple, a wisp of vapor rising from the shaft, and gathered my courage. It was time to act like a man, even if I wasn't one. Bobby Likens's crack about me being a wimp was still digging at me. It was time to stand up and be counted, even if I didn't know all the numbers. *All right,* I thought, *I'm a miner, so I might as well live like one, too.* I gathered my few pitiful things in a cardboard box and marched out of the house and headed down Main Street. This time, nobody picked me up. It was as if the passing drivers knew this was a journey I had to make on my own.

I arrived at the Club House, climbed up the stone steps, and went into the high-ceilinged foyer. The breeze from opening and closing the door caused the massive crystal chandelier overhead to tinkle. The warm aroma of fried food filled the air. Mrs. Floretta Carbo, a stout colored lady, emerged from the kitchen. She was the Club House manager and I knew her fairly well. She was in the choir at the Mudhole Church of Distinct Christianity, the Reverend Julius "Little" Richard's church. When I told her why I was there, she gave me a hard look but didn't argue. "This way," she said, her hands in the pockets of her starched white apron.

She led me up the stairs to the third floor and then down a long, dark hall. She produced a key from her apron and opened one of the heavy oaken doors to reveal a small room with a white porcelain sink, a narrow bed with a thin mattress, a round wooden table, and two straight-backed wooden chairs. A small window looked out on the road between the Club House and the Community Church. Down the hall, she said, was the bathroom, which included a bathtub and a shower.

"Rent is twenty-six dollars a month," she said, "which includes breakfast and supper. Breakfast is served six to eight. Supper's six to seven. Give me your bucket and I'll pack your lunch for an extra dollar a day. Anytime you're here, you get hungry, the kitchen's yours. Leftovers will be in the fridge or on the counter beside the stove. I'll do your laundry, a dime for each piece unless it's a pair of coveralls, and they're a quarter. There's a laundry bag in the closet with your room number on it. Leave it in the foyer on your way out. I don't make up your room. Make your own bed every day and keep your room straight. I'll be leaving you clean sheets every Tuesday, put the old outside the door that morning. There's a broom, a mop, a vacuum cleaner, and some dust rags in the closet down the hall. That's it. You want the room?"

"I'll take it," I said.

"You want me to pack your lunch?"

"Yes, thank you."

She studied me, her hands gathered in her apron. "Do you know what you're doing?"

I fiddled with the hand mirror on the tiny table by the sink. "No, ma'am. I just know I'm doing it."

"You want me to tell you what I think?" When I shrugged, she said, "Quit now before you get hurt. I know that's what your mother would want. She and I have always been special friends, I mean as best we can, her being the mine superintendent's wife and all."

"She's always spoken highly of you," I said, which happened to be true.

"What do you weigh?" she demanded. "A hundred and forty pounds or so, I'll bet. Those jobs they do down there, they ain't easy. Takes some heft to do them." Her face clouded. "My mister was killed in the mine. His motor flipped and crushed him. Everywhere you look, there's some tight place where you can get a leg or an arm took off."

I knew she was right. "My Poppy—my granddad—got both his legs cut off in the mine," I said.

"There you go. You'd better quit. It's not hard. Just walk across the road and tell Carol DeHaven you made a mistake."

"I swore an oath to the union," I said, reflecting on how nearly everybody who gave me advice, from college deans to the Club House manager, was always after me to quit. Apparently, I was making a career out of being wrong.

Mrs. Carbo wasn't done. "The union won't protect you from falling slate and mountain bumps," she said.

"No, ma'am, I guess not. But I can't quit. I have to keep going." I started to tell her why and even had my mouth open to do it, but, unfortunately, I wasn't certain of the reason myself. It was all a mush.

She cocked her head and sighed. "You may call me Floretta," she said. "If you're going to be a working man, might as well call me like they do."

"Yes ma—Floretta. Thank you."

She gave me a long study, maybe thinking to give me more advice, but then she shook her head and led the way back downstairs. She handed over the guest registry and a chit for a month in advance and I signed them both, leaving me in debt to Coalwood for another twenty-six dollars not even counting future laundry and lunches. I had been in town for less than a week but I was on a roll, not all that difficult when you're headed downhill.

10

THE ENGINETTE

THE THIN blanket on my Club House bed had not been enough to keep me warm through the night, even in June. I had discovered the wind tended to whistle down Snakeroot Hollow after dark, flowing over the Club House like a giant natural air conditioner. I climbed out of bed, trembling in the predawn chill, and drew on my new uniform of khakis and hard-toe boots. The smell of eggs and bacon beckoned me downstairs. As I reached the bottom step, Floretta came out of the kitchen, carrying a silver tray with covered dishes and a steaming coffeepot.

She gave me a curt glance. "You better go eat, boy, and get on up the road. You don't want to be late your first day at work!" Then she continued down the hall to where I knew Dr. Hale, the company dentist, kept his residence. When I'd been a newspaper boy, I had gotten the opportunity to peer inside Dr. Hale's quarters when I'd gone to collect my fee. Compared to my spartan room, it was an ornately decorated palace.

In the main dining room I found two men waiting with

forks and knives in their hands, paper napkins tucked in at their necks. There was a look of quiet desperation on their faces. I knew them immediately for junior engineers, the pride of the steel mills and the scourge of Coalwood. Junior engineers were sent down to Coalwood by the Ohio steel company that owned us, to get some seasoning and maybe learn a little about coal mining. After they were done with their stint, usually lasting about six months, they went back to Ohio to learn how to squeeze dimes, or some-such. The two boys gave me a look, dismissed me as unworthy of their concern, and resumed their vigil. Floretta soon rewarded them by appearing with dishes of scrambled eggs, biscuits, and bacon balanced on her arms. She was apparently working alone. She set the plates down, then withdrew as they fell upon the food like starved wolves.

In a minute, maybe less, not a morsel was left, leaving me with a still-empty plate. I scraped back my chair and went into the kitchen, carrying my plate with me. Floretta was all arms and elbows. "I know, I know," she said. "Those boys would eat a dead cat if I put it out." She tossed in a three-inch-thick slab of bacon with one hand, then cracked a half-dozen eggs open with the other. In a couple of minutes, she loaded up my plate and sent me on my way.

I withdrew to the far end of the table. Floretta rushed in behind me, laden with more grub. After a round of snorting and belching and slugging back about a gallon of coffee between them, the young men took a moment to consider me. "Are you a new miner?" one of them asked. He was a twirpy-looking boy with short blond hair.

I considered him for a moment, then said "Yes," and left it at that. Even though they were older than me and college graduates, junior engineers never rated a "sir" from anybody in Coalwood, no matter how lowly that Coalwoodian was. Now that I thought about it, I guessed there wasn't anybody in Coalwood much lower than I was.

"First day at work?" the young man demanded.

I chewed my bacon. "Yes."

The other junior engineer, a skinny youth with slicked-back black hair and a pug nose, eyed me suspiciously. "What's your name, boy?"

"Homer Hickam," I said. It was technically the correct answer.

The two looked at each other. "My, how you've changed," the blond one said. "No, really, what is it?"

"What's yours?" I asked, swigging from a steaming mug of coffee that, even though I'd liberally diluted it with cream, was still the deepest and richest I'd ever drunk. I figured I'd be awake for at least a week. Its caffeine molecules were already swaggering through my veins.

"I'm Ned Bean," he said. He nodded toward his companion. "Victor Vance. We're engineers," he declared with some pride. "You'd be advised to be nice to us. We're management, you know. Now tell the truth. What's your name?"

I decided to give him a straight answer, just to be nice, not because I cared about them as "management" or in any other way. I knew the rugged life they were living while going through my dad's killer boot camp for engineers. It had sent more than one junior engineer scurrying back to Ohio with his tail well tucked. "I'm Sonny Hickam," I said. "Homer Hickam's son."

"Homer's boy?" Ned looked me over, then squinted suspiciously. "What position do you play?"

"I'm not the one who plays football," I replied with a sigh.

Victor scratched his head. "Homer Hickam has two sons? I never knew that."

I wasn't surprised. Everybody in the county and the state knew my famous football-playing brother. Although winning a gold and silver medal at the National Science Fair had given me some fame, it had been short-lived. "I'm the illegitimate son," I said to stir their pots. "I've come back to claim my inheritance."

Victor and Ned leaned forward. "What inheritance?" Victor wondered.

For some reason, I had always enjoyed taunting junior engineers. Maybe it was because they were so simple or maybe it was because I was. "You don't know about the Hickam family fortune?" I demanded.

"No!" they chorused.

I made an attempt to look mysterious and went back to eating my breakfast, chewing very slowly. Some junior engineers were a challenge, but Ned and Victor were about as dull as butter knives.

Floretta came back into the dining room, carrying four lunch buckets, one of which I recognized as mine by its fresh store-bought gleam. She set them down on the table, then eyed the grandfather clock across the way in the parlor. "You boys better hurry, especially you, Sonny."

I wondered who the fourth bucket was for, but then I heard someone coming down the stairs. When I looked to see who it was, there, to my amazement, dressed in standard junior engineer's clothes—khakis tucked into knee-high lace-up hard-toe boots—was none other than—a *girl.*

And what a girl! I stared at her, and maybe that was why she put her hands on her hips and stared back, her eyebrows raised. Her thick black hair was pulled back into a long braided pigtail. The way she stood there in her high boots, I couldn't help but think of Wonder Woman, the comic strip heroine who flew around in a glass airplane. The wide miner's belt at her small waist was pulled in tight, and it looked to me as if she had tailored her khakis to fit all her curves. I guess I was gaping because as Floretta swung by to hand the woman a cup of coffee, she said, "Hey, boy. Be careful you don't catch no flies."

I shut my mouth so hard my teeth clicked.

"Maybe he's never seen a girl engineer before, Rita," Victor said. "I mean an enginette, of course."

"Be careful, Victor," the girl said. "You're going to find your tail jerked up between your ears."

Victor grinned and went into a very bad Humphrey Bogart impression. "I'm yours anytime you want me, sh-weetheart."

"Victor," she said coldly, "you couldn't handle it. Trust me."

I kept trying to figure out what was plainly in view. I'd heard of women engineers, of course, even guessed there were plenty of them, but I never figured to see one in Coalwood. Just by being there, she was challenging one of the strongest of all coal-mining superstitions: A woman in a mine caused death, desolation, disaster, and destruction, and that was just for starters.

"You ready for your day at the office, girl?" Ned asked in a needling tone. He looked over at me and gave me a wink. "Rita works in the office, shuffling paper and whatnot."

"I do what they let me do, snot-for-brains," she retorted. "I'm working on the design of the new preparation plant. What are you doing? Following a foreman around and getting in his way, no doubt. *Very* important work."

Ned's lip went out. "At least I'm underground."

Floretta came out of the kitchen, saw what was happening, and put her hands on her hips. "You children still here? Sonny, I'm telling you—get to work! You can't be late the first day. You'd embarrass your daddy all to heck."

"Who's your daddy?" the girl-engineer wanted to know.

"He's Homer Hickam's son of a bitch," Victor said.

Ned rolled his eyes. "He's his *bastard,* you moron. A son of a bitch is somebody whose mother is a dog."

Victor looked confused, but then, after a moment of reflection, he blurted out, "Boy, around here, you learn something *every day!*"

Floretta glared at the two young men. "Sonny Hickam is nobody's nothing except he's the second son of Homer and Elsie Hickam what's home from college and has ended up working in the mine just like any common miner—only if he don't get his tailbone moving, he's going to be out of a job on his first day. Sonny, this is Miss Rita Walicki, who is ten times the engineer than these two put together, only she's a woman and that means she's trying to do something nobody in this old place is ever going to let her do. Miss Rita, Sonny. Sonny, Miss Rita. Now everybody get out of my Club House and get to work! Except you, Miss Rita. Got your breakfast ready, honey. Set yourself down."

"Miss Rita" gave me the hard eye. "If I could get past your father," she said, "I could go into the mine."

"Good luck" was all I knew to say, and so I said it. I hefted my bucket, the water sloshing in the lower pan.

She wasn't through with me. "Do you have something against female engineers, Sonny Hickam?"

"No, ma'am," I said. "I like women and I like engineers so I guess putting them together doesn't trouble me."

"Then how about putting a word in for me with your father?"

"I'd be the last one he'd listen to," I confessed. It was true, but what I didn't say was that I had no intention of helping her. My entire life, I'd heard about the evil of women in the mine. I didn't believe it, of course, but then again, maybe I did. Somebody said one man's superstition was another man's religion, and I think he was on to something.

I plopped on my helmet and tipped its brim to Miss Rita Walicki, but she had already turned toward the breakfast table. Victor and Ned were watching her walk, wicked grins on their faces. It was a walk that was indeed something to admire, but I had no time for it. I had taken the company scrip and it was time to earn it. I struck out for the mine.

11

MARCHING IN THE LINE

HOW MANY times had I watched the stream of men going to and from the mine? When Dad took the Captain's job and we moved into his house, I claimed an upstairs bedroom that gave me a clear view of the mine and its tipple. Every day, three shifts of men marched from their homes up the Coalwood hollows to the man-hoist and back home again. At night while I lay in bed, the sound of clumping boots, clunking lunch buckets, and the low note of voices during the exchange of the hoot-owl and evening shifts were a comfort. I figured as long as the men of Coalwood were going to work, all was well.

Now I was one of the men trudging up Main Street. I swung my bucket with each step, getting the feel of it, the water in the bottom of the tin sloshing and pulling at my arm. My helmet felt heavy and tight, so I stopped to adjust it. I loosened the band inside, then plopped it back aboard. That made it too loose, so I worked on it some more. Men passed me by, grinning and elbowing each other. "Supposed to wear that thing, boy, not diddle with it," I heard someone say, but he was swallowed in the line before I could look up to see who it was.

I passed the vacant house that had been Tuck Dillon's. Its windows were dark, its porch empty. There had been a time in Coalwood when a house wouldn't have been left vacant for more than a day. That had been when the company owned all of the houses. Now, I supposed, there were mortgage companies to deal with and that slowed things down.

At the Captain's house, Poteet came racing to the fence, her long red tongue wagging. Dandy waddled behind her, his nose in the air. I detoured to say hello, but at the sound of my voice Poteet started barking. The men going past me laughed. "We're going, Poteet!" one of them said.

Barking was Poteet's way of encouraging Coalwood's men to get to work so she could spend the day lounging around the yard. I guess she was giving me the same message. Dandy stood back, his head cocked as if puzzled, perhaps because the sound of my voice was coming from outside the fence. I ached to open the gate and give the old boy a pat, but I felt the pressure of the line going past, almost as if it were a strong current, so I rejoined it, going single file up the narrow path that led to the mine. Poteet kept barking us on our way. When I walked past Dad's office, Mr. Woody Marshall came out on the porch. "Hold up, Sonny," he said.

I'd always liked Mr. Marshall, an easygoing man when he wasn't worrying about the mine with Dad. I guess he liked me well enough, too, although I'd almost drowned his daughter Sue about ten years ago. Just as soon as I'd gotten *Huckleberry Finn* under my belt, I'd built a raft and floated it down the creek, managing to turn it over with Sue on board. She had taken turns laughing and crying all the way home. I had dearly hoped she'd be in one of her laughing turns when she made it back home, but no such luck. Mrs. Marshall gave me a well-deserved swat on the seat of my pants and then Mom added another later for good measure. I heard later Sue's brother Billy was considering beating me up, too, but he never did. He probably forgot.

"Get on over to the lamphouse, Sonny," Mr. Marshall said, "and collect your tag and your lamp. Then get with Richardson. He'll be your foreman today." When I nodded and started to go, Mr. Marshall held me by my sleeve. "I think you should know your daddy's going to cut you off after this shift."

I was astonished at the news. "What for?"

Mr. Marshall patted me on my back and nudged me in the direction of the lamphouse. "Because he wants to," he said.

I refused to be nudged. "Then why'd he let me get this far?" I demanded. "I know he had to sign off on my papers."

Mr. Marshall shrugged. "He said he wanted to see how far you'd go."

I looked at Dad's open office door and started to head toward it. I was being picked on, in my opinion, and I wanted to say it out loud. "He's not there," Mr. Marshall said patiently. "He's already gone inside."

I stopped, frustrated and angry. I felt like bouncing my bucket off his wall the way one of my rockets had done so long ago. "This isn't fair," I said, but even as I said it, I knew "fair" didn't matter, not at my father's mine.

"Just go get your day in," Mr. Marshall urged, "then it'll all be over."

When I wheeled around, I found Bobby Likens standing there. He was wearing a pair of blue jeans tucked into his boots and a gray sweatshirt. He had a battery pack on his belt and a lamp clipped to his helmet. He might have been dressed up like a miner, but he still looked like Joe College to me. "I guess I'd better help you," he said.

"I don't need your help," I snapped. I was pretty much mad at the world.

He acted like he didn't hear me. "Let's get you a lamp and a tag," he said. "I've already been through the drill."

"You'd better go on, Sonny," Mr. Marshall said, this time putting his hand firmly in my back and gently prodding me in the proper direction.

Still so mad I could spit, I followed Bobby to the lamphouse, a grubby brick building just up the hill from the shaft. Inside was a rude wooden counter, and behind it were rows of batteries and helmet lamps. The odor of quietly fusing electricity hung in the air. "Sonny needs a lamp, Mr. Filbert," Bobby said, and the clerk behind the counter went down the line until he found one fully charged. He handed it over, saying, "You got a tag, Sonny boy?"

I confessed I didn't, and he pointed at a big board hanging on the wall. It was painted black and had rows and columns of numbered hooks. "You're going to be number fifty-three," Mr. Filbert said. "You get two tags with that number. When you get your helmet lamp in the morning, I'll give you a tag and you should put it in your pocket. I'll hang the other number 53 on the board beside that number. When you come back out and turn your lamp in, give me your tag and I'll take the other one off the board."

"Can you remember that?" Bobby asked.

"I don't know," I snapped. "It's so complicated."

Bobby apparently didn't recognize wit when he heard it. "Well, try your best," he said fussily. "It's so a foreman can check the board and see who's in the mine. In case of an accident, they can identify you with the tag in your pocket. Do you understand?"

I didn't answer. I had just remembered again that I was going to get cut off. The more I thought about it, the madder I got. *Cut off!* I thought suddenly of Lonnie Huddle. His daddy had been killed, and then he and his mama and his sisters had been cut off without so much as a thank-you from my dad and the company. For the first time, I realized how much I hated those two words. *Cut off!* Not me, I swore. *Not me!*

Bobby gave me a once-over. "Look, Sonny, I'm just trying to help you out here," he said reasonably. "You and me, we've got to look out for each other, that's the way I see it. And since I'm older than you . . . well, I guess it's up to me to keep you straight."

I decided at that moment that Bobby Likens was really about the most arrogant fellow I'd ever known.

"I see you bought a new lamp belt," he said. "Why didn't you borrow an old one like I did?"

"I didn't buy it," I said. "I found it in the trash."

Bobby gave me a doubtful look and then showed me how to clip my battery pack on the belt and how to thread the power cord up through a loop on the back of my helmet. "I knew how to do that," I said, even though I didn't.

Mr. Richardson, a pleasant-faced man, called me out of the crowd of miners by the man-lift. I was delighted to see him, anything to get away from Bobby Likens. Bobby said, "See you later, Sonny."

I turned my back on him. *I hope not* was my thought.

Beside Mr. Richardson stood a slump-shouldered giant of a man. The smell of his sweaty clothes reached me before he did. "You know Big Jeb?" Mr. Richardson asked.

I sure did. How could I not? Big Jeb was famous for being the strongest man in town, white or colored. It was said he could hold up the mine roof with his back and had done it a few times, too. He was married, so I'd heard, to two women up Snakeroot Hollow, and had two sets of kids, too. Big Jeb was wearing a ragged coverall underneath a coal-caked denim jacket. It looked as if he'd worn those same clothes for the last decade. He stared at me, his tiny eyes puzzled. I supposed he was trying to figure out who I was.

"You'll go with Big Jeb today, Sonny," Mr. Richardson said. "Setting timbers, ain't you, Jeb?"

Big Jeb's eyes flicked toward Mr. Richardson and then came back to me. "Yes, sir," he said, his voice a rumble from somewhere about a mile deep.

"You take this boy with you, you understand? Go back to where you were yesterday on West Main D. The hoot-owl shift should have left you a pile of timbers and shims to work with."

Big Jeb's eyes never left me. "Yes, sir," he said with about as much enthusiasm as a bear coming out of hibernation.

"Good," Mr. Richardson said, and then he was off running, barking orders to various men. I looked around and found Bobby Likens watching me. A miner I didn't recognize came up beside Bobby, slapped him on the back, and said something. Bobby laughed, and then the two of them turned and got on the man-lift. Big Jeb grunted something, and I followed him to walk out onto the lift platform, too. A bell rang twice, and the big bullwheel on top of the man-hoist tower began to turn. Although my stomach stayed where it was, the rest of me began to drop down the shaft.

At the top of the page, partial text is faintly visible but largely illegible.

1 2

BIG JEB

AS THE lift dropped, I kept hearing a wheezing noise that sounded like a broken accordion. After a while, I realized it was coming from Big Jeb each time he breathed. Then Bobby started yammering, talking about college and how much he was looking forward to medical school. When he was asked, he allowed as how he made pretty much straight A's all the time. He also said this was the second time he'd ever been in the mine, the only other time being a field trip when he was in the ninth grade. I just wished he'd shut up. My knees were quivering, and they might have even knocked together a couple of times. It was a long way down that shaft. I'd been down it twice before, once with my dad, another time with my friend Jake Mosby. This time, maybe because I was coming as a miner, not a visitor, I was scared, and Bobby's chatter punctuated by Big Jeb's wheezes weren't helping me any.

When we reached the bottom, I started to get off the lift, but before I could do it, nearly every miner on it said: *"Turn your light on, boy!"* They seemed to get a lot of satisfaction out of saying it. Sheepishly, I turned the knob on my helmet lamp. Bobby came over and shined his light in my eyes. "Sonny, you've got to pay attention or you could get hurt down here."

"I can take care of myself," I muttered.

"You'd better."

I'd just about had enough of Bobby Likens. "What's it to you?" I demanded.

He kicked the dirt. "I guess I have to tell you. Your mother called the house last night and asked me to keep an eye on you."

"What?"

"Your mother called—"

"I heard you." So Mom knew what I'd done. That explained for sure why Dad was going to cut me off. Mom must have burned up the telephone line to him and then called the Likenses. But why hadn't she called me at the Club House? If she knew I'd signed up to go to work, surely she knew I'd taken a room, too. The more I thought about my parents and their incessant battles and intrigues and manipulations, and how they tended to use me like a kickball, the madder I got. I contemplated jumping on the lift and going straight back up, but the men going off shift beat me to it. It rose out of sight.

"Look, Sonny," Bobby said earnestly. "We're not together today, so try to keep yourself from getting killed. Your mother would have my hide if you did."

I glared at Bobby and then stomped off looking for Big Jeb. He was pretty easy to find, since his back was about as wide as the mine. When I saw him climb headfirst into a man-trip car, I climbed in next to him. Though the car was built for four men, it was a tight squeeze for just the two of us. Big Jeb opened his lunch bucket, withdrew the top part, and tipped the bottom to his lips, taking a deep gulp of water. He then let loose a wheeze so long that I wondered if it would ever end. Then, as soon as he had his bucket back together, he smacked his vast black lips and promptly fell asleep, each breath a rumble. Then I remembered I'd left my own lunch bucket in the lamphouse.

The man-trip lurched once, the wheels squealing, and we were off. No matter what else happened this day, I had sentenced myself to a shift without food or water.

At least I didn't have to be with Bobby Likens. I could imagine what he'd have to say about my forgotten bucket. It would have been just like him to offer to share his lunch with me, too. I started a long, slow mental burn, and pretty soon I'd managed to transfer the worst qualities of mankind over to Bobby Likens, the conceited med school, straight-A's creature that he was.

The man-trip rumbled on into the darkness, its wheels squealing and grinding every time it turned. I could smell the heat coming off its powerful electric motor. After a while, we stopped to let men get off, but Big Jeb kept sleeping. How was I supposed to know when we got to wherever we were going? If Big Jeb stayed asleep, maybe we'd keep going and going and . . .

I worked to get hold of myself. It was all so crazy. *What in God's good earth was I doing in the mine!* We were picking up speed, really flying now. Shapes flicked by, wooden timbers white with rock dust. The man-trip rattled and squealed and lurched. At any moment, I expected it to jump the track and roll over and smash us all. I sure didn't see how anybody could sleep aboard it, but Big Jeb never stirred.

A half hour or so farther down the track, we stopped again. My tailbone felt like somebody had just spent that half hour kicking it. I didn't know what to do, so I didn't do anything. Coach Mams back at Big Creek had once said, "It's better to do nothing than the wrong thing." At the time, I thought his advice made a lot of sense. I was always pretty capable of doing nothing. But as I sat in the darkness stuffed inside a steel cage with a man who was not only the size of a grizzly bear but pretty much smelled like one, too, I began to wonder if doing nothing might sometimes be the wrong thing, after all. Philosophy seemed to come easy to me inside a man-trip, especially since my mind was the only thing that could move.

The beam from a helmet light suddenly hit my eyes. "Big Jeb? Sonny? You awake? Come on out of there."

"Yes, sir," Big Jeb instantly answered. Ponderously, he swung his bulk to clamber out, pretty much crushing me against the man-trip cab. After he was out, I climbed out, too.

"Turn your light on, boy," the man-trip driver said.

I hadn't realized I'd turned it off, so I fiddled with my lamp until I got it working again. The driver pointed down the track. "Richardson said this is where the hoot-owl shift got last night. There's posts, shims, and crib lumber stacked in the gob."

"Yes, sir," Big Jeb rumbled, and limped off, his head down, one huge arm behind his back, the other carrying his bucket.

Since I had no bucket, I put both my hands behind my back and plunged after him. After two steps, I straightened my spine slightly and promptly slammed my helmet into the roof. I was knocked to my knees, stars doing a little pirouette around my head. When they stopped spinning, I also saw that my lamp had gone off again. Before I could get to the knob to fiddle with it, the man-trip driver came over and helped me up. "Boy, if you plan on raising the roof of this old mine, you'll need something harder than your head." Then he added, with undisguised glee, "And you need to turn your light on, too."

I pulled away from him and lurched on, still fiddling with my lamp. Big Jeb had disappeared somewhere in the darkness. I heard the man-trip locomotive behind me crank up and then the squeal of its wheels as it trundled away.

I had no idea where I was. After the noise of the man-trip faded, it became very quiet. I could feel a slight breeze in my face. I peered around with the feeble light from my lamp, trying to catch sight of Big Jeb. When I didn't spot him, I held my breath and listened until I heard a distant wheezing. I headed in the direction I thought it was coming from and pretty soon found Big Jeb sitting placidly on a pile of thick timbers. By their size, I knew them to be the posts that were used to hold up the mine roof. "Yes, sir," he said as I came up to him. I was beginning to wonder if he ever said anything else.

"What are we supposed to do, Big Jeb?" I asked, but he made no reply. Instead, he pried his lunch bucket open and sloshed some water into his mouth. Then he just sat there, breathing heavily. He was sick with the silicosis, I supposed. That was when gob, a mix of coal and rock dust, coated your lungs. The silicosis was not uncommon in Coalwood, but usually when you got it as bad as Big Jeb, you stopped working. Maybe because he had two families, he had to keep at it.

After a while I assumed we were waiting for something or somebody, so I took a seat up on the lumber stack with Big Jeb. Then, just as I got comfortable, he said, "Yes, sir," crawled heavily off, and went wandering into the dark. I saw him stoop, and then he came up with an ax in one hand and a sledgehammer in the other. He walked over to a timber supporting the roof, ran his hand over it, peered at its top, then dropped the ax and swung the hammer into the timber as hard as he could. It fell down with a heavy thump. I waited for a million tons of rocks to fall on top of us, but, to my utmost relief, nothing happened. Big Jeb ran his hand over the lumpy stone roof, threw down the hammer, walked over to a stack of posts, and picked one off the top. Then he waited, still wheezing. When he looked over in my direction, I got the message.

I took one end of the post with both hands. He eyed me, then started walking, holding his end of the post with a single hand. I followed behind, managing a kind of bent-kneed waddle. When we finally got to where we were going, I dropped my end and stood up to stretch my back, and bounced my head off the roof again. Big Jeb didn't say anything, just set the post into its place, then shuffled away into the darkness. Rubbing my head, I waited until he returned with a triangular-shaped piece of wood. He inserted it at the top of the post, then whacked it with the blunt end of the ax blade. The wedge tightened the post against the roof. "Yes, sir," Big Jeb said, and then lumbered back to the stack of posts and sat down again. When I clambered up beside him, he was drinking more water.

I wistfully eyed the cool liquid. After he finished, he wiped his mouth with the back of his hand and put the bucket away. We sat until I became restless. Big Jeb kept wheezing. It occurred to me that maybe he couldn't do very much without getting out of breath. "How about I try my hand at putting up one of those posts, Big Jeb?" I asked him. "You just tell me which one."

Big Jeb snorted, then scratched his chin languidly. "Yes, sir," he finally allowed, and after a moment more of staring into the dark, he stood up and lurched off toward the line of posts going down both sides of the track.

I grabbed a post and waited for him to help me with it. When he didn't, I dragged it after him. "I'm coming, Big Jeb," I called.

My idea to do most of the work was apparently one that appealed to Big Jeb. For the rest of the morning, he would go to a post, swing his sledgehammer, knock it loose, then wait until I got the new one in place. Then he'd tap in the wedge and wait while I carted the old post away and picked up a new one. I kept forgetting the low roof. Pretty soon, my head took on a dull, permanent ache.

I don't know how many posts we'd set before Big Jeb said "Yes, sir" again and lumbered back to his lunch bucket. He started pulling out sandwiches wrapped in heavy gray wax paper. I leaned against a rock-dusted wall and closed my eyes and just listened to Big Jeb grunt and wheeze and slosh and chew. Then there was a long silence and I opened one eye and found his light shining into it. I couldn't see his face for the glare, but when I peered closer, I saw an apple in his hand, being tendered in my direction. I snatched it lest he change his mind and never tasted an apple so sweet! Then I saw he was also holding out the bottom pan of his bucket to me. "Thank you," I said as I gulped the delicious wet water down my parched throat.

Big Jeb silently took his bucket back when I was finished, then hunkered down. Soon I heard him snoring, each exhalation a raw wheeze. I watched him until I felt a certain urge in my bladder and intestines.

I got up and staggered back into the gob. There were no bathrooms in the mine. I knew that much. You had to find whatever place you could that was out of the way. I wandered on, turning this corner and then that one until I felt as if I had reached a place decently far away.

Just as I finished my business, my helmet lamp faded, then went off altogether. My heart knotted. I was immersed in a darkness so black that I could almost feel the pupils in my eyes stretch as they tried to find some light.

I fiddled with the knob on my lamp, but nothing I did seemed to work. I took a step, waving my hands in front of me. Then I took another step and another until I touched the cool, dusty surface of a wall. I didn't know which way to go. My heart started racing. I was lost for all time! Not only that, I was *hungry* and *tired* and *my head hurt* and soon, I thought, I'd be adding *dead* to that list. *Lost!*

I started yelling. "Big Jeb! My light's out! I'm lost!" The pitch of my voice started to rise. "Big Jeb!" I shrieked.

I listened, but I heard not so much as a sound, not even a scurrying rat, which, now that I thought about it, were supposed to be in the mine to the tune of about a million.

Would they be after me next? I started to sweat, a trickle of it wandering down my cheek and startling me into slapping myself.

My cheek still stinging, I decided I'd better give myself a little pep talk. I could figure my way out. All I had to do was think like an engineer and put two and two together and see if I didn't get four. I felt the movement of a whiff of air across my sweaty face. What did I know about the mine? For one thing, the giant fans on the surface pushed air down a multitude of shafts and kept the mine slightly above atmospheric pressure. I'd picked that much up just listening to Dad yell into the black phone over the years. Would they even bother to ventilate an old shut-down section of the mine? I doubted it. What I needed to do was move toward active air. That would be in the direction of the main line. That was my theory, anyway. I turned slowly, sensing the faint pressure of the air brushing my damp face. I kept turning. It was subtle, but I was pretty certain there was more air on my face in one direction than any other.

I walked slowly toward the air, stopping every so often to call out Big Jeb's name. Finally, my aching eyes picked up an atom of light. Then I saw another one, and then a flash that lasted a fraction of a second. "Big Jeb!" I yelled.

"Yes, sir," I heard him say, then I saw his massive shape coming at me. I'd never seen a more welcome sight.

"My light's dead," I said, my voice trembling.

Big Jeb slowly made his way to me, then, without warning, slapped the side of my helmet. He almost knocked me down, but my lamp came back on brighter than ever before. "Thank you, Big Jeb," I said, even though my ears were ringing. He said nothing, just continued past me. I guessed he was going to do his business. I went back to the pile of posts and collapsed on top of them. Oh, I was having a fine day.

When Big Jeb returned, we went back to work and kept

up the same routine all day. By the time the man-trip showed up, I was pretty much worn out. All I could do was thank the good Lord my dad was going to cut me off. I wanted nothing more to do with mining coal, even though, technically, I hadn't actually mined so much as a lump. I got on the man-lift and looked up the shaft. There was light up there somewhere. I allowed myself a little smile as we started to rise toward it.

My career as a coal miner was over, and that was fine by me.

1 3

CUT OFF

WHEN I stepped onto blessed open ground, Mr. Filbert, the lamp man, waved at me from his lamphouse. "Hey, Sonny, come on over here."

I didn't know what he wanted, but I had to turn in my lamp and give up my tag for the first and last time, anyway. Mr. Filbert led me to a wooden powder box in a dark corner. "Back here's the lost-and-found box," he said. "See anything in there you lost?" He was having trouble holding back his outright laughter.

Silently, I retrieved my bucket.

"Guess you got mighty hungry," he said, still laughing up his sleeve.

"Not a bit of it," I said. "I'm on a diet."

I headed outside, where, to my surprise, Big Jeb was waiting for me. "What is it, Big Jeb?" I asked.

"Yes, sir," he said, and fell in beside me.

"I'm supposed to go see my dad," I explained.

Big Jeb shrugged heavily and kept walking with me. At Dad's office, he sat down on the steps. "I'll be right out," I told him, since it looked like he was bound and determined to stay with me. He raised a hand and wheezed while nodding his head.

Wally glanced up as I came inside his anteroom. "Go on in," he said.

Dad was at his desk. At my knock, he waved me inside. "Shut the door," he said ominously.

I did as I was told. Dad got up and sat on the front edge of his desk. "All right, Sonny," he said tiredly. "You and John Dubonnet have had your fun but it's over. I want you to quit."

"Quit? I thought you were going to cut me off," I said.

Dad crossed his arms. "Sonny, I've got a problem. I want you to help me with it."

"Okay," I said, but I was instantly on my guard.

"I can't afford to train a couple of college boys just to have them leave in a few months. You understand what I'm saying? That means the only jobs you and Bobby Likens are going to get are the absolute worst and dirtiest ones in this mine. Why do you think Dubonnet agreed to this in the first place? It's because his union members don't want to do those jobs."

"Then why don't you just cut me off?" I asked.

His blue eyes went hard. "Because you're a union member!" He shook his head as if he hadn't yet quite grasped the concept. "If you quit, Dubonnet won't be able to say anything. So that's what you have to do."

"What about Bobby Likens?" I wondered. "Did you tell him he had to quit, too?"

"Yes. He just left."

"What did he say?"

Dad looked grim. "He said he needed the job. He didn't care if it meant he had to shovel gob twenty-four hours a day, he wasn't going to quit."

"Then I'm not quitting, either," I said.

"Bobby's parents can't pay his way through med

school," Dad said, his voice calm although I noticed his fingers tighten on the edge of the desk. "But you—you're on the gravy train. I pay every penny of your college tuition, your books, your uniforms, everything. You don't need this job."

I didn't have a good answer to that and he knew it. All I could say is what I said. "I'm not quitting." Then I thought—*Damn! That felt good!*

Dad glowered, and his voice tightened. "All right. Let's do it this way. You want to keep going to college? Quit, or you'll never see another dime from me."

My dander was totally up. For the first time in the entire history of my life, I was going toe-to-toe with my dad. "I don't care what you do," I said. "I'm not quitting. And if you give me trouble about it, I'll run to the union."

Dad's eyebrows went up so high I thought they were going to bounce off the ceiling. "You're just like your mother!" he sputtered. "If I see you at work tomorrow, you'll get no more money for college—ever. That's the deal. Take it or leave it."

"Well, I leave it, then," I said. My heart was pounding so hard, I thought it was going to leap right out of my throat.

Dad blinked, then took a sudden interest in the map of the mine that covered one side of his wall. "Get out," he said.

I had the sudden sense I'd embarrassed him. Wally was listening, even through the closed door. Everything we'd said would be all over Coalwood in a matter of minutes. "Dad—"

"You heard me."

I closed the office door behind me. Wally just stared. Big Jeb stood up as I came outside. "Yes, sir," he said.

Big Jeb and I marched side by side down Main Street. I felt weak-kneed and foggy-brained. Not only did my head hurt, every muscle in my body felt like it had been twisted into knots. It felt like I had blisters on my feet, too.

Between jolts of pain, it occurred to me that I had managed to get myself cut off, not from the mine but from college. What had I done?

At the Club House, I stopped at the steps. To my astonishment, Big Jeb put a huge paw on my shoulder. I winced, my shoulder a wad of cramped muscles. "You done good," he rumbled.

Startled, I gulped, "Thank you, Big Jeb."

His lips turned up in a smile and his tiny eyes fairly glowed. "You done *real* good."

Then Big Jeb removed his giant hand from my shoulder and, wheezing, lumbered on down the road. As I watched him go, it occurred to me Big Jeb was about as eloquent a man as I'd ever had the privilege to know.

1 4

WHUPPED

WHEN I entered the Club House, I found Floretta waiting for me. "You look like you're whupped," she said.

The grimace on my face probably told her I was in full agreement.

"Tell me what hurts."

"Everything."

She chuckled. "I think some of my special liniment might fix you up. Get on upstairs and take your shower. There's Lava soap in there. Scrub good around your eyes. We don't want you looking like Cleopatra."

I limped toward the stairs. "These new boots pretty much rubbed my feet raw."

"I got some salve for that, too. Go on with you, and I'll be right up."

I shuffled to the bathroom and sat down on a stool by the shower. I practically had to screw off my boots. There were two nice blisters on each of my feet, one on the heel, the other on my instep. I stripped off my sweaty, filthy clothes, perched my glasses on the window ledge, and climbed in.

The hot water beat on my back. I'd never felt anything quite so wonderful. I slid down to the tile floor and just let the water wash over me. When I started to feel a bit better, I crawled to my feet and got the Lava soap and started scrubbing. Lava soap, made of volcanic grit and beach sand, could peel a layer of hide right off you, but it did its job.

When I finished, I wrapped a towel around my waist and tottered to my room, falling facefirst on my bed. A little later, I heard a tapping on my door and Floretta came in without me saying anything. She was carrying a glass jar and a round tin can. When she opened the jar, the smell of whatever was in it burned my nose all the way across the room. "What is that?" I asked suspiciously.

"Floretta's Special Club House Muscle Liniment," she replied.

"What's in it?"

"Pine resin, mutton tallow, ginseng, pale bergamot, Gilean buds, pennyroyal, and John Eye's joy juice," she recited. "Along with a good dose of camphorphe'nique."

"Is it going to hurt?"

"Let's find out." Her tone was gleeful. She stripped my towel away. When I started to complain, she said, "I seen you when you was a baby and I still ain't interested."

I was too sore to argue. She dripped the liquid on my back and started kneading muscles. I yelped when she found knots and gave them a special squeeze. Her liniment burned like acid and I said so.

"That means it's working," she said, kneading even harder. "So did you get cut off?"

"Only from college."

She stopped her battering. "What are you talking about?"

I told her the whole thing, and she started to squeeze my muscles again, this time even harder. "I swan, you

Hickams! Sometimes you say things that don't mean nothing to nobody nohow. I can understand your daddy—he's been known to get puffed up now and again, but you, I figure you'd do some better."

"I'm sorry," I grunted. I didn't know why she was so mad.

She huffed, then seemed to subside. "How'd you like working with Big Jeb?"

"I never had so much fun." Then I asked, "Is it true he has two wives?"

"Big Jeb's business is colored folks' business," she said.

"But you talk about *me* all the time," I said. "Isn't that white folks' business?"

"Some roads go only one way."

"That's not fair."

"Who are you to say what's fair or not? Be careful or I'll slap you silly."

"I don't think I'd feel it right now," I confessed.

Floretta finished her kneading and put the cap back on the bottle of the foul-smelling liquid. Then she applied some salve from the tin on my foot blisters. It felt wonderful.

"What's that?" I asked.

"Possum grease."

"Really?"

She chuckled. "Why do you care as long as it works?"

"I was born curious," I answered.

"Curiosity killed the cat," she said.

"And the possum, too," I quipped.

She finished layering on the salve and pushed the top back on the tin. "That'll do you," she said. "I'll bring up a food tray later."

"You don't want me to come to the dining room?"

"The way you stink? I don't think so!" She laughed herself out of the room.

I WOKE the next morning to the shrill rattle of the alarm clock on my bedside table. It sounded like a giant metal hornet. I flailed at the thing and knocked it off the table, where it bounced once and happily kept ringing. I threw my blanket down to smother it. The little key in the back of the clock must have gotten tangled because it produced a strangled little *bing* and—thank the good Lord—stopped.

I waited until my heart stopped pounding, then eased my legs around to sit on the edge of the bed. I took stock of my body. It felt like somebody had spent the night hitting me with a board. I wrapped a towel around my waist and lurched into the hall, my thighs screaming bloody murder. My head also hurt and my feet announced they still had their blisters, too.

When I returned to my room, I found my work clothes, all washed and nicely pressed, beside the door. I was too stiff to pick them up, so I opened the door and kicked them inside. After much grunting and groaning, I managed to get myself dressed. Limping, my blisters complaining as they rubbed against my boots, I went slowly downstairs. I entered the dining room just as Floretta came in from the kitchen with a huge plate of steaming eggs, bacon, toast, and hashed potatoes. She set it down in front of Ned and Victor, who, surprisingly, just stared at it. "Did my liniment help?" she asked me.

"I don't know."

She frowned. "It takes a while to get the kinks out sometimes."

"I think I got more than kinks," I groaned as I eased myself into a chair. The junior engineers just stared straight ahead, their faces kind of green-hued. "What's with them?" I asked her.

She huffed. "Got themselves drunk as mules last night. I put them to bed myself. You boys need to stay away from that John Eye liquor, you hear?"

Ned and Victor nodded sadly, then both of them grabbed their mouths and rushed out of the room. I watched them go and then forgot about them. I had my own problems. I dug into breakfast. At least my appetite was alive and well.

After I'd finished off my second plate and was working on my third, I was surprised when the enginette—Rita—arrived and pulled up a chair opposite me. She leaned her elbows on the table and gave me a sweet smile. "Are you going to talk to your dad about me going inside the mine?" she asked, her tone as sweet as her smile.

"It wouldn't do any good," I answered.

Her smile faded. "Why not?"

I shrugged, or attempted to. It hurt too much for the full thing.

Her eyes narrowed. "Is it true you used to build rockets?"

"Yes."

"I'd love to see one fly," she said.

"You're a year too late," I replied, grimacing as a muscle in my back announced that it was still peeved about yesterday.

Floretta appeared, carrying a coffeepot. "You be eating with this old coal miner, honey?"

Rita shook her head. "He's a bit too grumpy for me. I think I might have liked him better when he was a rocket boy."

"Honey, everybody liked him better then," Floretta said. "He was a boy knew how to be a boy. Now he's a man don't know how to be one. That's why he's all grumped up."

Rita said, "I'll have my breakfast at my table, Floretta, thank you."

She went over to a corner table where I saw there was a rose in a vase. She got a cloth napkin, too. We at the junior engineer table got paper ones.

I kept eating. I just couldn't get enough food in me fast enough. When I was on my fourth plate, none other than Mr. John Dubonnet appeared and sat down opposite me. Maybe, I thought, I should start charging admission for the chair. "How'd yesterday go?" he asked.

"I was born to be a coal miner," I said.

My attempt at humor eluded him. "Sonny, I'm going to put my cards on the table." When he caught me looking, he said, "I don't mean literally." He twisted his lips over to one side, then drummed his long fingers. He was having trouble saying what he was about to say, whatever it was. "You see, it's like this. Your mother called the other day, said she wanted you to stay in Coalwood for a while, that you and your daddy needed to have some time together. She asked my advice and I told her to leave it to me, I'd see what I could do about keeping you here. Then you rolled your daddy's Buick and I struck upon the idea of offering you a job in the mine to pay for the damage. What better way to keep you in Coalwood? That was my thinking, anyhow. But I made the mistake of not telling your mom about it. I guess I can get too clever by half if I'm not careful. It's a trait you and I tend to share. Your mother nearly wore my ear out about it last night, and said I needed to get it straight. So I called your father and we agreed to let you quit, if that was what you wanted."

Of all the things he'd just said, only one seemed incredible. "You and my dad agreed on something?"

He took off his hat and laid it on the table. "All I agreed to was that I wouldn't fight it." He shook his head. "Lord knows I was a fool for getting mixed up with you Hickams."

I had to agree with him on that one. "I'm not quitting," I said, but even as I said it, I thought, *What a strange beast am I!* There was nothing I really wanted more than to get out of that old coal mine.

Mr. Dubonnet looked pleased. "Well, I have to say I'm glad to hear it," he said. "It's good for a boy to mine a little coal sometime in his life. There's a lot to learn down there. But what are you going to use for college money? Your dad said he was serious about cutting you off from it."

Again, I tried to shrug but ended up wincing instead. "I'm making good money in the mine. I'll use that."

"It won't be enough," he said. "Not even three months of work will cover a year of tuition, books, and all that. Homer's not done you any favors on this one, Sonny boy."

A question just popped out of me and it surprised me as much as it did Mr. Dubonnet. "Mr. Dubonnet, why do you hate my dad so much?"

Although I could tell I had startled him, his answer back was immediate, as if he was used to answering it. "I don't hate him. I just don't like him. There's a big difference."

"Still, I guess you'll be plenty glad if he loses his job over Tuck Dillon," I said.

His eyebrows plunged. "I don't like any man to lose his job!" he snapped.

I guess I looked taken aback, because Mr. Dubonnet's expression softened. He leaned in. "Sonny, does the name Amos Fuller ring a bell with you?"

"Talks like a machine gun and has a personality to match?"

"That would be him."

"Sure. He was the man the steel company sent down to sell off the houses. He even tried to put the rocket boys out of business while he was at it. Dad took up for us on that one."

Mr. Dubonnet nodded. "Fuller's the steel company's hatchet man. Whenever they've got something nasty to be done, he's their man to do it." His hand went to his hat and he stood up. "Fuller's been put in charge of the Tuck

Dillon investigation. He should be here any day. Thought you should know. I've already told your mom."

"What did she say?"

Mr. Dubonnet plopped on his old hat, running his fingers over the brim. "She had a few things to say, but I guess I'll keep them to myself."

His answer was no surprise. My mom was one for secrets and intrigues. "Can you help Dad, Mr. Dubonnet?"

He shook his head. "This is one I can't touch, Sonny," he said. "For a couple of reasons." When he saw me open my mouth to ask what reasons those might be, he said, "Coalwood business, son. I'm sorry."

After he left, I was just starting to contemplate Mr. Dubonnet's latest round of information—and lack of same—when Floretta came in from the kitchen to hurry me along to work.

"Floretta," I asked, "have you reserved a room for Mr. Fuller? He works for the steel company."

"I know who that rascal is," she answered, making an ugly face. "He'll be here next Sunday."

"He's coming to destroy Dad," I said grimly.

"That may be, Sonny," she replied, filling my hand with my lunch bucket and aiming me out the door. "But there's not a thing you can do about it. Go on. And this time remember to take your bucket inside with you!"

"Okay, Mom," I said, which seemed to give her some pleasure. She responded with a soft chuckle.

I WAS back in the line of men heading up the valley when I noticed a woman standing in the front yard of one of the smaller houses along Main Street. It was Mrs. Nate Dooley, the wife of Coalwood's secret man. She was wearing a pink robe, and was leaning on her fence, her hand languidly holding a cigarette between two upraised fingers. Blue and pink hair curlers covered her head. She lifted her thin, pale face at the sight of me. "Sonny Hickam," she called. "Come here."

I went to the fence. "Yes, ma'am?" I could smell the chemicals, sharp and bitter, on her hair.

"Where are you going?"

"To work, ma'am."

Mrs. Dooley frowned and took a puff on her cigarette, then threw it down and stepped on it with a pink bedroom slipper. "Next couple of days, come by the house. It's time for Nate's bath."

"Ma'am?"

"Are you deaf? I need help with Mr. Dooley's bath."

"How is he?" I asked stupidly.

She raised her eyebrows. "Dirty. That's why he needs a bath."

"I mean his wrist."

Her pale blue eyes rested on me. "It's better," she said at length.

"How did it happen?" I thought to at least get a report for Mom. Our next conversation, I figured, was going to be a knockdown, drag-out affair about me working in the mine, and maybe I could get her talking about Mr. Dooley instead. It was a slim hope but a hope nonetheless.

"What do you mean?" Mrs. Dooley asked.

"Did he fall?"

"No, he didn't fall."

"What then? I asked Doc Lassiter, but he said he didn't put on the cast. Who did?"

She shrugged and pushed back from the fence. "Come Saturday noon," she said. Then she went up on her porch, opened her front door, and went inside.

I puzzled after her for a bit and then fell back into line. As I neared the Coalwood School, I heard what sounded like somebody running in their boots thudding behind me. When I turned, I was surprised to see it was Rita Walicki, the enginette. She was carrying a canvas bag slung over her shoulder. She slowed to a walk. "Got to deliver some drawings to the tipple," she said, taking in a quick breath. "Mind if I walk with you?"

I didn't mind one bit. "Did you run all the way from the engineering office?"

"Sure. I like to stay in shape."

"You look like you're already in great shape to me!" I blurted out.

She laughed, and I noticed anew that she had a wonderful smile. "Thanks. I ran the mile in college. Held the women's collegiate track record for a couple of months."

I started to tell her I had been on the track team, too. Intramurals. I'd come in third place in the hundred-yard dash. Of course, there'd only been four runners in the race, so I had second thoughts about telling it.

We walked along. "How long have you lived in Coalwood?" she asked.

"All my life," I said, "not counting this past year in college."

She looked past me, to an abandoned house on School Mountain. All the glass had been busted out of its front windows and its porch sagged. "Who used to live in that house?" she asked.

I considered saying I didn't know. It was a sad story, and I'd had a part in it right before the last Christmas I'd spent as a Coalwood boy. But she seemed genuinely interested, so I gave her a condensed version of the story. A man named Cuke Snoddy had once lived there with a young unmarried woman. Dreama was her name. Because she was living with a man out of wedlock, and also because she was from Gary, most of the townspeople had rejected her as unworthy. Dreama wanted, more than anything in the world, to be a Coalwood girl, and, as it turned out, she'd gotten her wish.

She was now a resident of our town forever, the only white woman buried in the colored cemetery on the mountain behind the Mudhole Church of Distinct Christianity. Cuke Snoddy had murdered her. "Coalwood has its ways." I shrugged as I wrapped up the story.

"It sure does," she said. "For one thing, there seems to be a history of mistreating women around here."

I glanced at her. "I don't know about that. Women pretty much run Coalwood. The teachers tell everybody what to do, for one thing, and the wives keep their husbands on a short leash, for another."

"Sure," she replied bitterly, "as long as they stay teachers and wives. But you let one of them try to break out of that mold, and see what happens."

I didn't know what to say to that, so I fell silent. So did Rita. After a moment more of walking, she said, "How about taking me for a hike?" She nodded toward the mountains. "I've been thinking about going up there and having a look around but I'm not sure where I'd go. How about it? Floretta told me you know these hills better than just about anybody."

I considered her offer and couldn't find anything wrong with it. As long as I was stuck in Coalwood, I might as well do it in good style, especially with such pretty company. "We'll see," I said, but I was actually already thinking about where we'd go.

At the tipple, I pointed at the little machine shop. "You asked me about my rockets. That's where we first built them. A man by the name of Mr. Bykovski lost his job helping us."

Rita seemed interested, so I told her the rest of the story, how Mr. Bykovski had been banished to the mine after Dad had discovered what he'd done. "But Mr. Bykovski said he didn't mind. Helping us was the right thing to do."

"Does he still work here?" Rita asked.

"He was killed," I answered. "A mountain bump." There was a lot more to it, but I had settled that tragedy in my mind and didn't want to go any further. Mr. Bykovski's death had nearly made me stop building rockets, and nearly driven me to quit studying in school. Only Miss Riley had been able to pull me out of my dive to personal destruction. When I'd seen her in Welch, she'd reminded me of what she'd said then, that when I had a job to do, it didn't matter whether I wanted to do it or not. That was when a thought popped into my head. Maybe my real job this summer was to help my dad, even if he didn't want it! Mom had said I was supposed to keep him company, but that had never been a serious possibility, considering our history. How to help him, though, completely eluded me, except to be curious and find out all I could. *That* I could always do!

At the tipple office, Rita gave me a wave and went up the steps and inside. I watched after her. "You going to work?" Hub Alger asked as he went past. "Or are you going to just stand there and wait for that girl to come back out?"

"I know which one I'd do!" Pick Hylton crowed. There was general laughter from the crowd of miners streaming past. I was beginning to wonder what Coalwoodians did for laughs before I'd come back to town.

15

THE KETTLE BOTTOM

MR. RICHARDSON, a big chaw swelling his cheek, was waiting for me at the lamphouse. "You're not working for me today, Sonny. You're with Johnny Basso."

"What about Big Jeb?" I asked.

He spat a stream of tobacco juice into the gob. "Big Jeb has a quota of posts he has to change out every week. It's his lungs, you know. He can only do so much. He got a week's worth done yesterday. I don't know how he did it, what with you slowing him down."

"Big Jeb is a true whirlwind," I said.

He wrinkled up his nose. "What's that smell?"

"Floretta's special liniment," I confessed.

"I've heard it works if you can stand it," he said, moving upwind.

I set about finding Mr. Basso. He and his missus—Goldie was her name—lived up on Substation Row in one of the duplex houses above the Little Store. When we'd lived in our old house across from the Substation, he was one of the line of men who used to walk past our yard to and from the mine. Sometimes, he'd stop and ask me what I was do-ing, and I'd often confess to be acting out some scene in a book I'd read. I had a clear memory of telling him one time when I was about eight years old that I was Jesse James, and Roy Lee Cooke was my brother Frank, and we were trying to figure out how to rob the Big Store. Another miner, Bato Patsy, had joined us at the fence and we'd all put our heads together on the plot. As best I could recall, we decided we needed horses, which slowed our life as criminals down considerably.

Some years back, the Bassos had adopted a boy, the only adopted child, as far as I knew, who lived in Coalwood. It had prompted a lot of gossip across the fence-line as to why it had been necessary for them to go to an orphanage for a child. Mom said Cleo Mallett had been the one who'd started tongues wagging about it, and that she might've served Coalwood better had she visited the orphanage for her children, too. Since her boys tended to beat me up, I agreed.

Mr. Basso had also been one of our assistant scoutmas-ters. At the meetings, he liked to talk mostly about the gar-den he'd planted on the side of Sis's Mountain. Apparently, he was a pretty good farmer. During the summer, he'd swing by our house once or twice to offer Mom his surplus tomatoes, cucumbers, and peppers. She usually took him up on it, and though she always invited him in for coffee, he'd usually tip his hat and say he had other deliveries to make. Only once that I knew of had he come inside, and then only to admire Mom's famous unfinished mural of Myrtle Beach. Chipper had bit him twice before he'd taken three steps inside the kitchen.

I spotted Mr. Basso, all alone near the shaft. With his wide Italian face, majestic nose, and paunch that lapped over his battery belt, he reminded me of Vince Lombardi, the famous coach of the Green Bay Packers. I went up to him and said, "Hey, Mr. Basso," and then, "I'm supposed to work with you today."

He looked me over and said, "Sonny, how do." He didn't sound very enthusiastic. I could smell hot peppers on his breath. I saw that he was reading a small Bible, which he tucked away in his hip pocket.

A lot of coal miners were deeply religious, some of them "Holy Rollers," who thought it took wrestling with the Devil every day to get into heaven. I'd heard Mr. Basso was one of these.

Bobby Likens walked up. His helmet was shoved cockily on the back of his head as if he were the most experienced miner on the tipple grounds. "You smell like a locker room," he said to me.

I ignored him. "Where are we going, Mr. Basso?"

"East Main D," he said, and then, "Call me Johnny. I ain't no foreman." The man-lift warning bell rang and he walked onto the lift, fiddling with a sawed-off piece of broomstick he pulled from his belt. "It's a roof thumper," he said when Bobby asked him what it was for. "I can check on the rock over our heads with it. Good or bad, this old stick will tell its tale."

I merged into the men getting aboard the man-lift. The wooden floor rang hollowly under our boots. Beneath us was seven hundred feet of nothing. We were halfway down the shaft when Johnny turned to me and said, "Turn your light on." While I hastily fumbled with the switch, he went on to say we were going to change out posts all day.

"That's what Big Jeb and I did yesterday," I said.

"I got a tour of the mine," Bobby volunteered.

"I hope you didn't wear yourself out," I said caustically.

"I'll try to keep up with you today," he replied.

I stared at him. "You're going with us?"

"Sure am," he sang.

Mom's designated nursemaid was going to be watching after me every minute. "Wonderful," I grumped.

After we climbed aboard the man-trip, Johnny apparently got his first whiff of me. "Floretta's liniment?" he asked, and then nodded gravely when I replied in the affirmative. "Stuff stinks but it works, I swan."

It took about twenty minutes for us to get where we were going. Bobby turned out his lamp and lowered his head. Johnny kept his on to read his Bible. When the man-trip ground to a stop, he tucked the little book back into his pocket and hopped out and took off down a dark tunnel like somebody was chasing him. Bobby charged after him and I was close behind. Before we'd gone three steps, Bobby's helmet hit the roof, the familiar *pop* of plastic on rock, and he fell backward, causing me to trip over him. It took a few seconds to get ourselves untangled. We might have said a few curse words in the process, I shouldn't wonder. Johnny loped back and spotted us with his light. "Don't ever take the Lord's name in vain, especially in the mine," he said angrily. "It's terrible bad luck." Then he took off again, the spot of his light bouncing and weaving. Bobby and I scrambled to our feet and did our best to keep up. Finally, he stopped. "You boys get over here!"

Panting, we gathered around him while he patted a post. "Looky here. This post's rotten. See how it's splintered at the top?" He rapped on it with his knuckles. "Hear that? It sounds hollow because there's holes all through it. There's a bunch of posts on this section that are just like this one. We're going to find and change out every one of them today. But first, we'll say our prayers."

Johnny sank to his knees and turned out his lamp, lowered his head, then started mumbling something I couldn't hear. Then he looked up abruptly, saw Bobby and me staring at him, and said, "Turn off your lamps and get down on your knees."

"I don't believe in showing off my religion," Bobby said smartly.

Johnny glared at us and said, "Boys, there are only two things that are going to keep you alive in this coal mine. Me, and the tolerance of God."

I couldn't resist showing Bobby up. I went down on my knees and pressed my hands together. "Amen!" I said after pretending to fervently pray for a couple of seconds.

Bobby switched off his lamp and went down on one knee and said, "God is great, God is good, let us thank Him for our food."

"That's a supper prayer," I said.

Bobby stood up, smacked his helmet against the roof, and was knocked back to his knees. I laughed out loud. "I tried to tell you," Johnny said. "Tempt not thy Lord."

I carefully rose, wedging my helmet against the rock ceiling. "Here's how you stand up in the mine, Bobby," I instructed merrily. He was almost as much fun to mess with as a junior engineer.

Bobby got up slowly, then bent over and rubbed his head. He'd really cracked it.

"All right, boys, let's get to work," Johnny said.

I quickly discovered that what Johnny considered work was going as hard and fast as possible and then a little harder and faster on top of that. We quickly fell into a routine. Johnny would knock down a bad post and Bobby and I would manhandle a new one into place. Then he'd shim the new one while Bobby and I hauled the old one back to the rising stack of discards. The whole time, Johnny kept yelling at us to hurry up or spouting a sermon about how we'd better learn to listen to the Lord and how the Lord God Jesus should be in our every thought. I didn't know about Bobby, but I was having trouble thinking of much of anything past keeping my head low and trying to catch a breath.

"I wonder if he handles snakes in that church of his," Bobby said grumpily.

"He'd probably yell at it to bite him faster," I replied, and Bobby and I shared a laugh, the first one together. I was starting to think he wasn't such a bad old boy, after all, even if he pretended to be my nursemaid way too often.

When Johnny saw that Bobby and I had thrown the old rotted posts into a pile, he demanded that they be stacked into a nice square.

"How come, Johnny?" Bobby argued. "They're just going to get hauled away."

"Dwight Strong likes to keep his section neat as a pin," Johnny said. "And so do I."

"But it doesn't make any sense," Bobby said, his back bowed beneath a piece of low rock.

"It does to me," Johnny replied with narrowed eyes.

As the day wore on, I would occasionally allow myself a little moan. "What's wrong with you?" Bobby finally demanded.

"I'm sore and I've got blisters on my feet."

"You want me to look at them?"

"Are you a doctor?"

"Not yet."

"Then I don't want you to look at them."

"You really need to change your attitude," he said.

"Work, boys! No talking!" Johnny bawled.

"We weren't talking," I said. "We were arguing."

"About what?"

"Sonny's bad attitude," Bobby said.

Johnny worked his way over to us and squatted, the first time all day that he'd stopped. "Sonny, Olga Coal pays us to work. Do you understand that?" I opened my mouth to protest, mainly because I couldn't recall not working for more than a minute since the shift had started, but Johnny went on. "I don't cheat Miss Olga for my pay. That's something you boys got to understand right now if you want to work with me."

Bobby nodded. "I understand," he said grimly.

I didn't reply. Yet another thought had popped into my mind, as they tended to do. There was something going on that was just a bit off-kilter. Then it came to me in a flash. "Johnny, did somebody tell you to get rid of us?"

Johnny drew a red bandanna from his back pocket and mopped his face, leaving greasy black smears behind. "Boys, let me tell you a story," he said.

"I knew it," I said. "I thought I smelled a rat."

"What rat?" Bobby demanded.

"My dad, unless I miss my guess. I'm right, aren't I, Johnny?"

Johnny tucked his bandanna in his pocket, then rubbed the back of his neck, twisting his head around. His neck bones popped and it hurt to hear it. "Homer and I had a little talk last night," he allowed. "He said he was really worried about you boys, said he was afraid he and the union had made a mistake letting you down here. He asked me to watch you two close. If I thought you weren't worth anything, I'm supposed to chase you off."

Bobby's jaw dropped. I guess he'd been gone from Coalwood so long he'd completely forgotten how the place really worked. "I don't get it," he said.

"I'd be happy to explain it to you," I said smartly.

He ignored me. "What about the union?" Bobby demanded of Johnny. "We can't just be fired, can we?"

Johnny said, "If you boys can't cut the mustard, I'm supposed to report it to Dwight Strong. He'll tell Homer and then you're both gone for cause. Homer said Dubonnet won't likely fight it because a union member— that would be me—said you boys were a danger to yourselves. So it's up to me whether you go or stay, I reckon."

Bobby took off his helmet and rubbed what must have been a sore spot. "Johnny, I need this job," he said. "Don't take it away from me, please."

Johnny poked his light at Bobby and then at me. "I've seen a few worse miners in my days than you two boys." He swiveled his light back to Bobby. "But both you boys got to do exactly what I say when I say it. You hear me?"

"Yes, sir," Bobby replied between gritted teeth.

"How about that morning prayer?"

Bobby hesitated, then nodded. "I can say a prayer with the best of them."

"Praise God. How about you, Sonny?"

I shrugged. "Praying's always a good thing."

"I meant about doing exactly what I tell you."

"Sure," I said.

"Then let's get back to work."

Johnny raced back to the next post to be changed while Bobby and I picked up a new post and, bent beneath the roof, waddled after him. For the next two hours, we didn't talk, just changed out posts as hard and fast as we could go.

When it looked as if we were about to run out of rotten posts, Johnny decided he didn't like the piled-up rock and coal—gob—on both sides of the track and flagged down a passing man-trip to send a message up the line about it. Soon afterward, a locomotive brought in an empty car and left it on a siding. We started shoveling gob into it, an exercise that quickly identified some muscles I hadn't yet abused. We'd hardly sat down to eat lunch, it seemed, before Johnny was up again and yelling at us to come help him. Bobby and I threw down our buckets and scrambled to find him.

"How does he do it?" Bobby demanded when, just for an instant, he and I stopped to catch our breath and gulp some water.

"He can't keep it up," I said confidently. "He's got to be forty years old, at least. And that belly of his . . ."

"More like fifty," Bobby said. "And he might have a belly

but I'm guessing there's some hard muscles underneath. Adipose tissue isn't necessarily an indicator of sloth."

"What's adipose tissue?"

"Fat."

"Why didn't you just say fat, then?"

"I'm trying to learn how to talk like a doctor."

"How would you like it if I started talking like an engineer?"

"I'd be impressed," he said.

Unfortunately, I couldn't oblige him.

Later in the day, Dwight Strong, the foreman, showed up. Bent over beneath the roof, his hands behind his back, he watched us for a few minutes. I mostly kept my head down, but once I flashed my light in his direction. His round, friendly face was distorted by a big chaw in his cheek. He gave me a nod. Mr. Strong was one of Dad's favorite young foremen and had often visited our house to talk mining. I'd been impressed when he'd learned to keep Chipper at bay by picking up one of our cats for his lap. "Take it easy, boys," he said after watching us for a while. He knocked at the roof with his roof thumper, then walked away.

"What do you think, Johnny?" Bobby worried as Mr. Strong disappeared into the darkness. "Is he for us or against us?"

"I'll handle Dwight Strong," Johnny said.

"Praise God!" Bobby said, and Johnny grinned approvingly.

I was reaching for my end of a fallen post when I heard a sharp *crack,* like a rifle shot. I looked up and saw an oval slab, like the bottom of a big dirty egg, directly over my head. Johnny gave me a shove and then the floor shook with a solid *thump* as whatever it was came crashing down on the very spot where I'd been standing.

"Not a thing in the world held it up save evil," Johnny remarked while I crawled to my feet. "This is a kettle bottom, boys. It'll come down on you like a hammer."

"Johnny saved your life, Sonny," Bobby said unnecessarily. I knew it to be the truth.

I stared at the kettle bottom. It was a big black funnel-shaped rock, oval on the bottom and tapering to a point at the top. If it had hit me, no helmet in the world would have done me any good. My skull would have been shattered like an eggshell. I stammered my thanks.

"I should have seen the blamed old thing before you got under it," Johnny said, craning his neck to look up into the hole in the roof. He got out his roof thumper and rattled it around inside.

"It looks like an old tree stump to me," Bobby said, kicking at the thing.

"Can't be," Johnny said. "It's made out of rock."

Bobby knelt and rubbed the kettle bottom with his gloved hands. "No, it's a stump. You can see the corrugations of the bark. Millions of years of compression turned it into rock."

"The Bible says the world's only about five thousand years old," Johnny said, patting his pocket where he'd tucked his little book of gospels. "Praise God and all His wonders."

Bobby saw fit to argue. "You can't believe that. Look at the evidence all around you. Coal is made up of plants that grew a hundred million years ago, even before the dinosaurs. Compression and heat from the weight of the rock overburden gradually changed the plants into coal. Isn't that right, Sonny?"

"Leave me out of this," I said. The last thing I wanted was to get into an argument with a Holy Roller, especially one who had just saved my life.

Bobby frowned. "I thought you were studying to be a scientist."

"An engineer," I corrected him. "There's a big difference."

"What's the difference?"

I didn't know for sure, so I made something up. "A scientist would care if it was a fossil. An engineer wouldn't."

He went back to studying the kettle bottom. "Look here, Johnny. Growth rings. You can even count them. One-two-three—you see?"

Johnny refused to look. "The Lord God made everything in six days—coal, rock, kettle bottom, everything," he said.

While Johnny and Bobby were going at it, I took the opportunity to lean up against a rib of rock-dusted coal and rest my back. My cramped muscles sent a message of thanks. When they stopped arguing about the kettle bottom—pretty worthless, since neither of them listened to a thing the other one said—we got to work busting the nasty thing up. We took turns with the hammer. When it was my turn, I hit the roof on the upswing and the sledge came down on top of my helmet, almost knocking me silly. Johnny and Bobby tried not to laugh. At least, I think they did. It took me a while to get back my focus. When we'd finally finished breaking the thing up, we hauled its pieces back to the gob car. Getting rid of the kettle bottom took us nearly two hours. God, or the Devil, had booby-trapped the mine with one very dense chunk of rock.

When Mr. Strong came by again, Johnny showed off the hole the kettle bottom had left in the roof and then the two of them moved off to talk. Bobby and I kept shoveling gob until he leaned on his shovel and worried, "What do you think Johnny's telling him?"

I couldn't let him get ahead of me, so I leaned on my shovel, too. "Probably that you're an atheist and ought to be fired for that reason alone," I said.

"I need this job, Sonny."

"Maybe you should stop arguing with Johnny about religion, then. Why do you want to be a doctor, anyway?"

"So I can have tennis balls I can read."

"Is that supposed to make sense?"

Bobby pushed his glasses up on his nose. "My whole life growing up here in Coalwood," he said, "I never played a set of tennis except with used balls Doc Lassiter or Doc Hale gave me. They were so old, the writing was worn completely off them. I decided I was going to be a doctor myself someday so I'd be able to afford to buy new ones."

"I'm sure your patients will be glad to hear you're their doctor because you want fuzzy tennis balls you can read," I said.

His light flashed into my face. "That's not the only reason. I want to heal people, too."

"Uh-huh," I replied with a doubtful smile.

"You really need to change your attitude," he said.

I lost my smile. "What's wrong with my attitude?"

"You're a pessimist. And nearly a cynic, unless I miss my diagnosis."

"I thought you were going to be a doctor, not a psychiatrist."

"I hope to be a general practitioner, but I wouldn't mind some psych work."

"Don't start with me."

Johnny's light caught us. "You boys stop leaning on those shovels and use them!" he barked.

We got back to shoveling. When Johnny returned, he said, "I told Dwight you boys are a mite slow but you're catching on."

For a second, I thought Bobby was going to hug Johnny. I was less enthusiastic but still pleased that I was going to keep my job. For the first time ever in the history of my entire life, I was making my way without help from anybody. It was a pretty good feeling.

When Johnny announced the man-trip was on its way, I squatted on my haunches and took a deep breath. *Thank the good Lord this shift is over* was my thought. All I could think about was a hot shower, that and wondering if I could convince Floretta to layer on some of her special liniment again.

But Johnny hadn't announced the man-trip to tell us we were done for the day. He just wanted us to know we needed to hurry and clean things up. "It ain't right to leave a workplace dirty, boys." He pointed out the trail of chips and splinters we'd left, hauling the posts.

I squinted at the debris. "Who'll care if we leave a bunch of splinters in the gob?" I asked.

Johnny said, "I will." Then he said, "You should."

There was no use arguing, so Bobby and I pushed the gob car along and shoveled debris into it until Johnny announced he was happy with the result. I couldn't see a bit of difference but kept my opinion to myself. After Bobby and I pushed the gob car into a siding, we returned to find Johnny had used spit and his bandanna to polish our shovels and the sledgehammer until they gleamed. He fussed around our work site until finally the grimy yellow man-trip ground up beside us, its brakes squalling. I was sure glad to see it.

Johnny and Bobby got into a car together, but I jumped into another one where I could be alone. I wanted to take inventory of the new set of bumps, bruises, blisters, and aching muscles I'd obtained. Then I thought about the kettle bottom. My second day in the mine and I'd nearly been killed. I had a hunch I'd see that kettle bottom in my nightmares for a while.

At the lift, I thought to ask Johnny a question that had been lurking in the back of my mind all day. Bobby was off talking to somebody else, so it was a good time to get my question in. "Mrs. Dooley wants me to come by and help her give Nate a bath," I said. "But I can't figure out why she asked me."

Johnny took his helmet off, scratched around his ears, then peered upward into the darkness of the great shaft. "Nate can be a handful, so I hear."

"But why would she ask me to help her?"

"I don't know."

"Well, who's been helping her until now?" I demanded.

Johnny pulled on his nose, coughed into his hand, wiped it on his pants leg, and lowered his voice. "Tuck Dillon," he said. "He was Nate Dooley's best friend."

I felt a chill go up my spine, don't ask me why.

16

IN THE GRAVEYARD

WHEN I limped back to the Club House, any hope I had for another therapy session with Floretta disappeared when I heard a commotion in the kitchen and saw another aproned lady go through its swinging door with a tray of utensils. I recognized her—Lula Pearl Carpenter, a lady from up Snakeroot Hollow. She was apparently helping Floretta get ready for a function of some kind. I poked my head inside the kitchen, and Floretta shrieked at the sight of me. "Get your dirty coal miner self out of my kitchen, boy! What are you thinking?"

She was stirring a pot with one hand and shaking a pan with another. The delicious aroma of chicken-fried steak wafted over. "What's all the excitement?"

"Mr. Bundini sent Carol over to tell us he had guests and wants to bring them here tonight for supper. Waited until the last minute, that rascal, so I had to rustle up Lula Pearl to come help me. Your mama called."

It took me a second to process her last nugget of information. "She did? What did she say?"

Floretta paused long enough to wipe her hands on her apron and consult her memory. "Let's see. Something about you'd better call her tonight if you knew what was good for you but not too early because she's got some no-good roof contractor she has to yell at first."

I gulped. "That's it?"

"We talked some but not for your ears. Now get out of my kitchen!"

I got out and headed for the shower. I was in a sweat. I'd waited too long to call Mom. Now she'd tracked me down, probably built up to a fury for all my shenanigans. For all I knew, she'd hired someone, maybe one of the Mallett boys, to pop me a good one. I ventured back downstairs after I got cleaned up. Lula Pearl, a tiny woman who had burn scars down half her face from a kerosene lantern explosion years ago, drew me aside. "Reverend Richard sure would like to see you, Sonny," she said, tugging my shirtsleeve.

"I sure would like to see him, too," I said, regretting that I hadn't already gone to see him since my return. It seemed as if everywhere I turned, there was old Mr. Regret standing there, grinning at me. The Reverend had given me counsel and advice a lot of times while I was growing up in Coalwood, and I knew I could stand a little more right now.

I ate supper off the stove and slipped out before the Bundini family and their guests arrived. I liked Mr. Bundini a lot. He was a good general superintendent and had fit in well with Coalwood citizens. My dad admired him, too, had said more than once he was one of the best overseers Coalwood had ever had. Still, I thought it wise to avoid him, just in case his guests were from the steel company. I suspected Dad hadn't advertised that one of his sons had joined the union, and Mr. Bundini was sure to introduce me if I was seen. It was sad to have to think of myself as an embarrassment to my father, but I was, and there was no use pretending otherwise.

I headed on down the road to see the Reverend Julius "Little" Richard. His Mudhole Church of Distinct Christianity was just past the old mule barn at the mouth of Mudhole Hollow. The church was a tiny wooden building with a stumpy steeple, and round windows in front. The Reverend had designed the windows himself, saying they represented the potter's wheel written about in the book of Jeremiah, a wheel that God used to shape us any way he liked.

The church was empty, so I limped up the hollow between the row of little wooden houses that lined the dirt road until I reached the Reverend's place. There was no answer to my knock at his door. A huge woman dressed in a vast blue dress and a snowy white apron came out on the porch of the house next door and hailed me. I recognized her as Mrs. Pauline Faye Anderson, the piano player at the Reverend's church. "He's up there, Sonny," she said with a nod of her head toward Mudhole Mountain. When I looked blank, she pointed to the fence behind his house. "Go through the gate, honey, and follow the path." She spoke kindly and carefully, as if talking to someone rather slow. Colored people often did that with me, I'd noticed over the years.

I thanked Mrs. Anderson and trod the path that I found starting at the gate in the backyard. It plunged into a mass of thick green rhododendron and then went nearly straight up. I grabbed roots and trees to help me along, noting as I went how dry the dirt was. It hadn't rained, now that I thought about it, since the night I'd come back to Coalwood.

The trail flattened out after a bit, then wound through some shagbark hickories before coming upon a grove of pin oaks twisted by age. I passed through them and then entered a clearing that went all the way up to the ridge. I climbed until I emerged into a small meadow of sweet-smelling wild sage, wilted flower patches, and tombstones. A number of cats, their tails hanging down like furry vines, were lounging on top of the tombstones. A few of them jumped down at my appearance, but most of them just gave me a solemn glance and then went back to what they were doing, which was nothing.

The Reverend Richard, dressed in his black frock, was sitting on one of the tombstones, his pointy shoes drawn up to press against the front. In his hands, he held his old, cracked Bible. "Hello, Reverend," I said.

The Reverend was deep in thought or prayer, I couldn't tell which because, I suppose, sometimes there isn't much difference. His eyes cut in my direction. He blinked, then his mouth fell open. "Sonny Hickam. In all my borned days. Is it really you?"

I agreed that it was, indeed. He climbed down from his marble perch and opened his arms and I gladly fell into them. His thick black hair, smelling of pomade, brushed past my cheek, which was, to my surprise, suddenly damp with my tears. When he released me, his cheeks were wet, too. "Sweet Jesus, how I've missed you," he said as another tear slid down past his nose and into his thin mustache. "Let me look at you."

I let him look, all the while drinking him in, too. All of a sudden, there was nobody more important in the whole world to me than Reverend Richard. During my entire year at VPI, I had not deigned to write him so much as a letter. Now I regretted it—*Hello again, Mr. Regret*—and I think he saw it in my eyes.

"You and me, Sonny, we don't need to see each other because we know how we feel, eh?" He put his hand on my neck and drew me in again. "I am so proud of you, Lord, so proud, even if you nearly flunked out of college, rolled your daddy's car, and went to work in the mine against everything your mama ever stood for."

"Thank you, Reverend," I said, happily accepting his absolution. He'd already pretty much given me everything I'd come for. "I'll try to do better."

He released me. "I know you will, Sonny. The Lord has always had a special plan for you, don't you think He don't. Did you go to church down there in that college?"

"Yes, sir, some Sundays." It was even the truth.

He nodded. "The Lord likes to see you in His house every so often. Don't need to be all the time but enough so He can count you amongst the flock."

"Yes, sir."

The Reverend beckoned me to two tombstones close together. I sat on one and he sat on the other. I told the Reverend about my job at the mine and how Dad had first let me take the job and then had tried to fire me. Of course, the Reverend knew all about it, since the Mudhole Church of Distinct Christianity was another stop on the gossip fence-line. "You did a proud thing, Sonny," he said. "As long as you remember to go back to college this fall."

I told him that Dad had cut me off from college funding. "Mr. Homer will do right," he said. "I wouldn't be too worried."

"I'm too sore to worry," I replied, which was nearly the truth.

The Reverend grinned, his gold tooth flashing in the light from the sun just as it set behind the mountains. Orange and pink spokes of light emanated from the point behind the ridge where it had gone, and a drifting cloud looked to be made of spun gold.

"It sure is pretty up here," I said, petting the calico cat who occupied my tombstone.

"That's why we put these fine folks to rest in this place," the Reverend replied. He eyed me. "So what else you got going on, Sonny?"

I filled the Reverend in about the kettle bottom and my near miss. I could tell by the way he raised his eyebrows that he hadn't heard about it. "I'll say a prayer of thanksgiving," he said. "And give God special thanks for Johnny Basso. He is a most humble Christian man."

"Being with Johnny was my dad's idea," I said. "He was supposed to chase me and Bobby Likens off."

"Your daddy's got a lot on his mind these days, I swan," the Reverend said.

I knew the Reverend was referring to Tuck Dillon. "Dad just acts like there's nothing happening," I said.

"That's the way innocent people are supposed to act," he replied while petting a black cat that had just jumped up on the stone beside him.

"But he needs to fight what people are saying, doesn't he?"

"Maybe he just needs to pray."

"Dad's never been much for praying."

"Then I shall pray for him—and also that your mother will soon return. Homer's just not Homer without Elsie."

"I don't think she's coming anytime soon," I said.

"You've talked to her lately?"

"I'm supposed to call her tonight," I said. "She's going to blister me good for going to work in the mine."

"And you're afraid?"

I thought the question over. "Not afraid, just sorry I've disappointed her and Dad, too. I figured to really vex them by showing how I'd grown up and could do anything I wanted to do. Now I feel bad about it. So I've really gotten myself into a crack, Reverend."

The Reverend pursed his lips. "You have, indeed," he said. "Anything else?"

I told him the reason why I'd come back in the first place—Mom's directive for me to be with Dad during his time of trouble. "But I can't figure out how to help him or even what's happening," I confessed. "All I see is a tangle."

"Let me give you a line from Proverbs, Sonny," the Reverend said. "'It is the glory of God to conceal a thing; but the honor of kings to search it out.'"

I contemplated the eloquent ancient words. "So it is an honor for me to be curious and look into all this?"

"An honor often comes disguised," he said. "It might just as soon be a harlequin tramp as the president of the United States."

"I'll take the tramp any day. Presidents seem more trouble than anything. President Truman tore up Coalwood with the navy and now President Kennedy is heading for the moon before I can get ready to help him. That's got me worried."

He shook his head. "Don't you concern yourself about that old moon. You'll get there on God's own good time and not before."

Since I was unburdening myself, I decided to complete my list. I told him Mrs. Dooley had asked me to come help her with her mister's bath.

"You should do it," he replied.

"But why me?"

"Maybe Mrs. Dooley just likes you," the Reverend answered. "Some people do, you know. Take Miss Dreama sleeping over there beneath the willow tree. She liked you a great deal, Sonny. She trusted you, too."

The Reverend climbed off his tombstone and led me to Dreama's grave. She was, as I had told Rita, the only white person in the colored graveyard on Mudhole Mountain. Dreama had finally become the Coalwood girl she had wanted to be, and for all eternity.

I bowed my head in front of her grave. Red clover surrounded it, their scarlet blossoms waving in the mild breeze. A half-dozen cats lounged nearby. One of them got up and rubbed its head in a clump of woolly green plants that grew beside Dreama's stone. I plucked off a leaf, rubbed it between my fingers, and put it to my nose. "Catnip," I said, recognizing its tangy scent.

The Reverend reached over to pet one of the cats, which set it to purring. "The Mudhole kitties love to come up here," he said. "They get drunk on the catnip, then sleep on the graves in the sun. They're keeping the folks up here company, Sonny. That's a blessed thing."

Dreama's view stretched all the way up the valley to Coalwood Main. She could watch the town going and coming, something I knew she'd like. "You did good for Dreama, Reverend," I said.

"I did my best," he said. "As you will do yours."

Beside Dreama's grave, the Reverend and I talked more of many things, of the people of Coalwood, and of my mother, and my father, and even, when I mentioned the addition to Mom's mural, the little fox named Parkyacarcass, whom he remembered. "Your father did not kill it, that much I know," he said. "He's not a man who would do such a thing."

"I sometimes think that was when all their troubles started," I said. "The stories of their life together are wonderful and happy until they get to Mom's fox. Then there aren't any more stories at all, just arguments."

The Reverend gave me a nod. "To your father, it was a fox of trouble. To your mother, it was a fox of joy. But what did the fox think of itself?"

"I don't know. Maybe he just thought he was a fox."

Reverend Richard laughed his slow laugh and put his hand on my shoulder. "Let's leave the kitty cats to mind the graveyard," he said, "and go back to the living. There is much for us to do, according to the expectations of others."

I nodded agreement and, together, in the gathering darkness, Reverend Richard and I walked down the path to the small houses in the hollow, just beginning to glow with the first lamps of the evening. Along the way, I kept thinking of the Reverend's proverb. The truth of what had happened with Dad and Tuck Dillon was well hidden, whether by God or, more likely, what Mr. Dubonnet called Coalwood business. Honor or no, I suspected it would take a squadron of kings to penetrate even the smallest of the secrets that ran like a murky river through Coalwood. If it was truly my job to do, I sure didn't see any way to do it.

17

SQUARED AWAY

I PEEKED in the dining room from the Club House porch and saw Mr. and Mrs. Bundini and a man and a woman I didn't recognize seated at a table laden with silver serving trays of chicken-fried steak, butter beans, mashed potatoes with brown gravy, and corn on the cob. Floretta appeared out of the kitchen with a bottle of wine and topped off their glasses all around. She smiled serenely at something Mr. Bundini said to her, no doubt a compliment on the food and drink.

It was a warm, lazy evening, so I decided to stay out on the porch, selecting the wood-slatted swing as a good place to listen to the gentle eeping of crickets in the yard punctuated by the low thrum of frogs in the creek behind the machine shop.

I heard the door open and close in the company office building across the road. In a moment, boots thudded on the concrete steps to the porch. It was Rita, in her junior engineer outfit, complete with shiny white helmet. She peeked in the window, then spotted me. "Do you want some company?"

"Sure!" I said, standing up.

She chose a rocking chair near the swing. "Sit down, please," she said. She sounded tired. "I'm just a junior engineer, after all, the lowest of the low."

I settled back into the swing. "You're also a woman. Mom worked hard on my manners and I guess she wouldn't like it if I didn't use them."

"I've heard your mother is an independent woman."

"Some people say she's mostly stubborn."

"What do you say?"

"*Unique* is the word that comes to mind."

Rita smiled, though a bit wanly. "Maybe that would describe me, too," she said. She looked over her shoulder through the window into the dining room. "The Mastersons," she said.

"Who are the Mastersons?"

"Frank Masterson is the chief bean counter for the steel company. My father tried to get him fired sometime back— there was some kind of irregularity in the books—but Frank's a survivor. His wife, Jill's her name, is nice enough. She used to be his secretary until he got her pregnant. Father always said Frank marrying her was the only decent thing he ever did."

"Your father works for the steel company?"

"He's not an active player anymore," she said, a defensive tone creeping into her voice. "He just owns a lot of stock. And he didn't raise a finger to get me this job, if that's what you're thinking."

"I wasn't thinking that at all," I lied.

"I guess your dad didn't help you get your job, either," she said.

"That would be a safe assumption," I replied, trying not to laugh and succeeding. It would have been too much to explain to her, and she probably wouldn't have been interested, anyway.

She looked over her shoulder again, then frowned. "I wonder what Frank Masterson is doing down here?"

"People in Coalwood figure anybody from the steel company's pretty much a dime squeezer," I said. "Maybe he came down to tell Mr. Bundini to squeeze a little harder."

"Could be," she said. She settled back into the chair, rocked a little, and peered into the darkness. "Nice night," she said, though she didn't sound convinced. Fatigue dragged at her voice.

"That's why I'm out here," I said. "Just enjoying the breeze and the sounds. By the way, where'd you go to college?"

"Why?" she asked suspiciously.

"Just wondered," I replied, which happened to be the truth.

It turned out Rita had gone to the Colorado School of Mines. She had picked it because it was one of the best mining engineering schools in the country and also because she happened to love skiing. While she was there, she said, she had almost made the American Olympic ski team. "One tenth of one second faster and I'd have been on it." She fell silent, though I could see the muscles in her jaw working. Then she said, "God, I hate to lose."

"At least you came close," I said, fascinated to imagine her so near the glory of the Olympics.

Rita looked over her shoulder again. "Close isn't worth anything." She removed her helmet and turned it in her hands. Her hair was tied up in a bun, though a black tendril fell down alongside her cheek. "If you get used to losing, pretty soon it gets to be a habit. I made up my mind a long time ago to never quit anything I start—and that includes beating this idiotic superstition about women in the mine."

"Have you made any progress?"

She huffed a breath. "No. Every time I send a message to the front office about it, they just say it's up to the mine superintendent. Your dad," she added unnecessarily.

"Dad knows miners," I said. "They're a superstitious lot."

"How about him?"

"His mine tag number is thirteen. That might tell you something. No, Dad's an intellectual, doesn't believe in the supernatural. But he also knows he has to keep his miners happy and if they believe something, especially when he's got no reason to change it, he'll support them."

Rita shook her head. "I'd give anything to get a good report from your father. You know how many junior engineers ever got a good one from him?"

"Zero would be my guess," I said, shrugging.

"Two. I was shown those reports before I was sent here. 'Rita,' my boss said, 'go on down and show Homer Hickam what kind of engineer you are.' But your father's never given me a chance!"

"Tell me about your folks," I said, figuring it wise to move to another topic.

"Mother died when I was born," she said in a neutral voice. "My father was my best friend growing up. He always said I was the light of his life."

"We have something in common, then," I said. "My mom always said I was the light of her life, too. Dad said if that was so, she was following a mighty dim beacon."

Rita gave me the reward of her dazzling smile. It was so sudden it nearly took my breath away. "You got that hike planned?" she asked.

"How about Sunday?" I suggested eagerly.

"How about Saturday?"

I told her there was a lady asking for my help and I'd promised to come on Saturday to do it. I didn't tell her it was Mrs. Dooley. If Rita's father owned part of the steel company, she didn't need to know a man was on the company payroll who didn't do anything.

Rita said, "Sunday it is, then. Say about one o'clock?" She looked over her shoulder once more, then put on her helmet. She tucked the tendril of hair up inside it. "They're about to wind up in there. I guess I'd better go do my duty and say hello to the Mastersons. Plus I'm starved. I haven't eaten yet."

I stood as she got up from the rocker. "See you Sunday afternoon," I told her.

She nodded, but she was paying most of her attention to the people in the dining room. After taking another look, apparently gauging their momentum toward the door, she went inside the foyer. I heard a shrill cry of greeting, apparently coming from Mrs. Masterson. I edged into the shadows, watching through the screen doors. Rita was being hugged by everybody, including Mr. Bundini. I still didn't want to get introduced, so I went around to the back of the Club House and climbed the fire escape up to the second floor. My plan was to wait until the parlor was empty, then slip down and call my mother. I would have almost rather stood under an unsupported kettle bottom, truth be told, but it was past time for me to endure her righteous wrath.

VICTOR AND Ned wound up their evening watching *The Bob Cummings Show* on television and then vacated the parlor. I waited until I was sure they'd gone upstairs, and then I dialed Mom's Myrtle Beach number. She picked up after one ring, and I immediately threw myself on her mercy. "Forgive me," I said. "For I knew not what I was doing."

I waited for her to start yelling, but she remained perfectly calm. "I intend to kill you the next time I see you," she said evenly. "All I hope is that you have written your will to my satisfaction."

"I'm leaving everything to you," I said.

"Good. If I sold it all at ten o'clock in the morning, it would keep me going until at least half past noon."

I started babbling apologies, and Mom seemed content to let me do it, not interrupting once. I went through all my excuses: how I'd been trying to help out Bobby Likens, and how I needed the money to pay for the car, and how Mr. Dubonnet had skunked me. "That's the long and the short of it," I concluded.

"So 'tis," she murmured, as if she'd not paid much attention to anything I'd said. "I presume during all your peculiar adventures in Coalwood this summer, that you have taken at least a minute to spend some time with your father?"

I told her that indeed I had, neglecting to mention that so far it had been time spent mainly arguing and yelling at each other. Mom, however, was too sharp for my half-truth to slip by. "What do you talk about?"

"Mostly the best way to mine coal," I prevaricated.

"Be careful in that old mine," she said.

Her warning surprised me. "Be careful? You don't want me to quit?"

Her sigh filled my ear. "That's the one thing your daddy and I've always agreed on, to raise you boys not to be quitters. No, I don't want you to quit a thing you've started."

I decided to ask her then if she planned on coming back to Coalwood anytime soon. I thought maybe she would confess she was never coming back and I could send it around the gossip fence and people would stop asking me about it. But she said, "We'll see. The remodeling is a slow go. They don't know how to do things in South Carolina like we do them in West Virginia. Law, I never seen men take so many breaks."

"Maybe it's too hot down there," I said.

"Maybe they're just lazy."

"Maybe they don't like working for a woman, either." It was just a suggestion.

"Are you smart-mouthing me?" she demanded.

"No, ma'am." I really wasn't.

"Maybe I better get you squared away."

I thought: *Uh-oh. Now I've done it. Here it comes.*

"I expect you to not get yourself killed in that filthy hole."

I said "Yes, ma'am" and continued to do so as she went down her points.

"Do everything Johnny Basso tells you to do. He'll keep you safe."

I repeated my affirmative, reflecting that I hadn't mentioned Johnny's name. Who were Mom's informants? Floretta was at the top of my list, but there were at least a dozen more ladies who'd have been glad to tell her everything they knew, plus a little extra.

"I expect you to work hard and do the best you can.

"I expect you to keep your eyes and ears open and help your father whether he knows it or not.

"I expect you to not go dragging around with a long mouth like you're prone to do. And I expect you to stop fussing with Bobby Likens. There's never been a better boy to come out of Coalwood, you included.

"And I expect you to keep me informed of everything."

Her litany seemed to be over, so I said, "Mrs. Dooley asked me to help her give Nate a bath."

"Do it. You owe Nate Dooley your life. The least you can do is help keep him clean."

"Yes, ma'am."

"Are you squared away?"

"Never squarer."

"Good."

And with that, after a routine utterance of undying motherly affection in my direction coupled with another threat toward my continued existence if I made any more mistakes in Coalwood, she hung up, leaving me convinced that my mom was up to something, though what it might be remained a puzzle. When it came to concealment, I suspected God had some competition from the woman in Myrtle Beach.

18

A SKY MADE OF STONE

WHEN I next stepped aboard the man-lift, Johnny pulled me aside. "You ready to work like a bull?" he asked. "A certain fellow asked me."

I knew he meant my dad. Since I was not only squared away with my mom but had also received general absolution from Reverend Richard, I was in a free and easy mood. Not only that, but my muscles had nearly stopped complaining. "I wonder if we can get a heavier sledgehammer," I told Johnny nonchalantly. "That five-pounder's mighty puny."

That made him chuckle. "Turn your light on, boy," he said.

At the bottom of the shaft, I saw a miner who didn't have his lamp switched on walking toward the man-trip. "Turn your light on, boy," I said, and was rewarded by seeing him, after a startled look, do it.

"Not bad," Bobby admired.

I looked around to see if I could observe any more offenders and slammed the top of my helmet into a protruding roof bolt. "Nice try, but they already drove that ol' bolt in 'bout as far as it would go, Sonny," somebody said. Heavy laughter echoed down the man-trip line.

I laughed with them. They could poke fun all they wanted, but I thought I was getting the hang of mining coal, even though I still technically hadn't mined any.

Later that day, when Bobby had to stop for a pee break, Johnny started thumping the roof with his broomstick. "They need some roof bolts in here," he said.

"How do you know?" I asked.

He pointed at some fine lines that ran like a brown spiderweb through the rock. "That's mud. Makes it weak. A little squeeze, the whole shebang'll go to pieces." He took a piece of chalk from his shirt pocket and made a big "X" on the spot. "I'll leave a note for the hoot-owl shift foreman to look for my mark," he said. "His crew'll put in a bolt."

I studied the roof again, running my hand over it, feeling the tiny fissures. "It's funny," I said. "I've been looking up at the sky ever since *Sputnik* got launched four years ago. Now my sky is five feet high and made of stone."

The circle of Johnny's light played across the rock. "See the mica? See how it sparkles? This old gray rock is right pretty in its own way."

I looked closer and I could see what he meant. Millions of minute silica flakes glimmered in our lights. "A sky of stone with stars of mica," I said, trying to put out of my mind that it was also about a trillion tons of rock supported only by wooden posts and the occasional steel roof bolt.

"Most people think you got to know coal in the mines, but it's rock you got to know if you want to stay alive," Johnny went on. "I know a little about it but not like your daddy. He can tell you everything about this rock just by looking at it. You take the average engineer, all he knows is what he's read in a book. Your daddy, he don't need no book. He can smell bad rock."

I looked at Johnny. "Why are they blaming Dad for what happened to Tuck?"

"I can't talk to you about that, Sonny," he said. "It wouldn't be right."

"I'm going to find out sooner or later. I'd rather hear it from a man I respect."

Johnny's light hit me in the eyes, then flashed away. "I swan," he said, sniffing. He reached into his back pocket for his bandanna. "That's a nice thing to say."

Besides being superstitious, miners were a sentimental lot, too. Johnny honked his nose in his bandanna, then tucked it back into his pocket. "What I've heard, Sonny," he said, "your daddy's problem is that he let Tuck go inside by himself that night."

"Is that against the rules?"

"No, but what they're saying down at the Union Hall is it's against common sense. Your daddy and Tuck were there together at the man-hoist, getting ready to go inside and inspect Tuck's section. But Tuck went and your daddy didn't. What some folks are wondering is maybe if they'd gone in together, your daddy would've stopped Tuck from driving his motor into that fire damp."

"But Tuck was a good foreman, wasn't he? I mean, he should have known to be careful."

Johnny squatted on his haunches and stirred the gob with his roof thumper. "Tuck Dillon was the finest foreman in this mine."

"Then why did he blow himself up?"

Johnny's voice was flat. "That's what nobody can figure." He got up, stretched his back, then thumped the roof, took a step, thumped it again. "You listen for a low note to come back," he said. "That's a safe roof. You hear something that sounds high, like tapping on a stack of dishes, that's rock with a crack. Don't get under it."

"I won't," I said. "Johnny, why do you think Tuck went in alone?"

His light swept back. "I don't know, but I'll tell you this," he said. "If I was still a gambling man—which I ain't—I wouldn't bet against your daddy." He studied his boots. "Something else I got to say, Sonny. Your mama, she needs to come home. That's what everybody's saying, too. Homer Hickam without Elsie ain't the man he's always been. It's like without her his luck's drained away."

"She says she's not ready," I reported.

Bobby's light flashed as he came from between two posts. "Hey!" he yelled. I guess he couldn't see us.

"Over here," Johnny said.

"Thank you," I said to Johnny as Bobby made his way toward us.

"You boys ain't nothing but trouble," he replied, but I could tell he didn't mean it.

AT MY knock, Mrs. Dooley appeared and pushed open the screen door. "I hope you've been building up your muscles," she said.

I followed her into the tiny living room. When my eyes adjusted to the dim light, I saw an apparition sitting on the sofa. It was a man, gaunt as a dead hickory tree, dressed only in baggy underwear shorts. The few wisps of hair on his head floated up, reeds in the light wind coming from a small electric fan in the corner that emitted a low hum. A long, mottled scar ran across the top of his skull.

"Where's his cast?" I asked Mrs. Dooley.

"His wrist is healed. I took it off."

"By yourself?"

"What do you care?"

"Mom's worried about him, said I should be, too."

"Thank your mom and tell her he's doing just fine."

"But—"

"Nate," she said, raising her voice, "it's time for your bath."

Mr. Dooley's cheeks, gray with whiskers, puckered in, as if he were catching his breath. Mrs. Dooley looked at me. "Are you going to help me or just stand there?"

"What am I supposed to do?"

"I'll start drawing his bath. You stand him up, help him into the bathroom. Go on. He won't bite."

I edged around the coffee table and took Mr. Dooley's right hand. It was damp. A slick sheen of moisture was formed above his lips. His pale blue eyes looked drained.

"Ask him to stand up," Mrs. Dooley called from the tiny bathroom just off from the living room. I heard the water running.

"Stand up, Mr. Dooley," I said gently. He didn't move. Beads of sweat were on his forehead.

I turned to call Mrs. Dooley. "He's not mov—" which was the last thing I said for a while because Mr. Dooley launched himself from the couch, catching me chest-high with his bony shoulder. We fell across the coffee table.

"That's it!" Mrs. Dooley cried, not bothering to come out and look. "You got him!"

Mr. Dooley was all sharp knees and elbows. I grappled with him while he flailed and grunted. And laughed. He was laughing big horse-laughs, gasping for breath in between. "Come on, Mr. Dooley!" I straddled him and pushed his hands to the floor. "You want to take your bath, don't you?"

"He should!" Mrs. Dooley crowed merrily. "Been over a month!"

Mr. Dooley went suddenly limp, although he still giggled as I worked around to get my hands under his arms and drag him to the bathroom. I just about had him through the door when he suddenly scrambled to his feet and twisted away. I dived after him—it was like tackling a skeleton—and we fell into an easy chair, which tipped over. Then he fell limp again. I lifted him by the armpits and started walking backward. His bare bony feet bumped behind.

When I got him in the bathroom, Mrs. Dooley closed the door behind us. "Let me get off his drawers," she said.

She did and I picked him up and sat his rump on the edge of the bathtub. I was breathing hard. She swung his feet around into the water. "Let him down easy. Be careful and don't bump his head. There you go."

Mr. Dooley, sighing, slid like a wet rag into the tub. Mrs. Dooley went down on her knees, picked up a folded washcloth from the side of the tub, dampened it with tub water, and rubbed some white soap on it. She picked up Mr. Dooley's right arm and began to slide the cloth over it, the soapy water leaving a gleaming trail behind. "Mrs. Dooley," I asked, still trying to catch my breath, "do you want me to stay?"

Mr. Dooley's face seemed to coalesce. It took the sheerest of moments. Where there had been blankness, there was sudden cognizance. "Sonny Hickam," he said. "I'd know your hide in a tanning factory."

Mrs. Dooley sputtered out a short laugh. "Nate, you old fool."

"I might be a fool, woman, but I know Sonny Hickam when I see him, although I guess it's been a while."

He fastened his eyes on me. They were suddenly a bright and lively blue. Mr. Dooley held up his left arm, and Mrs. Dooley wiped it down. She did it with lovingly long strokes, a small, gentle smile on her lips. "You over that scarlet fever, Sonny?" he asked.

I closed my mouth, which had fallen open. "Pretty much, sir," I gulped.

"That's good to hear. It kills a lot of babies." He gave me a warm look and subsided into the water, blowing bubbles through his pursed lips. When he raised up, he said, "You a monkey."

I didn't think I'd heard him right. "Sir?"

"You an ol' monkey," he said again, and then cackled at

what he took to be a joke. I noticed he was missing a front tooth, an incisor. "You an ol' monkey and got a tail. I'm gonna tell on you to your mother."

Mrs. Dooley had lost her smile. She was scrubbing his narrow chest while he squirmed. "Hold still, Nate!" she snapped at him. "Sonny, come here, push down on his shoulders."

I came around to the end of the bathtub and did as she said. His shoulders were horizontal bones, the skin wrapped around them soft as velvet. "I said hold him!" she barked.

I held him. "Please, Mrs. Dooley. What just happened?" I asked.

She kept scrubbing, going up under his hips to make a thorough job of it. He was twisting, trying to get up, scrabbling his feet against the end of the tub. I knelt down, got a better hold of his shoulders, and felt him subside against me, giving in to my strength.

"Nate comes back in his mind every so often," she said. "I never know when. It doesn't last long, but more than once he's even gotten himself dressed and gone off to work. The men are always on the scout for him. They call Tag to come bring him home."

She reached to pull out the plug in the tub. The water gurgled as it drained away. "Stand him up, Sonny. It's all right. The fight's gone out of him."

I put my arms under him and lifted. "Your old man's a bastard," he hissed.

"Nate, don't cuss," Mrs. Dooley said, and he fell silent. "He doesn't know what he's saying," she apologized.

After she got him toweled off, she sat him down on the toilet and slid a pair of clean shorts up his legs. She made him stand and she pulled them the rest of the way up. Then she told me to take him across the hall to the bedroom. I held his hand and he shuffled behind me. I pulled the quilted covers back from his bed, and he crawled beneath them. Mrs. Dooley put a finger to her lips and beckoned me back into the hall. "He'll sleep most all day now. Are you staying at the Club House?"

"Yes, ma'am."

"I'll call you when I need you."

I nodded. "Ma'am, when he gets . . . right again, will you tell him something for me?"

"I guess."

"Tell him I said thanks for making that navy doctor give me penicillin."

"I'll tell him." Her voice was flinty, as if she blamed me for something. Maybe, for all I knew, she blamed me for everything.

I let myself out the door and walked back down Main Street. I heard a car coming behind me, but I didn't turn around. I didn't want to be picked up. I just wanted to keep walking and thinking about what I'd just seen and heard. The car eased on by and I saw it was the Buick, roadworthy once more. Dad braked. Reluctantly, I climbed inside.

"Sonny," he said.

"Dad," I replied.

We didn't speak all the way to Coalwood Main. He parked in front of Mr. Bundini's office, across from the Club House. "How's your room?" he asked.

"I like it," I said.

"Enjoying the food?"

"Yes, sir."

"Floretta's a great cook."

"She sure is."

He drummed his fingers on the steering wheel. "Got a meeting to go to," he said.

We both got out of the Buick. He put on his hat. "See you," I said, and started to walk across the street.

"Hey!" he called, and I stopped. "Johnny Basso tells me you're a pretty good miner."

I turned about. Had he actually sounded proud? "I'm pretty sore," I confessed.

"It'll pass."

"Yes, sir."

He nodded, then went inside the office, and I climbed the steps to the Club House porch. Someone was sitting on the swing. It was a squat little toad of a man with a crew cut. I knew him all too well: Mr. Amos Fuller. "What time is it?" he demanded. He held his watch up to his ear. "Damn thing's busted!"

I wasn't wearing a watch, so I shrugged. He glared, but didn't seem to recognize me. He grumbled something I couldn't hear, then got up and went inside, the screen door slapping behind him.

Then I heard a familiar voice in the direction of the Big Store. A tall, rangy young man dressed in starched khakis was talking to some miners sitting on the Big Store steps. After he finished his conversation, he walked across the street toward the Club House. I recognized him immediately. When he'd been a junior engineer, Jake Mosby had taken up for the rocket boys, more than once. He'd even set up a telescope observatory for us on the Club House roof. After I'd graduated from high school, Jake had gone back to Ohio to work as a manager for the steel company. I hadn't realized how much I'd missed him until I saw him again. I cried out like a happy little kid as he came up the porch steps. "Jake!"

"Sonny boy!" he yodeled. He clutched my shoulders, pushed me and pulled me, turned me around, and gave me a complete once-over. "Damn you've grown!" he said, squeezing my shoulders. "Feel those muscles, too! I heard you'd taken up coal mining. You'll make lots of money. Then back to school, eh?"

"We can only hope," I responded. "What are you doing here?"

Jake's grin faded. "Tuck Dillon," he said. He cleared his throat. "Sonny, I'm on the investigating team."

My grin disappeared, too. I asked, "Does Dad know this?"

He shook his head. "We're going to be fair, Sonny. It's an honest investigation to find out the facts of the case."

He had called it a "case." That made Dad sound like a suspected criminal. "Jake," I said, my stomach tightening, "don't be a part of this."

"It's my job, Sonny," he said stiffly. "I didn't ask for it but I got it because I know Coalwood."

Mr. Fuller came back out on the porch. "Let's go, Jake," he said.

Jake shrugged. "Sonny, I'll talk to you later."

"Sure," I said. I watched him join Mr. Fuller on the porch steps, then walk down the sidewalk and across the road. Then I remembered something. "Hey, Jake," I called. "Where's your Corvette?" Jake had always driven a cherry-red Corvette. To me, it symbolized who he was, a man who knew how to squeeze fun out of life.

Jake turned and walked backward a step. "Sold it," he called back. "Got me a good, hardworking Nash." Then he turned around and went up the steps with Mr. Fuller and into Mr. Bundini's office, leaving me openmouthed in astonishment.

Mom gone, Dad in trouble, me working in the coal mine, and Jake without his Corvette. If the world got any more peculiar, I didn't think I would recognize it at all.

1 9

WATER TANK MOUNTAIN

FLORETTA PACKED a lunch for my Sunday picnic with Rita. "Peanut butter and jelly sandwiches might be fine for you but ain't right for Miss Rita," she said.

She handed over a wicker basket. When I hefted it, I figured she had enough food in there to feed a half-dozen junior engineers, or a regiment, which was about the same. "We're going hiking, Floretta," I said. "I can't carry all this heavy stuff up a mountain."

Her voice was dangerous. "You be careful with Miss Rita up there, boy. She may think she's a coal miner but she's still a girl underneath all that. I want her back here in the same condition she left." She eyed me. "What's that on your belt? A nasty old army canteen! Has it ever been washed?"

Now that she'd mentioned it, I didn't guess it had, not since my uncle Robert had brought it back from the Italian campaign, anyway. I had used it all through childhood to carry water up in the mountains during my adventures there. Floretta held out her large, flat hand. "Give that thing to me. I'll run some hot water and soap through it and try to get some of the scunge out."

I dutifully unclipped the canteen and handed it over. I heard the sink run fast and furious for a minute, then Floretta came through the swinging kitchen door and handed it back. "The water in it was as brown as dirt," she said, sounding triumphant.

At the sound of footsteps coming down the stairs, Floretta vanished into the kitchen. It was Rita and she was wearing her khakis and tall lace-up boots. She gave me one of her delicious smiles. "This is going to be so much fun," she said. She let her eyes rest on the basket. "Is that as heavy as it looks?"

"It's just what we need," I replied, nodding at the kitchen door behind which I knew Floretta was listening. Lugging the basket with both hands, I walked Rita toward the double screen doors that led to the porch. "Don't worry," I whispered. "I have a plan."

"Where are we going?" she whispered back.

I lost my whisper. "Water Tank Mountain. There's a nice view from up there. I want to swing by my house first. I've got a backpack in the garage and I can unload this stuff into it. And, if you don't mind, I'd like to take Dandy and Poteet along. I think they'd like the exercise."

"Dandy and Poteet?"

"My dogs. They won't be much trouble."

Before we got off the porch, a familiar voice asked, "Where you folks headed?"

Jake was sitting in the porch swing. He was wearing Bermuda shorts and a T-shirt, his feet clad in sandals. "Hello, Rita," he said, not bothering to get up.

"Jake," she said.

Jake smiled, then gave me a wink. "Rita and I have something in common, Sonny. Our fathers both own a percentage of the steel company."

"I'm sure Sonny is fascinated," she replied. "And how is your father, the *real* Mr. Jake Mosby?"

I was surprised to learn that Jake was a junior, like me. All the years I'd known him, that had never come out. "As fine as a watch, Rita," he said. "I presume your father is the same?"

The screen door smacked open and Mr. Fuller came out on the porch, crossed over to the other side, and sank into one of the metal chairs. Rita's eyes cut toward him. "Let's go," she said.

I did so, gladly, muttering something in the way of a good-bye to Jake. When we got out of earshot, Rita said, "Where do you know Jake from?"

"He used to be my friend, even helped me with my rockets. He's here with that other fellow on the porch—Fuller's his name—to do the Tuck Dillon investigation."

"I know Amos Fuller. My father's had a run-in with him more than once. He knows what I think of him. Are you worried about the investigation?"

"Dad could lose his job," I said, shrugging.

She looked back at the porch. "Your dad's smarter than both of those two put together."

"How do you know Jake?" I asked.

She tossed her head, her long black hair falling down her back. "We grew up together, practically. When my father would go to Ohio for the board meetings, we'd usually stay at Jake's parents' house. I spent one summer on their farm in Kentucky. They had horses. Jake and I used to go riding all the time. But we never really got along. He was too childish even though he was older than me."

We climbed into her car, a white Ford Thunderbird with little round portholes in back. I stowed the basket in its minuscule trunk. There was barely room, but the little car was flashy and suited her. The interior smelled of leather and her perfume, a scent I would have been happy to inhale for the rest of my life. She went smoothly through its gears but left a little rubber on the road in front of the Club House. I saw Jake had stirred himself out of his chair and was leaning on one of the porch pillars. He had an odd half smile on his face. He raised his hand, but I didn't give him one back.

On the way up Main Street, heads turned in our direction at nearly every porch and yard. We were leaving behind a lot of wagging tongues, that much was for certain. At the corner of Tipple and Substation Rows, I directed Rita into the alley behind our house. Dad's truck was gone. He was up at the mine, I figured, even if it was a Sunday afternoon. She parked the T-bird, and I went inside our garage and returned with a canvas backpack. Like the canteen, it was an artifact of my uncle Robert's World War II Italian campaign with the United States Army Signal Corps. I opened it up and packed Floretta's sandwiches, some little tubs of coleslaw, a few boiled eggs, and a tablecloth. I left behind everything else—the thermos and the cloth napkins and silverware and the vase with the rose wrapped in wax paper.

I rattled the back gate, and, as expected, Poteet came bounding out of the basement with Dandy waddling close behind. I let them out and introduced them to Rita. "Won't they get lost?" she wondered.

I laughed. "All I have to do is tell Poteet to go home and she's better than any compass."

"I've never owned a dog," she said, taking a step back when Poteet sniffed her knee.

"Then you've missed one of the pleasures of life."

We crossed the road to Water Tank Mountain and climbed up to the dirt road that led to the Coalwood School. When Dandy reached the road, he was panting and his head was down. I went over to him. "You all right, boy?"

"What's wrong with him?" Rita asked.

"He's fifteen years old."

"Is that old for a dog?"

I worked to keep the surprise at such a question out of my voice. "Yes, very old. Mom always said it's about seven dog years to every human one. That makes him a hundred and five."

Rita absorbed the information. "Father would never let me have a pet of any kind. He said he was allergic to fur."

I had never heard of such a thing and immediately suspected her father was lying for his own convenience. I didn't voice my suspicions, though, it being impolite. I pointed, instead, to a break in the foliage. "There's our path."

"I didn't even see it," she marveled.

"It's easier to find in the winter. It's steep at first, then there's a fire road that'll take us out to where it's clear-cut. Then we'll angle up the mountain to the water tanks."

"Lead on, Hawkeye," she said.

I hitched the backpack on my shoulders and scrambled up the steep hillside. I grabbed trees where I could to help me climb. Rita slipped a couple of times but then caught on to the natural rhythm of going up a West Virginia mountain: dig in your toes, grab a tree and pull, and then keep climbing.

We reached the fire road, and Poteet took off, her nose to the ground. She soon discovered a patch of milkweed that made her sneeze. A puff of white, drifting seeds rose around her. Dandy panted up beside her, his nose in the air. When he sneezed, Poteet nuzzled him. Then he sat down on his haunches, looking puzzled. I squatted beside him and moved my hand back and forth in front of his eyes. Rita came up alongside us. "He's blind or nearly so," I said. I hugged him, and he shivered even in the heat of the day. Rita knelt and let her fingers graze Dandy's head. She jerked back when he moved. "He won't bite you," I said.

"Dogs scare me."

"Most dogs just want to be loved," I said. "It's only the

ones who don't get any attention who get mean. Dandy and Poteet, they're loved and they know it, pretty much."

She touched him again, and Dandy arched his head. "He likes it," she said.

"He sure does. You have a way with him, Rita. Dogs know things about people. He knows you're nice."

When I looked up, I found Rita watching me. "You're an interesting fellow, Sonny Hickam," she said.

"How so?"

She stood up. "You wear your heart on your sleeve, for one thing," she said.

"Some people think that's a failing," I replied, wincing. It was true. When I'd been so much in desperate love with Dorothy Plunk in high school, Roy Lee had told me the only way to win a girl was to pretend you didn't like her, at least at first. Because I just couldn't fathom why such a thing would be true, I could never manage it.

We continued our hike, working our way to the end of the overgrown fire road where a narrow path began. It led into a wide clearing, a swath cut by Appalachian Power and Light to make room for the electric power lines that led down to the mine. The company had widened the swath even more when it had chopped down hundreds of trees, both hardwoods and pines, to use as posts, headers, and cribs.

Every time we stopped to catch our breath, we could see more of the valley and the encircling mountains. "It's beautiful," Rita said as we stopped beneath some crab-apple trees and drank some water out of my canteen.

"I just wish it would rain," I said. "It's been almost a month. It doesn't take long for all this brush to dry out. If it goes on much longer, a little heat lightning, or somebody playing with matches, and the whole county could go up."

Rita made no response. Then I realized she wasn't admiring the mountains at all. Her eyes were on the Olga Number One tipple.

The tipple complex was a black scar in the valley. A huge brick chimney dominated it. A hundred feet high and long dormant, the chimney stood in a lake of coal dust and gob. Behind it sat Dad's grimy office and the shabby lamphouse and bathhouse. The man-hoist, a black iron structure with twin bullwheels on top, was a forlorn skeleton against the green of the mountains. Up until 1957, the man-hoist had been part of a much larger and more active complex—properly called a tipple—used for lifting, sorting, and dumping coal into miles of railcars lined up on four sets of tracks. All that work had been moved across the mountain when a new tipple and preparation plant had been built in Caretta. The Coalwood tipple wasn't really a tipple at all anymore, just a place for Coalwood miners to go in and out of the mine. "That's Dad's little slice of heaven," I said of it.

She studied me. Our eyes met. "You resent all the time he spends there, don't you?"

"I used to," I confessed, looking back toward the mine. "From way up here, it seems pretty small and dirty. Not much for a lifetime of work."

"Maybe you need to look at it a different way," she said. "More like an engineer. Look at how the grounds are laid out. It's easy to see the plan from this vantage. The lamphouse is perfectly situated to get the men in and out in a hurry. The bathhouse is set back so the shifts won't be bunching up in front of it. Your dad's office is placed so he can watch who's going in and out of his mine. I can see where the old tracks used to be and also the foundation of the tipple. See how it's angled perfectly to match the contours of the valley? And have you looked at the masonry work on the lamphouse and bathhouse? It's very fine."

"They were built by Italian stonemasons," I said. "Mr. Carter brought them all the way from Italy. They put in the foundation of the Club House, too, and the wall in front of it. One of them was Johnny Basso's father."

"I've never been able to understand," she said, "what some people think is ugly. To me, if something works according to its design, that's true beauty."

"Spoken like a true engineer," I said.

"I'm proud to be an engineer, Sonny," she said in a voice she could have used for praying. "I've always loved mechanical things. That's not very girllike, I know, but that's the way I've always been. Father came home one time from a trip to Europe—I guess I was about five years old—and I'd taken apart every mechanical and electrical device in his apartment. I just wanted to see how they worked." She smiled at the memory. "Father and the housekeeper tried to keep radios and clocks and whatnot away from me after that. But I'd get to them when they weren't looking. Sometimes I'd take them apart and put them back together and they never knew. I learned a lot doing that."

"I never had that kind of curiosity about how machines worked, not until rockets came along," I admitted. "I was more curious about people. Otherwise, I just liked to read."

"Engineers don't read," she said, chuckling. "Except maybe technical manuals."

I shook my head. "I couldn't get by without a good book."

"The last book I read was *Moby-Dick* in college."

"You're kidding!"

She shrugged. "I don't like to be bored." I fell silent, at a loss for words. Then she said, "I'm going inside the mine before this summer is out."

"Good luck."

Her eyes flicked toward me, then away. "You don't think I will?"

"No."

"Then you're wrong," she said.

We stayed on the path until we reached a clearing on the highest ridge. It held the two structures that gave the mountain its common name, a pair of cylindrical wooden tanks that held Coalwood's water supply. The water in them was pumped up from a vast underground lake beneath the mine. There was no cleaner or apparently healthier water in the world. There was something in it—I'd heard about a natural fluoride—that kept Doc Hale a pretty happy dentist, even though the miner's habit of chewing tobacco still gave him plenty of work.

Poteet and Dandy skirted the water tanks and then went over the ridge to the other side of the mountain. Poteet had picked up the trail of some animal, most likely a rabbit. I set my pack on a big flat rock that had boulders equally spaced around it. Years before, I had been one of a group of boys who had worked for days to position the big stones. Many the summer day I had sat there with Roy Lee Cooke, Benny Brown, Jimmy Evans, or Roger Lester, happily eating peanut butter and jelly sandwiches and swigging water from our old canteens. That had been a grand time. Every morning when I was a boy, I was eager for the new day.

While Rita spread the tablecloth on the rock and emptied the pack, I sat on a boulder and let myself admire her. I think she must have felt my eyes, because she looked over her shoulder and smiled. I looked away, but I'd been caught. I almost didn't care. It was a warm, lazy day, and I'd brought a beautiful woman to a beautiful place to share it. There couldn't be anything wrong with that, could there?

After we finished eating Floretta's feast, Rita said, "I feel like lazing around a bit. Do you mind?"

It sounded good to me. We laid out the cloth on the grass and sat on it. I watched a few small clouds float by in the crystal-clear blue sky, then plucked a blade of grass and sucked on it. Rita drew her legs up to her chest and wrapped her arms around them. "What will people say when they hear about our hike?" she asked, her head resting on her knees.

"They've already said it," I said. "I doubt if there's a

soul in Coalwood who hasn't already chewed it over with their neighbors on both sides of the fence at least once, and maybe twice."

She chuckled. "And what are they saying, Mr. Know-it-all?"

"They're wondering what in the world Sonny Hickam is doing taking a full-growed woman up in the mountains. Some of the women will make something out of it, say we're up to sinful things. The men will say it's not so. They know you from the mine and know you're way above me."

"Am I? Way above you, I mean?"

"As far as Coalwood is concerned you are," I said. "To them, I'm still a boy."

"I thought there was nothing lower in Coalwood than a junior engineer."

"I think you fall in a different category."

"And I think you're a bit more than a boy," she said teasingly.

I shrugged. "I'm working on it."

I felt oddly exhausted from our conversation. I couldn't contend with all the things that were rattling around in my mind. Rita had to be at least five or six years older than me. She was a college graduate, and usually the junior engineers worked at the steel mill a year or two before they were sent off to Coalwood to learn something of mining coal. How did that song go? *Born too late.* I whistled a few bars of it and let out a long sigh.

"What is that you're whistling?" she asked.

"Nothing."

"No, it's something." Then she giggled. "Wait, I know what it is."

She sang, a bit off-key:

> *Born too late for you to notice me*
> *To you I'm just a kid*

That you won't date.
Why was I born too late?

"The Poni-tails sang that. Pretty stupid song." She looked at me. "Hey. What's wrong?"

"I'm mortified," I said. And I was, too. My face felt hot. I was pretty certain I had turned as red as a beet.

She kicked her boots out and started laughing so hard she finally had to hold her stomach. "You're cute."

"Thanks." Cute. That was me. Cute like a kid.

Her mirth subsided. She turned her face toward me. "Hey."

"What?"

Her hand stole to mine. She had long, strong fingers that laced in between my own. At her touch, my heart started to race. "Look, Sonny. I don't guess it matters how old you are. What matters is how you feel about somebody."

I looked straight ahead, not daring to look at her. My heart was throttled up to a mile a minute.

"But right now," she said, taking her hand back, "I've got to concentrate on my work. I'm here to learn everything I can about mining."

I was intoxicated. Whatever it took, I decided I was going to win Rita Walicki. Everything else was just details.

"Are we okay, you and me?" she asked.

My thoughts were already in another solar system. All I needed was a plan to conquer her, a campaign. It would take careful thought to map it out. What should I do first? What did Coalwood boys ever do when they wanted to impress a girl? The answer was easy. First thing: *show off.*

"You ever swing on a grapevine?" I asked.

"A what?"

"Come on."

MY MEMORY served me well, and we found the grapevine right where I'd last swung on it, years before. It was a two-inch-thick sinew of muscadine vine hanging from a stout hickory. At one time, the ground beneath it had been worn away by the feet of boys. I cleared the brush away to give us room for a proper swing.

"So this is how you spent your childhood," she said, her hands on her hips.

"Every chance I got!" I boasted as I readied for a test swing. I gripped the vine with both hands and pushed off. It all came instantly back to me, the wonderful feeling of swooping out over the mountain, the trees all around a blur. I was instantly eight years old, yodeling like Tarzan. I swung back and pushed off again. I looked into the sky, laughing with my mouth open.

Rita eagerly grabbed the vine when I swung back and handed it to her. "Take it easy until you get the feel of it," I advised.

"You don't know me very well, do you?" she said, and then pushed off as hard as she could, whooping as she arced out over the mountain. She was an incredible athlete. She swung as far out as anybody I'd ever seen. When she finally handed the vine back to me, she was breathless with excitement. Our hands touched when she gave me the vine, and I felt nearly an electric shock. She bounded away, laughing. "That was so much fun!" she hooted.

I started really showing off. I went through all kinds of grapevine-swinging variations: one-handed, feet over my head, twirling.

I guess I shouldn't have done the twirling. The old vine gave it up, broke with a sharp snap, and my jungle cry died in mid-yodel. I fell like a dead pigeon into a bush of hard-scrabble thistles. Stunned, I sat for a moment while I mentally went through my body, searching for breaks and cracks.

Rita came after me, laughing so hard I saw she was

actually crying. "That was soooo funny!" Tears were leaking down her cheeks. She finally covered her mouth to keep me from seeing her so joyful at my misfortune.

I shakily climbed to my feet, pushing my glasses up on my nose. Nothing seemed broken, amazingly enough. Then I lost my balance and nearly toppled over. Rita put her arm around my waist to catch me. I leaned against her, breathing in the sweet aroma of womanly sweat and perfume. "Are you all right?" she asked.

I put my arm around her waist. It was small, tight, smooth. I desperately wanted to put both my arms around it. "I am now," I gulped.

She pulled away, gave me a serious look. "You know, you could be trouble."

"I hope so," I replied.

"But she didn't do you any favors, did she?"

"Who?"

"Your mother," she said. "I think she made you into a nice boy, Sonny Hickam."

"I thought nice was good," I replied a bit defensively.

"Usually it is," she said, "but mostly it's not."

Apparently satisfied with her contradictory statement, Rita headed down the mountain. I watched her for a moment and then climbed up to where I'd left my pack. Poteet and Dandy ran past, then frolicked around a tree before chasing on. I could hear Rita calling far below. I hurried to catch up with her in every way I could.

20

A TRACK-LAYIN' MAN

IT DIDN'T take long before getting my tag and my lamp and riding the man-trip into work seemed almost routine. Johnny, Bobby, and I mostly changed out posts in different sections of the mine, but one day we were sent up to the face to help the roof bolters. When the continuous miner stripped a gear and its crew stopped to work on it, Johnny found us some shovels. The shuttle car rumbled up next to us, and we started shoveling coal into it as fast as we could go. "Boys, you're real coal miners now!" Johnny cried joyfully. After a while, we were so covered with black dust all I could see of him and Bobby were their teeth. That night, the shower drain got clogged with all the dirt that came off of me. I was proud of it.

As I started out the door to work the next morning, whistling and swinging my bucket like I was in charge of the world, I offhandedly asked Floretta where Rita might be. She gave me a long study and said, "Don't be falling for that girl, Sonny Hickam."

My face registered innocence. "I just wondered where she is."

"If that's all, she's gone to Dehue to see some mining engineers about something." She gave me another look. "Rita's full-growed, boy. Don't forget that."

"I'm eighteen years old," I said stoutly. "Since February the nineteenth."

"That don't mean you understand a thing about women."

"Like what?"

Floretta glanced at the grandfather clock in the parlor and then pushed me through the screen door onto the porch. "Sonny, you're just like every other man when you're around a good-looker. You see all those curves and start thinking about a play-toy. But Rita's no toy. She's a serious woman and she means to put her mark on the world. Don't you be trying to get in her way."

"I'm not going to get in her way," I said, miffed at being fussed at so early in the morning.

"She don't have no time for a boyfriend," Floretta insisted.

"Who said I wanted to be her boyfriend?"

"You did, maybe not in so many words but in the way you look at her. I seen you with them puppy-dog eyes."

"I'm innocent of all charges," I said, even though I knew she wouldn't believe me. I didn't believe myself.

Floretta wrapped her arms around herself in the cool morning air and muttered something I couldn't hear. We walked side by side down the stone steps to the sidewalk. Miners were quietly going past in clumps of twos and threes. "Hey, Floretta," Pick Hylton called as he slogged by. "Don't forget to kiss your little boy good-bye."

"You just mind your own business, Pick," Floretta snapped. She pushed me into the line. "Get on with you, Sonny, and don't forget what I done told you!"

I got on, but I instantly dismissed Floretta's worries about me and Rita. *Rita Walicki, Rita Walicki.* How I loved my newest song. I couldn't imagine why Floretta would think there was a thing wrong with it.

THE WEEK wore on. I just kept working, eating, and sleeping. There wasn't much else to do. I supposed I was making some money, although I hadn't seen any of it yet. I dragged myself out of bed every morning, dug into breakfast like I was starved, which I nearly always was, and then headed for the mine. Before I even got to the tipple, my stomach was growling. It was like I had a hollow leg. My shirt was getting tighter, but my pants at my waist were getting looser. I didn't know what to make of it, but at least my aches and pains had almost gone away. It had taken a while but maybe I was finally getting the kinks out.

I saw nothing of Dad, and Mom didn't call. It was as if I had been cast adrift, and I kind of savored the feeling. One evening at supper, Ned and Victor took note of my solitude. They were good old boys, in their simple way. "Come on with us, Sonny," Ned said, straddling a chair alongside me. "Victor and me, we're headed over to Cinder Bottom. One of those girls over there will fix you right up."

"Sure," Victor added, leaning on my table. "Why, we'll even let you pay our way. There's this girl over there—"

"The one with the peroxide streak in her hair?" Ned asked eagerly.

"Yeah, that's the one. There's this girl who—"

"And has rings on her toes?"

"Yeah, she's the one. Now, Sonny, this girl—"

"And a rose tattoo on her back?"

"Yes, Ned!" Victor spat. "What of it?"

"Didn't she say she was going to slap your face if she ever saw you again?"

Victor gave Ned a look. "I'm trying to talk to Sonny, Ned. If he wants to pay my way with a girl, even if she's mad at me, who am I to argue?"

I picked up my plate and moved to another table. "I'm not paying anybody's way anywhere and I'm not going to Cinder Bottom," I said over my shoulder.

"Well, thanks for considering it," Victor said in an aggrieved tone. When I saw him start to follow me, I picked up my plate and went up to my room, the only place I figured I could get any peace.

One morning while we waited for the man-lift, Mr. Marshall walked over to Johnny, Bobby, and me. "Come on over to the office," he said. "There's something you need to hear."

Johnny said, "We've got work to do. Cribbing down on West Main—"

"Right now," Mr. Marshall interrupted, "your work is to follow me."

We looked at each other and then followed Mr. Marshall into Wally's anteroom. "You can watch from out here," Mr. Marshall said.

I peeked into Dad's office. I saw a sea of white helmets. All of Dad's foremen looked to be in there. Mr. Marshall took a seat in one of the folding chairs in front of the big desk. Dad was on the black phone. Wally slid past me carrying a green folder. He handed it to Dad, then came back and took up his usual station, shuffling papers.

My ears were tuned to Dad's voice. "Listen, Clarence, for all the coal that section loaded, the lot of them could have stayed at home. If I hear about another wreck on his section, you tell Stubby he's going to be looking for another job, understand?" He listened for a short second, and added, "Tell him I said he's no good and never has been any good. Tell him, Clarence! How's a man ever going to get good if he doesn't know he's bad?"

There was a commotion behind me, and my jaw came

unhinged when I saw Rita coming inside the anteroom. She was dressed in her engineer khakis and boots, and her hair was tucked up under her pristine white helmet. Coach Gainer, Big Creek High School's legendary football coach, would have said she had her "game face" on. She looked all business. Tucked under her arm were some poster boards. She glanced at me but made no sign she even knew me. She went into the office and positioned her poster boards on an easel. Somebody handed her a wooden pointer and she tapped it impatiently against her leg, staring at Dad, who was still rattling away on the phone. I had deduced he was talking to his brother, my uncle Clarence, who headed up the Caretta operation.

When Dad slammed the receiver down, he took a second to rub his damaged eye. He glanced at me for a moment, then at Rita. "All right, Rita," he said. "Let's see what you've got."

Wally put his hand over his mouth. "What she's got," he tittered.

Rita went to the big map of the mine that was tacked to the wall. She tapped her pointer along a line that ran from one end of it to the other. "Mr. Hickam, I've finished the study you asked me to make of the main line. Of course, I had to do it with secondhand information, not being allowed to go inside and make a thorough inspection myself."

Dad nodded but made no comment. She waited a beat longer and then ran the pointer along the line. "This is the main track, as you well know," she said, her voice a degree frostier. "It was constructed over a forty-year period. The only sections of it that have been replaced are the ones that have been severely damaged by an accident. As a result, it is in various stages of disrepair."

Dad's shoulders raised slightly. "Right. So what?"

If Dad meant to rattle Rita, it didn't work. "As you *also* know, sir, I asked that workers be sent to randomly remove ties from the track."

"Miners," Dad said.

"Sir?"

"They're miners, not workers. I don't have workers in my mine. I have miners."

Rita took a breath. I sympathized with her. Interrupting on an irrelevant point was just one of Dad's techniques of dominating a conversation. She plowed on. "Every tie the *miners* brought back was rotten. My conclusion is that the only thing holding some parts of the main line track together is impacted breccia and gob."

Rita waited a beat, perhaps to let Dad and the foremen absorb her conclusion, and then walked to her poster boards. She took off the blank one on top, revealing a carefully lettered chart with all the sections of the mine listed vertically, and out from each a percentage number. I looked for 10 West, the section where Tuck Dillon had died, and saw a percentage of 30. Over the list of percentages was an abbreviation: *Est. L/T (%)*.

"Because of the rough shape of the track," Rita said, "trips have gradually slowed over the years. A series of interviews with all section foremen"—she tapped the chart with her pointer—"confirms that fact. Each of these numbers represents the estimated lost time percentages. In some parts of the main line, the motormen slow to a crawl. The time lost from production is formidable."

She pronounced the word for-*mid*-able, which seemed to me a wonderful way to say the word. Her next chart was "a statistical prediction of man-hours lost on the main line and the probability of future accidents." My admiration for Rita soared. She had a way of putting across complex ideas in just a few words.

Bobby nudged me. "Why are we here?" he whispered.

"To see a real engineer at work," I whispered back, most proud just to know her.

He looked around at the foremen. "They don't look very convinced," he said.

"She only has to convince Mr. Hickam," Johnny whispered. "And she knows it. Smart girl."

"Pretty girl, too," I said.

Bobby put his hand on my shoulder. "Be careful," he said. "That's a woman there."

I glanced at him, just to be sure he hadn't turned into Floretta.

Rita continued. Her voice was cool and dispassionate, as befitted an engineer. "I spent a few days with the supervisors at the Dehue mine to confirm my figures. They, too, had an old main line that, until a few years ago, severely hampered their operation. I factored in their data. The lost-time number is far bigger than even I thought it would be, but I've checked and rechecked my numbers."

When nobody said anything, Rita said, "Gentlemen, we're losing at least two hundred man-hours a day because of the condition of the main line. Using a conservative figure of five dollars per man-hour, that comes out to one thousand dollars a day. Figuring an average production year of two hundred days, that means two hundred thousand dollars a year. Add in the lost time for accidents and we have another one hundred thousand dollars, as a minimum." She looked around the room, and then back at Dad. "There's more, if you want to hear it."

Dad waved his hand toward the map. "All right, Rita," he said tiredly, "we hear you. So what do you think we ought to do about it? You know it's one thing to identify a problem, quite another to fix it. Right, men?"

If Dad expected a chorus of agreement, he was disappointed. His foremen, apparently impressed, stayed silent, their eyes locked on Rita. She had their full attention. "Here's what we do to fix this situation," she said, turning to her last chart. "We bite the bullet and change out the entire main line."

The chart had a list of materials—ties, rails, spikes, and labor hours. She quickly went through her calculations.

Dad frowned. "Do you have a plan?"

"Get in there, do it as fast as we can."

"Why not a little bit at a time, spread it out over a couple of years?"

"It's simple, Mr. Hickam," Rita said, still cool as a cucumber. "If we do it gradually, we'll end up causing lost time over a longer period. The smart thing to do is to do it all at once."

The corners of Dad's lips twitched. They almost turned up to a smile. Almost, but not quite.

"By all at once," Mr. Marshall interjected, "do you mean we start at one end and go to the other?"

"Yes, sir. Since the Coalwood shaft isn't used to bring out the coal anymore and is the oldest track, I suggest we begin here. Coalwood men can enter from the Caretta side during the months the work is being done."

A discussion followed among Dad's foremen. All the while, I watched Dad. So did Rita. He was looking at the map of the mine, his finger tapping the big blue blotter on the desk. When he cleared his throat, the other men instantly stopped talking.

"Here's how we're going to do it," he said. He looked around the room from one man to the next. They all leaned in to hear what he had to say, and I confess I felt proud of him, the way he commanded their attention.

"We'll start at both ends and work toward the middle," he said while holding up his hand in Rita's direction. "I know it's not the most efficient, Rita, but it's the way my miners will like it. Coalwood men are used to going inside from Coalwood, and Caretta men from Caretta. Miners have their routines and they're a comfort to them." He shrugged. "No use getting them upset. The two teams will work the day shift. They'll wait until the man-trips go in, then tear out the old track behind them and put in the new trackage before the end of the day."

While Dad was speaking, I couldn't help but notice Rita

irritably tap the pointer against her leg. When he stopped to take a breath, she said, "The evening or the hoot-owl shift would be preferable, Mr. Hickam. That way there'd be less interference with production."

Dad glanced at her with raised eyebrows, then continued without skipping a beat. "The hoot-owl shift will handle all the logistics. They'll stockpile the track layers and have them ready to go each morning."

Rita turned and gathered her posters, putting them back on the easel. She'd lost her audience, except for me.

Dad was the focus of everybody's attention now.

"How do we get the coal out on the Caretta side during the day shift?" Mr. Marshall asked.

"Set up a route along the new north track," Dad said. "It'll take a little longer, but not much more than it does now."

"What if there's a problem and the miners have to get out in a hurry?" Mr. Nordman asked. Mr. Nordman, another one of my former scoutmasters, was the company safety man.

"Set up an alternate route for every section and make sure each foreman is briefed," Dad replied. "Make some practice runs."

Everybody bent over their notebooks and scribbled Dad's orders. Then Dad nodded to Mr. Strong. "Dwight, I'm putting you in charge of changing out the track. Get with Rita, figure out the logistics of this thing."

At the mention of her name, Rita turned around. I could see her eyes glistening. She'd been near tears. The pointer tapped again against her leg, this time an eager movement.

"Got it," Mr. Strong said, nodding to Rita, then scribbling furiously in his daily notebook. "We've already got a good stockpile of ties. If it's all right with you, we'll get the hoot-owl shift to start moving them in tonight."

"Since it's my plan, I'll need to directly inspect the work," Rita interjected.

Dad smiled. "Nice try, Rita."

"Who's going to be my track layers?" Mr. Strong asked.

"A three-man team on both ends," Dad said. "I want Johnny Basso in charge on the Coalwood side. He's the best track-laying man we've got over here. He can pick any other two men he wants."

Bobby and I traded glances. It seemed as if we were going to get another boss. But Johnny quickly said, "I'll take Bobby and Sonny, Dwight."

I was amazed that nobody saw fit to argue with him, not even Dad. Bobby winked at me. I had to admit to feeling sort of proud, while being a little worried, too. I'd walked along a track or two in my boyhood, and one time we rocket boys had dug cast-iron pipe out from beneath an abandoned spur to sell as scrap. But laying track was something I'd never done, or imagined doing. I'd heard it was a pretty hard job, too, maybe the toughest in the mine.

"How about the Caretta end?" Mr. Strong asked.

"Use the same team that just put down the north track," Dad said without a moment of hesitation. I knew then he'd already thought through the entire thing, even before Rita's presentation. "Garrett Brown and those two boys."

"Delmar Crouch and Chinky Pinns," Mr. Marshall said.

"That's them," Dad said. "They're strong boys and they're fast."

They were, indeed. Both of them had been star players on the Big Creek High School football team the same year I'd graduated.

Dad turned to Rita. "This is your project, Rita. You ride herd on it. You know how to do that, don't you?"

"Yes, sir, I know very well," she said.

"Then that's it," Dad said, reaching for the black phone. "We've jawed enough. Get to work!"

Rita, her eyes still on Dad, reached quickly for her posters and knocked them all to the floor. When everybody started to laugh, I pushed inside and helped her gather them up. I didn't say anything, just stacked them on her easel, and went back to my place. When I turned back around, I found her eyes on me, saying thanks.

Bobby tugged my arm. "Come on, Sonny. Johnny's already on the man-lift."

On the way down the shaft, Johnny explained our new job. We'd be pulling up the old rails, inspecting them, digging out the old ties, then after the bed was properly prepared, putting the ties and track back in place, all under the low roof of the main line. "We'll do it, boys, better'n it's ever been done before, or my name's not Johnny Basso."

"It sounds hard."

"You'll earn your pay, that's for sure," Johnny said. "You boys game or not?"

Bobby narrowed his eyes. "I'm game." He looked at me. "Sonny? How about you?"

"I was born game," I said. I also figured it would be good to work on Rita's project. It would give us something to talk about.

Johnny nodded. "Boys, prepare to sweat buckets like you've never sweated before."

JOHNNY'S PREDICTION turned out to be pure truth. The next day, we descended on the main line like we were going to war. Johnny was the general and Bobby and I were the raw recruits. He gave us a quick run-through of our tools, the spike pullers, the rail carriers, and the sledgehammers. "Listen to me, boys!" he demanded fiercely. "This is serious work. Once we pull up a track, we've got to put it down just right or the man-trips could wreck and somebody could get killed. Do you understand what I'm saying?"

Bobby and I nodded uncertainly.

"All right, then. Set to."

We set to. We pulled the spikes, then pushed the heavy rails off into the gob. Then we grabbed picks and shovels and pry bars and dug out the old ties until we hit draw rock.

Johnny said it wasn't enough to go down to the rock. We had to keep shoveling until every particle of dirt was gone. Only then could we set a tie in place. We learned to man-handle a tie into the groove we'd dug, then stomp it down until it was as level as we could make it. Then, while Johnny used a bubble level on the tie to get it perfectly flat, Bobby and I grabbed our pry bars and shovels and got after the next tie. It was slow going, made all the harder by the low roof. We couldn't just throw the dirt over our shoulders. It would bounce back into our faces. Everything was done at an awkward angle. More hidden muscles, apparently dormant for the entire history of life, started complaining.

After the ties and rails were set in place, Johnny showed us how to drive spikes. We had to work on our knees to avoid hitting the low stone slabs overhead. The first time I took my turn, I threw the hammer up and it bounced off the roof right down on top of my helmet. It nearly drove it over my ears. Johnny laughed and Bobby did, too, though he denied it later.

Another hazard was much more serious. A trolley cable stretched down the main line, and it carried a powerful electric charge. When we got on station, Johnny called on the mine phone to get the wire turned off. But there was no way to look at it and tell if it was dead or alive. If it was alive, one touch with our hammer and "Katy, bar the door," as Johnny put it to describe the pile of smoking flesh we'd become.

All day, we fought the track with Bobby and me learning as we went along. At the end of the shift, I fell into the man-trip, *whupped* in a whole new way. Bobby looked done in, too. Johnny didn't seem at all any worse for wear. In fact, he was whistling and talking about doing some gardening that night with his son.

When we got off the man-lift, a cluster of men stood in front of the lamphouse, eyeing us hard. Bobby and I must have looked like prisoners of war—haggard, slump-shouldered, our boots dragging in the gob. When Johnny noticed the stares, he said, "These boys have been laying track." I caught a glint of respect in their eyes and managed a bit of stiff-legged swagger. All the way down the valley, I walked proud and then I got a little prouder when I re-called that John Henry, the steel-drivin' man himself, had been a West Virginian. How had the ballad gone?

> *John Henry told his captain*
> *A man ain't nothin' but a man*
> *But before I let your steam drill beat me down*
> *I'll die with a hammer in my hand, Lord, Lord!*
> *I'll die with a hammer in my hand.*

After a while I took on the opinion that the women who were at their fences were there to watch me go by, as were their open-mouthed children. I couldn't much blame them. I deserved their honor and awe. I had taken on the roughest, toughest job in the coal mine. I made up my own song and sang it to myself all the way to the Club House:

> *Sonny Hickam told his daddy,*
> *I'm not a boy but a man*
> *Your old mine ain't never gonna beat me down*
> *I've become a track-layin' man, Lord, Lord!*
> *I've become a track-layin' man!*

21

BOBBY'S ADVICE

NEARLY EVERY evening, Rita, still dressed in her work clothes, joined me for supper in the Club House dining room. Usually, she'd arrive straight from the engineering office. I'd visited her there once, just to see what kind of place the company had made for her. She was in the hall with a drawing board, a stool, and a filing cabinet. The top of the cabinet was stacked with her books. She kept an olive-drab canvas bag at her feet. When she opened it to pull out her slide rule, I saw only a hairbrush and some tissues in it. Just down the hall from her station, Ned and Victor shared a cramped closet of an office, but at least it was their space. They even had their own black phone. If Rita wanted to make a call to one of the foremen to talk over a project, she had to use the black phone in the meeting room. Usually, she said, either the phone was busy or the room was being used. Sometimes, she'd sneak up front to Mr. Bundini's office and Carol would let her use her phone there. She also had to go all the way up front to go to the bathroom.

At supper, Rita always wanted to know about my day. I told her how Johnny would yell *Praise God!* when he swung his hammer and Bobby would call out *And pass the spikes!* I told her how Johnny had thrown his hammer up and hit the trolley line and then fallen, shaking like he'd been electrocuted, and how Bobby and I had run around in circles trying to figure out what to do, until Johnny sat up and laughed at us.

"I don't see what's so funny about being electrocuted," Rita said.

"He was *pretending* to be electrocuted," I explained. "It scared us, but when we saw he was only fooling, it was funny."

Rita crooked her mouth and shrugged. "It must be a man thing," she said.

Maybe it was. I told Rita how Johnny had sent me and Bobby running back down the line to the tool car to find a rail stretcher after a rail was found to be too short. Dwight Strong had chanced along to find us there, pawing through the equipment and arguing on what a rail stretcher looked like. Mr. Strong laughed so hard when we told him what we were after, I thought he was going to bust a gut.

"I can't imagine how anybody would think there was a hand tool to lengthen a rail," Rita said. "Surely you must have had some inkling Johnny was pulling your leg."

"Johnny knows everything, so we trust him!" I explained. "I mean, Bobby and I both just charged off, determined to find that tool."

She looked blank. "And this was funny?"

"You had to be there," I said weakly.

I told her how we had gotten back at Johnny by getting Mr. Bolt to make us a wooden spike. "Johnny reared back with his hammer and let fly and all you could see was a cloud of sawdust. His eyes were as big as saucers! Then Bobby said, 'Gol, Johnny, you must be the strongest man in the mine!'"

Rita blinked once, then sighed. "And then all three of you laughed over this . . . this prank?"

"Johnny and Bobby did," I said. "Not me."

"Uh-huh" was her skeptical response.

After my daily dose of anecdotes, none of which seemed to amuse her much, Rita got down to cases and quizzed me closely on technical matters—such things as the quality of the ties and spikes, whether Johnny was getting a proper level on the track, or how many rails we were putting down each day. "I've got everything perfectly mapped out," she said, gnawing on her lower lip. "All Dwight Strong has to do is follow my list."

Since she seemed to need reassurance, I told her that all seemed to be going along just fine. Every morning when we got on shift, the hoot-owl boys had stacked fresh ties where we'd left off and provided new kegs of spikes. We were going as fast as we could, which, truth be told, wasn't all that fast. Bobby and I still had a lot to learn about laying track.

One night, after I'd told her yet another funny story she didn't bother to laugh at, she asked, "Have you seen your dad? Do you think he knows how well things are going?"

"I haven't seen him," I said. "But I'm sure Mr. Strong keeps him up-to-date on how things are going."

"It would be better if I could brief him personally," she fumed. She picked through her food. "This has got to go perfectly."

"I'll make sure it does," I told her.

Rita provided me with a smile, the first one in some time. "I'm counting on you," she said. Then her smile faded. She took a memo pad from her shirt pocket and jotted down a note. "I just had an idea for a simplified application of the Hardy cross-ventilation algorithm," she said in an urgent tone.

I had no idea what she was talking about, but I kept it to myself. Rita wasn't a patient teacher. She'd started talking one evening over dessert about a plan she had for pulling pillars to avoid converging zones of pressure and I interrupted her to say I didn't understand a thing she was saying. She'd put down her fork, muttered something to herself, then refused to talk about it or anything else the rest of the meal. I'd learned my lesson, at least about asking her questions.

After we finished eating, Rita excused herself, saying there was a project back in the drafting room she had to finish. "I'm charting a new approach to multiple face advancement," she said, picking up her still-unmarred white helmet. "I intend to prove that shuttle loading and conveyor belts can work in tandem to simplify the echelon driving sequence."

"That sounds like a great idea," I said, though I'd only understood every other word—at best. I watched her from the dining-room window as she walked across the road. She stopped once, got the memo pad out of her pocket, made another note, then kept going. I admired her anew. As soon as I could figure out a plan to make it happen, I was sure it was going to be so much fun to have such a smart and good-looking woman as my girlfriend. Maybe we could even go see a movie together at the Starland Drive-in Theater in Welch. Floretta's admonition about Rita being a serious woman too busy for a boyfriend drifted up into my brain and just as quickly went out of it again.

I was pondering the door through which Rita had disappeared, when Victor and Ned came up to my table. "We're heading over to Cinder Bottom again," Victor said. "Going to get our ashes hauled."

"Have fun."

"You got to ease up, boy," Victor said. "Come on with us."

"We don't usually take long," Ned said. "In and out, that's us."

"No," I said.

"Well, could you loan us forty bucks?" Victor asked.

"No!"

Victor and Ned left, shaking their heads. Floretta came over and swept up my empty plate. "You should have gone with 'em."

My mouth dropped open. "You think I ought to go to Cinder Bottom?"

"Don't get persnickety with me, young man. I ain't saying to go whoring. I just think it would be a good idea for you to keep Victor and Ned company, that's all. Be good for you to see how silly they act around those girls."

"Why?"

"It never hurts to look in the mirror even when it ain't exactly you looking back."

She had lost me with that one. She shook her head, mumbled something about a boy and his brains and gonads getting all mixed up, and headed back to the kitchen.

Late that night, Ned and Victor returned, clambering up the stairs with exaggerated shushing sounds. I heard them a full five minutes before they thumped up against my door. I threw it open. "What now?"

"We got one for you, Sonny boy," Ned said, leaning against the doorjamb. His breath almost knocked me down. It smelled like pure Keystone rotgut.

"Her name is Sucrose," Victor said. His shirt was buttoned one button off all the way down.

"Sucrose?"

"Yeah, sweetest little girl you ever seed. We told Sucrose all about you."

"Sucrose?"

"Well, hell, she wanted a name that told her customers how sweet she was, but one of the other girls already took Sugar," Ned said.

"She asked us for help, us being college graduates and all, so we named her," Victor slurred, though proudly. "We know our chemistry."

"But Sucrose is an awful name," I said. "Why didn't you name her Candy? Or even Cookie?"

Victor frowned. His lower lip started to tremble. "You rat bastard! If you'd have gone with us, that pretty little girl wouldn't be stuck with that awful name!"

"You really are a lousy friend, Sonny," Ned said, tearing up. "You know we ain't creative. We're engineers! Now poor little Sucrose is gonna hate us her whole hussy career."

I closed the door in their ruddy, sweaty faces. Shortly afterward, I heard twin thumps in the hall and crawling sounds.

DURING THE man-trip ride inside one morning, it occurred to me that Bobby was four years older than me and might, as a result, have a tad more experience with girls. Of course, that wasn't too difficult. Any experience was pretty much more than I had. Maybe that was what Floretta was getting at, that even an experience in Cinder Bottom was better than nothing.

I decided to question him during lunch. We were sitting on a stack of ties. Floretta had packed me three sandwiches, and I was already worrying they wouldn't be enough. Fortunately, she'd also thrown in two Twinkies, a banana, an apple, and two boiled eggs with a wax paper packet of salt. The way my stomach growled all the time, I figured I'd need every bit of it to get through to supper. It was occurring to me lately that maybe I had some kind of disease. I'd read about them, where men ate all the time but still faded away to nothing. I'd have gone to see Doc Lassiter, but I was always too hungry to take the time.

"So, Bobby," I said. "What do you think about Rita?"

Bobby wiped his mouth with the back of his hand, leaving a slimy smear of black streaks around his lips. He pushed his glasses up on his nose. "She's a fine-looking woman."

"But what do you think about her and me—together, I mean."

"You and Rita?"

"Me and Rita."

"You really want my opinion?"

"I really do."

He shrugged. "Not likely. She's got experience in places you don't even have places."

He might as well have slapped me in the face. "What does that have to do with her falling in love with me?" I demanded.

Bobby frowned behind his mask of gob dirt and sweat. He took off his helmet and ran his hand through his sandy hair. "Are you saying she loves you?"

"Not yet," I said, "but all I need is a plan. I thought maybe you could help me figure one out."

Bobby slumped against the ties and shook his head. "Love's not the same as laying track, Sonny. Or building rockets, for that matter. You can't make it happen by working hard. Forget it and find yourself a girl your own age. That's my advice."

Johnny had gone off behind a crib on down the line to eat his lunch. I guess he needed to get away from Bobby and me every so often, don't ask me why. We heard his footsteps coming back and then the sound of spikes being pulled. "Gaw," Bobby moaned. "Where does he get his energy?"

I didn't know. I squashed my sandwiches into my mouth and then stuffed in my Twinkies, too. I'd eat the fruit and eggs when it wasn't my turn on the hammer.

On the way to the track, Bobby asked, "Are you going to take my advice?"

"No," I said.

"Then why did you ask me for it?"

"I hoped you'd tell me something I could use."

"No," he said. "You hoped I'd tell you something you wanted to hear."

"I just need a plan."

"If there was a plan that would win over a woman, every man in the world would pay you good money for a look at it."

"So I should just quit?" I complained. "That's your advice? Just give up?"

Bobby stopped and dropped his chin on his chest. "It doesn't matter what I say. You're not going to listen, anyway."

"Boys!" Johnny bawled. "Time's a-wasting! You say your prayers? Lunch would be the right time for the onliest one *you* know, Bobby! God is great, God is good, let us thank Him for our food! Haw! Come on, let's get the lead out!"

Bobby groaned. "He isn't human," he said.

"*Boys!*"

"On our way!" we chorused.

THE NEXT day before we got going on the shift, Johnny drew me aside. "Something I heard in the union meeting last night, Sonny. There's going to be open testimonies in the Tuck Dillon investigation."

"What does that mean?"

"Anybody can attend."

"Is that good or bad?"

"You should come to the union meetings. You might learn something."

"I meant to come but I fell asleep."

Johnny nodded tragically. "Jake Mosby was there and made the announcement. He said the decision had been made so that the men would know the mine was still safe."

"Does that mean my dad will testify in front of God and everybody?"

"It does."

A flash of anger surged through me. It wasn't right that

Jake should have such power over my dad! "Did he say when the testimonies were going to be held?"

"Nope, but he said where. The Club House parlor."

That, at least, explained why Floretta had been in a dither that morning. I'd heard her muttering something about "new drapes."

"Thanks, Johnny."

"What are you going to do?"

I mulled his question over. "Attend the testimonies, I guess. And then call my mother to tell her what I heard."

"I wish your mama would come home," Johnny said. "Don't seem right in Coalwood without her."

I agreed with him and said so. But the more the summer wore on, the more I was convinced she never would. She'd painted her fox on the kitchen wall, a declaration of her independence, and headed south. If there was anything that could bring her back, I surely didn't know what it was.

22

THE BET

IT WAS toward the end of June when I came off the man-lift into the bright sun, looking forward to a long, hot shower followed by supper with Rita, when, all of a sudden, Johnny's hoarse voice boomed across the black dirt. *"What do you think you're doing, Garrett Brown?"*

Johnny took off, pushing through the miners queuing up at the shaft. Bobby and I looked at each other, shrugged in unison, and followed him until we arrived at a big flatbed truck beside the lamphouse. The truck had a stack of railroad ties on it, and beside them, a big man, his fists on his hips, stood laughing.

"Those are our ties, Garrett!" Johnny yelled. "Put 'em back where you found 'em!" The man only laughed even harder.

At the back of the truck stood a couple of boys I recognized as Delmar Crouch and Chinky Pinns, classmates of mine at Big Creek High School. Although they'd been star football players, they hadn't been good enough to get a college scholarship. To them, that meant their choices were either the military or the mines. They had obviously chosen the mines, at least until the draft caught up with them.

Garrett Brown, the leader of the Caretta track-laying crew, looked like a tank with legs. "We ran out of ties on our end, Johnny," he boomed, "so we came over to get some of yours. You boys are so slow, you don't need 'em."

"You must be doing a fair sloppy job to be going so fast, Garrett," Johnny growled, his hands reflexively balled into fists.

Garrett laughed. "We know what we're doing. Not like you and these college boys."

A crowd was gathering around the back of the truck, not only miners coming off the man-lift but the ones who were supposed to be getting aboard for the next shift, too. Several foremen came over for a look, pushing their white helmets back on their heads and frowning at the delay.

"These boys can lay track as fast as any men in this mine," Johnny said.

Garrett had a laugh like rolling thunder. "You willing to lay some money down on that?"

I recalled Johnny telling me that gambling had been the hardest thing he'd had to give up when he'd become a Holy Roller. Now I watched him hesitate, struggle for words. "Get thee behind me, Devil," he finally muttered.

"Come on, Johnny," a miner said. "You got to put your money where your mouth is."

"What's the bet?" asked another man, his face plastered with coal dirt.

"Johnny's college boys here against Garrett's football boys!" came the reply from a clean-faced evening-shift worker.

A chorus of hoots and cheers rose from the assembly. Even the foremen joined in. Everybody seemed to be having a lot of fun. Bobby leaned against the bathhouse wall, his arms crossed. His eyes were narrowed behind his glasses, taking everything in. In my estimation, he looked dangerous.

"How do we call it?" asked one of the foremen, Mr. Early Smith.

"We measure the main line," Garrett said, "then figure out where the middle is. Whoever gets there first wins!"

"Ain't a proper bet," somebody said. "Look at Delmar and Chinky. Those puny college boys'd never have a chance!"

Bobby suddenly became energized. He jutted out his jaw and strode into the clearing of men behind the truck. "Who said that? Who said I was puny?" He surveyed the men. "Come on, let's hear it."

I sidled up next to him. "Leave it alone, Bobby," I whispered out of the corner of my mouth.

Bobby's blood was up. "I say we can kick their tails, no problem," he said, pushing his glasses back up on his nose with his finger.

I pushed mine back up, too. "Are you kidding?" I hissed. "Look at those Caretta boys!"

He ignored me. "You hear what I said?" he yelled. "We can beat anybody laying track in this mine!"

Johnny kept balling his fists and unballing them. His lips were moving, but I couldn't hear what he was saying. He looked as miserable as anybody I'd ever seen.

Garrett Brown jumped down from the truck bed. "You heard Bobby Likens, folks! He says he can beat us. I say he can't. Let's start tomorrow to find out! The hoot-owl shift can measure tonight to find the center and make a mark on a post. Then we race to it. How about it, Johnny?"

Johnny looked up abruptly, then opened one eye. It was fierce. "You know I've given up sin, Garrett Brown!"

"Come on, Johnny, this is just a little sport," a voice

urged from the crowd. "No evil going to be done. Why, we're all churchgoers here, ain't we?"

A flurry of nodding black-and-white helmets indicated that only God fearers, Bible-thumpers, and pew sitters were at the scene.

"My uncle will set up a line," somebody said. It was Teddy Blevins, John Eye's nephew. John Eye's Snakeroot Hollow emporium would take a bet on nearly anything.

"A hundred dollars is my bet, Johnny," Garrett said, and put out his hand. "That's a personal bet between you and me. The rest of you men can set up your own game."

Dollar bills and bags of scrip instantly appeared in various hands. Why the miners carried money into the coal mine was beyond me, but they did. Maybe I would've carried some, too, if I'd had any.

Teddy produced a little spiral notebook and pencil and started to write down the bets. A friend of his stepped up and took off his helmet. Pretty soon, it was filled with money.

Johnny was eyeing Garrett's outstretched hand. When he didn't grab it, Garrett took it back and spat in it and stuck it out again. "There, sealed with spit, Johnny, just like we did when you and me were kids over in Gary."

Johnny's jaw twitched. He was struggling mightily with himself, there was no doubt about it. Then, as if a surge of internal electricity got too much for him to hold it in, he spat fiercely into his right hand and grabbed Garrett's big paw. *"Done!"* he said, a strangled look on his face.

"Done!" Garrett laughed, and the crowd cheered.

Bobby started laughing. I didn't see what was so blamed funny. Johnny Basso was surely going to lose his one hundred dollars, and since I was the weak sister of our crew, it was probably going to be my fault. The fence-line could go a lot of days with that kind of Sonny Hickam jerky to chew on.

Delmar lumbered up and stuck his face in mine. I could smell the Red Man on his breath. "I'll bet you six hundred dollars, college boy," he said.

I'd surely heard him wrong. "Did you say sixty dollars?"

"Six hundred and not a dollar less," Delmar growled. "Or are you too chicken?"

Money had started to mean a lot more to me now that I needed it for college. Grinning miners crowded around us. I had to say something. "One hundred dollars!" I blurted out, instantly regretting it.

"Chicken!" Delmar snapped. "Five hundred dollars, then."

More men crowded around. I looked at Bobby, hoping he'd stop me, but he had adopted a cocky smile. I felt like belting him. He'd gotten me and Johnny into this! "Two hundred," I said, gulping. What else could I do?

"All right, Mr. Chicken. Three hundred dollars and not a penny less!" Delmar spat in his hand and stuck it out while the crowd cheered. His arms were as thick as mine posts.

The sight of his hand did it. I couldn't let such a challenge pass me by, no matter what it cost in blood or money. I spat on my hand and slammed my palm into Delmar's. *"Done!"* I roared.

And then I looked up and saw Dad standing in the doorway of his office. He was watching me, his brow a puzzled furrow. I held his gaze for a long second, then raised my spit-soaked hand to him in salute.

Don't ask me why.

23

JOHNNY'S TEAM

THE PHONE rang once, and Mom picked up on the other end. I identified myself and was met with silence. I waited her out. "I have run out of words," she said finally.

It didn't surprise me that somebody had beat me to her with news of the bet. It didn't matter who. "I know it was a dumb thing to do, Mom," I said. "Floretta thinks maybe I need a psychiatrist."

"He'd be working on the wrong end of your anatomy," she replied.

I rushed to agree with her. Then I said, "Come home, Mom. I need you. Dad needs you. Coalwood needs you."

"Do tell," she said with a noticeable lack of enthusiasm. "Certainly, it makes wondrous sense for me to leave the house I've always wanted in the clutches of these thieves who masquerade as contractors down here in the Palmetto State."

Wisely, I resisted saying that I could have been there helping her with those contractors.

"I love you, Sonny," she said suddenly.

"I love you, too, Mom, and I'm really sorry for being an idiot."

"It might come natural, I don't know," she considered. "Your ground-daddy was always a gambler. One time he came home with a wad of cash in his pocket after a poker game and Mama found it and burned it all up in the cookstove. She said she'd have nothing to do with money that came from sin. Daddy started hiding his gambling money out in the barn after that. Good thing, too. He won a lot of it. Kept us kids in shoes. I always thought there was a bit of my daddy in you. I guess it's finally come out."

"I'll resist my gambling urges from here on," I promised fervently.

"That would be a good thing. Did you give Nate his bath?"

The change of subject was welcome. "Yes, ma'am. For a minute, he even knew who I was."

I described the entire experience. Then she said, "Anything Mrs. Dooley wants, you give it to her."

"I will," I promised.

She said, "Anything I can do for you?"

"I already mentioned coming home."

"Anything else?"

"Can you get my college money restored?"

"Your dad still holding to that?" She sounded nearly nonchalant about my desperate situation.

"He hasn't mentioned it lately, so I guess so."

"Maybe you'll win your bet and have plenty of money for college."

"What if I don't?"

"I guess you should have thought about that before you gambled," she said. And then, "What's this about you hanging around with an older woman?"

I told her about Rita. I couldn't help mentioning how wonderful I thought she was. "You should talk to Bobby

Likens," she said. "He always had a hand with the ladies. Listen to what he says."

"I already have. He says I should run."

"You don't need to get serious about any girl right now, anyway," she said. "Plenty of time for women later in your life."

I fell silent. "Later in life" for Mom, I suspected, was when I was about forty years old.

She said, "There's one thing you can do for me, Sonny."

"Anything."

"I'm just going to say it once."

"I'm listening."

"Win that bet!"

THE NEXT morning, someone had erected a chalkboard and placed it near the entrance to the man-lift. COALWOOD VS. CARETTA was written at the top. A horizontal line represented the main line and vertical tick marks showed the relative progress of the two teams working toward the middle. Below the line was space for the relevant statistics: the number of rail sections each team changed out the previous shift, the average rail sections changed per shift, and the number of rail sections to go until the midpoint. At the bottom of the board was another statistic that was pretty depressing: Since the changing out of the track had begun, Garrett and his boys were changing out a steady average of eight rails per shift. We were averaging a little more than five. We were well behind before we'd even got started.

Aboard the man-trip on the way in, Johnny got Bobby and me squared away. "Okay, boys. We'll go as fast as we can but we ain't gonna skimp on nothing! The main line's gotta stay safe."

"But what about Garrett?" I demanded. "Who's going to keep him honest? He and his boys will throw their track down as fast as they can."

"Every night, your daddy sends an inspector to see what we've done," Johnny said. "He'll be looking at Garrett, too, don't you think he won't. Garrett'll get caught if he tries any dirty tricks."

When we got to our section, Bobby drew me aside while Johnny was off praying. "We've got to put our heads together and figure out how to win."

"Why? You didn't bet anything."

"I couldn't, Sonny," he explained. "I need every penny for medical school. Why do I have to keep reminding you? That doesn't mean I don't care about this bet. My reputation is at stake."

I shrugged. "I don't know what else to do except work like the Devil."

"All I'm saying is we need to think about it."

"You boys through praying?" Johnny demanded.

"Amen!" we yelled back in unison.

He worked his way to us, then thrust a spike puller in my hands and a shovel in Bobby's. The expression on his face was fierce. "Let's go!"

"Wait a second, Johnny," Bobby said. "We've got to figure out a way to be more efficient."

A scowl crossed Johnny's face. "You mean like a time study?"

Bobby snapped his fingers. "A time study! That's what we need!"

"What's a time study?" I asked.

"It's a waste of time, that's what it is," Johnny growled.

"No, it isn't!" Bobby replied. "A time study is where you break a job down into its different elements, then you put a stopwatch on them. You study the results, figure out where the delays are, and then you know how to do the job faster, cheaper, better."

"It's some lazy bum watching a man work, that's all it is," Johnny groused.

"Can you get us a stopwatch?" Bobby asked him.

Johnny wasn't giving in. "The union's against time studies. They burden the working man."

"But they're legal in this mine, aren't they?"

Johnny reluctantly nodded. "I guess."

"I can get a stopwatch," I volunteered. "Rita will get me one from the engineering office if I ask her."

Bobby hesitated. "I don't want you to get into debt with her."

"Mind your own business. Do you want me to get that watch or not?"

"Of course I do."

"If I get it, I want to operate it."

"It was my idea," Bobby groused.

"Maybe so, but it'll be my stopwatch."

Johnny drew his bandanna and honked into it. "Boys, I'm not gonna let any one of you stand around with a stopwatch. I'm telling you, it would be a waste of good time!"

"It's scientific, Johnny," I said.

"See if that scientific spike puller fits your hand," Johnny replied. "And you"—he pointed at the tool Bobby was holding—"get busy with that scientific shovel!"

"Johnny . . ."

"Let's go, boys! *Go, go, go!*"

Bobby and I went. We pulled spikes, rolled the rails to either side, then started digging out the old ties. Then we put the rails back in place and spiked them in, one at a time. Bobby kept thinking. "How about we skip lunch?" he proposed. "We can eat while we work."

My stomach growled at the idea of missing a meal, but such was my ardor to win the bet, I said, "I'll go along with that."

Johnny just kept wrenching. Bobby and I rolled the rails into place, and Johnny used a level to make sure they were set correctly. "Good" was all he said.

Bobby, on his knees, swung the hammer to drive in the new spikes. "We could use—*umph*—another—*umph*—

hammer," he said, grunting with each swing. "That way—
umph—we could get—*umph*—these rails in twice as fast."

Johnny finished with another fishplate, threw the
wrench down. He came trudging over, bent under the
roof. Bobby and I stopped what we were doing and looked
at him, our lights two bright circles on his sweaty face. "All
right, boys," he said quietly. "All right."

"Johnny, we don't mean to be disrespectful," Bobby
said.

Johnny held up his hand, a signal for Bobby to be silent.
"Sonny, can you get a stopwatch, like you said?" he asked.

"I can."

Johnny pivoted, walked a step, pivoted again. "And you
boys want to skip lunch, work right through it. That right?"

"Yes, sir," we chorused.

"And you want another hammer?"

"Yes!"

"You really want to beat those Caretta boys, don't
you?"

"Yes," we chorused again.

"Why?" He looked from Bobby to me and back again.
"This is important. Why do you want to beat them?"

Bobby and I looked at each other, our lights in our eyes.
I was about to blurt *So we can win our bet!* but, fortunately,
Bobby answered first. "To prove to everybody in
Coalwood and Caretta that we're as good as any other
miner in this mine, that's why," he said. Then he added,
"Even if two of us are college boys."

Johnny nodded. "You're right, Bobby. Sonny, do you
understand that? It's not the bet. It's because they've said
we're less the men than they are. That's why we're going to
beat them."

"I understand," I said. "We're a team."

"We're Johnny's team," Bobby amended. "You tell us
what to do, Johnny, and we'll do it."

Johnny wiped his forehead with his sleeve, leaving

behind a sweaty black smear. "Go get your buckets. Eat when you like, drink when you like, but this team don't stop for nothing!"

"*Yes, sir!*" Bobby and I went off at a run.

THAT NIGHT I sat down with Rita at supper. She looked as exhausted as I felt. She fiddled with her food while I tossed mine down. As usual, I was starving. Finally, I asked, "Could you get me a stopwatch? We want to time-study ourselves while we're laying track and see if we can get more efficient."

She studied me tiredly, then said, "Sure." If there was any enthusiasm in her voice, I failed to hear it. I knew she'd been keeping awfully long hours at the engineering office.

"Thanks," I said.

"Did you know John Eye has a betting line on me, too?" she asked.

"No. What's the bet?"

"Whether I'll go into the mine this summer or not. Odds are ten to one against me, so I hear."

I would have put the odds at about a million to one, but I was smart enough not to say it out loud. Sometimes a leisurely tongue can save the unwise.

"I put a hundred dollars on myself," Rita advised, leaning forward so no one else could hear. The top button on her canvas shirt was undone. I got a whiff of the perfume that seemed to escape from that shadowy, warm place, and my head swam.

"How about we help each other win our bets?" she asked.

I heard her question, but it didn't register. I was just trying to breathe normally.

"How about it?" she asked again.

I looked up from my heavenly vista and almost immediately sank into her eyes. "How about what?"

"We help each other."

Help each other? I was willing to help Rita Walicki do any-thing she wanted to do! Why, I'd climb the highest mountain, swim the widest sea, walk across the driest desert, endure the—

"Sonny?"

"Huh?"

"What do you say?"

"Yes!"

"Good," she said with a wink.

I puzzled over her wink for a moment, but then decided to just enjoy it. "Did you know there are mines in the Andes, high up in the clouds?" she asked. "I want to go there, engineer those mines. Then I want to go to the Australian outback. There's coal there, and also copper, iron, and aluminum. You name it, I'll mine it."

"I'd like to do that, too," I said.

She looked at me approvingly. "Would you?"

"We could do it together," I said, starting to warm to the concept. "We could start our own company."

"A consulting company," she said. "But I thought you were going to be an aerospace engineer."

Before I could answer, hard footsteps thudded into the dining room. It was Jake Mosby. He came over, nodded to Rita, and said, "Just thought you ought to know, Sonny. We'll start testimonies soon. I'd like to talk to you before we do."

"Why? I don't know anything about what happened to Tuck," I said.

"Background is all I'm looking for," he replied. When I didn't respond, he rocked in his boots and then said, "Rita, you and I need to have a conversation, too." He glanced at me. "This isn't about the testimonies. It's about the company festivities on the Fourth of July."

She raised her eyebrows. "Are you asking me for a date, Jake?"

I gulped. *Was he?*

"Not hardly," he said to my everlasting relief.

She shrugged. "Call Carol and make an appointment. You know how much in demand I am around here."

He laughed. "You always have a comeback. You're a good kid, Rita. I enjoyed that summer you came to the farm, even though you rode our horses pretty hard."

"Why do anything halfway?"

"That's one thing about you. You've never done anything halfway in your life. That's why I think you're going to be interested in my idea for the Fourth." Jake cast his gaze my way. "Sorry, Sonny. Not for union ears, I'm afraid."

"I don't care, anyway," I lied.

"Talk to you soon, Rita," he said.

"Can't wait." Her voice, I was happy to note, was as cold as a block of ice.

Thoroughly dismissed, Jake withdrew, sitting down with Victor and Ned.

"Amazing. He's still jealous," Rita told me in a low voice. "We used to race and he never beat me, not one time, even though he had the faster horse. He wasn't willing to smack his horse's rump. You have to get their attention, make them hurt a little. He never could understand that. He just wanted his horse to like him." She shook her head as if Jake Mosby were the dumbest creature on earth.

I nodded in agreement with her, although the truth was I was more sympathetic to Jake's position. I spent the remainder of my supper with Rita in silence, mulling over my misunderstandings, misinterpretations, and miscalculations as regards Miss Rita Walicki, all the while believing them to be utter truths.

24

SIMPLE THINGS

RITA DISAPPEARED the following weekend. When I got up Saturday morning, her T-bird was gone. Because I didn't want anybody to notice how infatuated I was with her, I argued with myself a little about it, then gave in and asked Floretta if she knew where Rita had gone. I knew Floretta was going to make me suffer for asking, and I was correct.

"My, oh, my," she said, filling up the kitchen sink with hot water to start the long process of washing all the dirty dishes we left her after breakfast. Soapsuds piled up, making their tiny popping noises underneath the rush of the water out of the faucet. "Why don't you just volunteer to carry her things around for her, Sonny? Be her private butler, huh? Maybe you could keep up with her that way."

I nodded but didn't say anything. Floretta would get to an answer eventually, I knew.

"Miss Rita said she was going up to Bluefield to see some kind of mining machinery, that's all I know," she said. "She's got a friend up there she goes to see, too."

My face dropped and colored at the same time. I couldn't help it. Of course, Floretta noticed.

"A *girl*friend, Mr. Jealous. The green-eyed monster has really grabbed you by your tail, ain't it?"

Floretta was absolutely right. I was horribly jealous of anybody else who spent time with Rita. To get some distraction, I watched a baseball game on television with some contractors in the parlor, then went outside for some fresh air. I was on the verge of moping, if I wasn't careful. On the porch, I found Mr. Fuller slumped down in one of the wooden Adirondack chairs and chewing on an unlit cigar. I walked over to the other side of the porch to have a look at the tennis court opposite the Community Church. Doc Hale, the company dentist, and Bobby Likens were battling each other swat by swat. A small crowd of boys and girls watched them, hanging by their little fingers to the chain-link fence around the court. Occasionally, a cheer would go up when one of the players made a good shot. While I was watching, Doc Hale jumped over the net and shook Bobby's hand. Bobby returned the favor by jumping over the net to the other side. Everybody around the court clapped, and some little girls ran off chasing little boys in games of tag.

"Bucolic, ain't it?" Mr. Fuller demanded from his throne.

I looked around, hoping there was somebody else he was talking to, but I was it. "You might say so," I answered.

He chewed on his cigar, its tip going up and down. "Do you know what the word means, son?"

"Rustic, countrified, and pastoral," I answered, educated product of the Coalwood School, Big Creek High, and Virginia Tech that I was.

He moved the cigar over to one side of his mouth. "How you like being in Homer Hickam's boot camp?"

I realized Mr. Fuller thought I was a junior engineer. It

was just too good an opportunity for some mischief for me to let it pass. "Homer Hickam is as mean as a snake, sir," I said. "He makes us work like common miners."

Mr. Fuller grunted. "I have never understood why the steel company lets him get away with the mistreatment of you fine young men. Him, with not so much as a scrap of paper from a college. I will be glad to see it stopped, sir. I can tell you that."

"So you believe his days are numbered?" I asked. I strolled closer and leaned against one of the supporting porch pillars, trying not to betray the intensity of my interest.

Mr. Fuller squinted at me. "Do I know you? Who's your boss?"

"You probably don't know him," I said. "He's kind of low-level."

"Try me."

I'd heard Dad over the years talking about a Mr. Battlo Jones, an Ohio man who seemed to be in charge of frustrating Dad's attempt to purchase large mining machinery. I named him.

"Battlo? You work for Battlo?" Mr. Fuller nodded approvingly. "You're with the best, young man. The very best."

"Yes, sir. Nobody can squeeze a dime like Battlo Jones."

Mr. Fuller grunted a proud affirmation.

"So you think that rat bastard Hickam is out of here?" I asked.

Mr. Fuller shrugged but got a distant look on his face as if he were watching angels fly by.

"What do you have on him?" I congratulated myself on my own craftiness.

"I'm working several angles," he replied.

"But you're going to get him," I said. "That's the important thing."

Again, Mr. Fuller shrugged.

I kept probing. There was nothing, beyond good sense, to keep me from it. "Do you have proof?"

"I've got a witness," he said.

I searched through my brain for a clever way to get the name of the witness out of him. What I came up with was "Who is it?"

Mr. Fuller's lips curled up into as near a smile as he could manage. "Homer Hickam himself," he said. "He's the only witness I need."

I STROLLED up Main Street to see the dogs. While there, I thought maybe I could warn Dad about what Mr. Fuller had said, but he wasn't home—no surprise. I saw Mrs. Sharitz across the fence, and she said she thought she'd seen him walk up to the mine a little earlier. I talked with her for a little while, agreed with her that we all wished Mom would come home, and then played "throw the tennis ball" with Dandy and Poteet. Dandy mostly watched from the back steps while Poteet showed her stuff. She was capable of flinging herself into the air and catching the ball in her jaws while still on the fly. She was an amazing athlete.

After I'd let Poteet work up a sweat, I sat down beside Dandy and scratched his ears. He crawled into my lap, and after a bit, fell asleep. Poteet came over and draped herself over my boots. Every so often, she'd let out a big sigh, as if something was worrying her. "It's okay, girl," I said. "Dandy's fine."

We sat on the steps for a long time. I looked up sharply, thinking that somebody was watching us, and then I realized it was just the old mountains. They were always watching. I had the sudden urge to climb them, maybe go up to Pine Tree Valley where Sherman and I had once found the dying fawn. There was wisdom up there. I only needed to climb and then be quiet and listen. Maybe I might even see Mom's fox, or its descendants. If I spied kits with half-silver tails, might that solve what had happened to Parkyacarcass? Maybe he had just gone looking for a mate, and found her. It was a fantasy, and I knew it. The answer to what had happened to Mom's fox wasn't on Sis's Mountain. I didn't know where it was, but it wasn't there.

On my walk back to the Club House, I stopped by the Dooley house. Mrs. Dooley appeared at the door. "Do you need me to do anything?" I asked.

"Garden needs weeding," she said. "Beans need picking."

"I'm your man," I answered, and went into the backyard to get a hoe and a basket from her toolshed.

Mrs. Dooley followed me. "Our garden's just up to the right behind the Hardin place," she said. "I got a scarecrow up."

"I'll find it," I answered.

"Fill the basket full of string beans. Nate likes to snap them."

"Yes, ma'am," I said, and climbed up the mountain.

I returned with a basket filled with beans. I'd enjoyed my time in the Dooley garden, doing honest work with the hoe and stoop labor over the bean vines. The sun was warm, and the trees on the ridge above me were rustling with the light breeze. They seemed to be having as much fun as I was. It was a pleasant thing to work, and sweat, in a place where I could stand up without hitting my head on a slab of sandstone. It helped me get the kinks out of my joints, too. I stopped from time to time and listened to the mountain. What I thought it said was *All is well.*

"Stay for supper?" Mrs. Dooley asked when I brought the filled basket back.

"Yes, ma'am. I'd like that."

"Nate's on the front porch. Carry that basket around to him."

Mr. Dooley was sitting in a rocking chair on the front porch. He put his hands out when he saw the basket. I handed it over and then pulled up a stool. "Can I help you, sir?"

"You an ol' fox," he said, but didn't object when I picked up a bean and snapped it, one—two—three.

"Nate likes you," Mrs. Dooley said, coming out on the porch.

I snapped another bean. "I like him, too, Mrs. Dooley. I wish I'd known him before he got hurt."

She sat down on the porch swing. "He was a good man. He loved to go up in the mountains. He hunted a bit for meat on the table, trapped for spending money. He didn't like killing the animals, but sometimes you do what you have to do."

Mr. Dooley looked up sharply. "Shut up, you ol' cat."

"You shut up, Nate," she replied, but there was no sting to her voice. "He's into cats and dogs these days, heaven knows why. Better than monkeys, I guess."

"He called me a fox," I said.

She laughed, and we kept snapping beans. It was the happiest I'd been in a long while, and I didn't even wonder why.

25

THE FIRST TESTIMONY

ON THURSDAY, June 29, 1961, the first testimony concerning the death of Tuck Dillon was held. I'd seen Jake go into the Club House kitchen that morning, and when he came out, Floretta was at his ear. "Tonight, Mr. Jake?" she asked, her hands fluttering.

Jake was perfunctory and unsympathetic. "Just set up some chairs, Floretta," he said, sitting back down to his breakfast and shaking out his napkin. "That's all we need."

Floretta kept hovering. "People will want to eat, and they'll want iced tea by the bucket."

"Floretta," Jake sighed, "those men you checked in last night are state and federal inspectors. They're here for testimony and I've got to get some in before miners' vacation. This is in no way a social occasion."

"Then you don't know Coalwood, Mr. Jake." Floretta huffed back into her kitchen.

On the man-trip ride in that morning, I told Johnny and Bobby about the coming testimony. I also showed them the stopwatch Rita had slipped me at breakfast. Bobby snatched it. "A first-rate piece of machinery," he said, giving it a test run.

He handed it to Johnny, who turned it over a few times, grumbling something under his breath, before I managed to retrieve it.

"I won't let it slow me down, Johnny, I promise," I said.

"You better not or I'm taking it away from you."

All day, I stayed on double duty, working and clicking the stopwatch and writing down the results with Bobby giving me advice every step of the way. Johnny gave me hard looks but didn't say anything.

Later in the day, Mr. Dubonnet showed up and watched us work for a while. "You been over to see the Caretta boys, too, John?" Johnny asked.

"Just came from there," he said. "They're having a terrible morning. Seems they got delivered the wrong size spikes and their stack of ties was late, too."

"Do tell?" Johnny responded. "Well, boys, you hear that? The Lord's helping us."

Mr. Dubonnet squatted in the gob. "I need to talk to your boys, Johnny."

"Make it quick."

Bobby and I went over and knelt beside the union chief. "Boys, I want you two to play on the union softball team this Fourth of July," he said. "Word's out management's got a hot pitcher. I don't know who it is but I figure I better get some young blood to match him."

"I'll play first base," Bobby said.

"You got it. How about you, Sonny?"

I hesitated. I'd never been very good playing any kind of ball, and I was surprised Mr. Dubonnet didn't know it. Then I thought—maybe he did know it and he was up to something, such as embarrassing Dad by showing off the fact that I was on the union team. Then I thought—why would he do that? Dad was about to be plenty embarrassed in the testimony that very night. Then I thought—

"Sonny will play right field," Bobby said, interrupting my ricocheting thought process.

"That's fine," Mr. Dubonnet said, shining his light in my eyes. I shined mine back at him. We looked at each other for a moment, and then he reached over and slapped me on the shoulder. "I'm proud of you, son," he said. "You're doing good work down here."

"I haven't been paid yet," I replied. He was the chief of the union, after all.

He chuckled. "End of the month's coming right up. Let me know if they shortchange you."

Mr. Dubonnet went off to have a word with Johnny. "Why did you get me into this?" I demanded of Bobby. "I'm going to be embarrassed all over the softball field."

"Don't worry," he said. "For some reason, my dad's always liked you. He and I will give you some coaching."

"Can you give me some hand-and-eye coordination while you're at it?" I said under my breath.

Bobby heard me. "There you go with that negative attitude. You really need to get past that."

That afternoon on the man-trip ride out, Johnny wrote down our progress. We'd laid seven sections that day, a record for us. When we stepped off the man-lift, we took a look at the bet board. Caretta had also managed to put down seven. We'd at least tied them. That was a first. "We're making progress," Bobby said.

Johnny looked doubtful. "They had a bad day, boys, and we had a good one. You can call it progress if you want to. I call it a crying shame."

I patted the stopwatch in my pocket. "I'll work on my figures, Johnny. That'll help."

He shook his head. "It better."

Floretta met me at the door of the Club House. "I don't want you fretting tonight, Sonny, what with your daddy's trial and all."

She had said out loud the word everybody was thinking. This was a trial, no matter how they tried to soften it by calling it a testimony.

"You know you've been known to get a little scatter-brained when you get fretted," Floretta continued. "That's not good for you, especially down in the mine. You got to keep your wits about you."

"How's Mom?" I asked.

Floretta studied me. "You think you're pretty smart, don't you?"

"Well, I know you either talked to Mom today or you're starting to sound just like her."

"She said for you not to worry about what happens tonight, Mr. Smarty-pants. That's what she said."

"She didn't say she was coming home anytime soon, did she?"

"She ain't ready," Floretta said. "I'm going to need help setting up the parlor."

"Can I take my shower first?"

"Go right ahead and then get back down here."

I was still setting up chairs when Cleo Mallett, the wife of the union's second-in-command, arrived along with the other women of the Coalwood Organization of Women. It had been Roy Lee, back in 1959 when the C.O.W. was formed, who first noted that its initials pretty much described its membership.

Mrs. Mallett gave me a sharp look as she came into the parlor, then proceeded to ignore me. I was just a common miner, after all, even if I was the son of the mine superintendent and, until recently, a college boy.

Mrs. Mallett had always believed she had married well beneath herself and aspired to be the town's social leader, which meant, as far as she was concerned, meddling in everybody's business. What Tag said about her described her best: *an ignorant woman who knew everything.*

Mrs. Mallett and the other C.O.W. ladies selected the chairs up front and plumped down in them, calling to

Floretta for iced tea. "Testimony ain't going to start for another whole hour, Miss Cleo," Floretta answered from her kitchen door. "And I ain't ready to serve."

"Floretta, dear," Mrs. Mallett answered in the high-pitched voice she used when dealing with someone she thought inferior, "the ladies and I require our iced tea. A slice of lemon in our glasses, too." Then her voice broke to her usual growl. "Right away, dear, if you know what's good for you!"

"What's good for you ain't on my menu," Floretta muttered. But soon the sound of the tinkle of a spoon on a glass pitcher from the kitchen told the C.O.W. ladies they were getting their way. They relaxed into gossip.

I kept working, carrying more folding chairs in from the storeroom in the back, but I couldn't help but hear what the ladies were discussing. It seemed there was a certain somebody's husband down in Frog Level who'd been observed in a certain somebody else's house on Substation Row while the certain somebody else's husband was working the day shift. I tuned them out, mainly because they weren't mentioning any names.

More folks were wandering in. Some miners, fresh off shift and still in their work clothes, filled some chairs. Then Jake came in, perused the gathering crowd, and announced: "Ladies, I'm sorry. The chairs on the front row are for the witnesses and the federal and state inspectors. I'll have to ask you to move."

"Jake Mosby, we're not moving anywhere," Mrs. Mallett said. She was holding a glass of iced tea in one hand and in the other a fan imprinted with a logo that read *Fanning Funeral Home, Welch, West Virginia*. The others of her ladies were similarly composed.

Jake caught my eye, and rather than hear any orders out of him, I went ahead and solved his little problem. "I'll put more chairs up front," I volunteered.

A tumult of voices in the parlor announced more

visitors, mostly Olga Coal Company officials. Mr. Bundini followed them, talking to a big-bellied man I didn't recognize. Another man, so skinny he was nearly cadaverous, came inside and peered into the parlor, taking it all in. He limped in such a way I deduced that he had a wooden leg. I'd never seen anybody with a wooden leg before, and I couldn't help but stare. The C.O.W. ladies also took note of the men and began fanning themselves faster and talking a blue streak. I heard them say the two men were the federal and state inspectors, the ultimate judges of Dad's fate, I supposed. The plump man, I would later learn, was Mr. Arlo Mutman, the state inspector. The skinny one, the federal inspector, was Mr. Percy Amsteader. I would also learn that he'd lost his leg in a mine accident.

Mr. Fuller took up station at the heavy oak table I'd moved up front. He asked for something to bang the proceedings to order, so Floretta went back into her kitchen and came out with a steel soup ladle. Mr. Fuller took the ladle, tapped it on the table for practice, and nodded his acceptance of the device as adequate to his needs.

Pretty soon, the parlor was packed and I had no more room for chairs. I asked Floretta if she wanted me to set some up in the foyer. "And scratch my floors? I don't think so," she said. She continued to ignore the C.O.W.'s waving their empty tea glasses at her.

Rita came inside, spotted me, and came over. "How'd the stopwatch do?"

"Great. Can I keep it for a while?"

A smile started that didn't quite make it. "You help me, I help you," she said.

I puzzled over her answer, but before I could say anything, Mr. Fuller vigorously tapped the ladle on the table. "Let's have order," he announced, and then banged harder when nobody paid him any mind.

Rita said, "I'm not going to be able to stay. I have some specs to work up for a project." She gave my arm a squeeze.

"You're really building some muscles." Then she was gone. It took nearly a minute for my heart to stop pounding.

Mr. Fuller began the proceedings with an announcement. "I would remind all here that this is not a trial and that we have no duty under the law. However, just as in a trial, our purpose is to find the truth. Accordingly, we will ask all who come forward to swear on the Bible."

"Is that an Ohio Bible?" a voice from the back of the room called out. I recognized it as Troy Hartman, a rock duster on the hoot-owl shift. "Best get a West *by God* Virginian one!"

Laughter erupted in the parlor while Mr. Fuller glowered at Troy. He banged down the soup ladle. "We will have no outbursts! Where is Tag Farmer?"

Tag had been leaning against the portal between the foyer and the parlor. He raised a laconic hand. "Right here."

"You will remove any person from this assembly who speaks out of turn or causes any disturbance. Is that understood?"

Tag reddened. "If that's what Mr. Bundini wants. He's my boss, but you ain't."

Mr. Bundini turned in his chair. "Go ahead, Tag."

Now it was Mr. Fuller's turn to turn crimson. "Martin, if I am to run this investigation, I will need at least the credibility of a judge. I can't have all my decisions second-guessed every time I make one!"

Mr. Bundini gave it some thought. "All right, Amos. Make your decisions and I'll back you up, every one."

Mr. Fuller gave Tag a dirty look. Tag just stared back in his most baleful manner. "Thank you," Mr. Fuller said after the staring match, pretty much a draw, was completed. "Now let's get down to cases. We're here to take testimonies concerning the killing of Tuck Dillon."

"Killing, Amos?" Mr. Bundini interrupted. "I believe 'accidental death' is what you mean."

Mr. Fuller shuffled his papers. "Accidental death, yes."

He nodded to Carol DeHaven, Mr. Bundini's secretary. She had taken a seat near the table, a steno pad held in her hands. "Mrs. DeHaven will take notes during the proceedings." Then he picked up a slip of paper and waved it around. "I have here a list of the men who will be giving testimonies this evening." He looked around the room. "How about Bill Nordman?"

Mr. Nordman was the mine safety director. At his raised hand, Mr. Fuller nodded. "And Jack Caulder?"

"I'm here," Mr. Caulder said. Jack Caulder had been the man-lift operator on the evening shift the night of the great storm.

"And Homer Hickam." Mr. Fuller looked around the parlor. I looked, too, even though I was certain I'd have noticed Dad's arrival.

"Homer Hickam?" Mr. Fuller called. "Where's Homer Hickam?"

"Where he always is," Troy averred from the back of the room. "Digging coal!"

The room erupted into laughter. I joined them. Mr. Fuller used his soup ladle on the table, then pointed the kitchen utensil at Troy. "Tag, remove that man!"

Tag unlimbered from his slouch against the doorjamb. "Come along, Troy."

"Well, hell, Tag," Troy said. "The man asked an honest question. All I did was give him an honest answer."

"Come along," Tag said, and this time there was steel in his voice. Troy meekly complied. Tag whispered something in his ear as he went by, and whatever it was kept Troy going, fully out the door. I heard a stir of conversation among the people standing on the Club House porch. Troy was giving them his side of things, I suppose, not that it mattered.

"Martin," Mr. Fuller said, "I must have Homer here to give testimony."

Mr. Bundini shrugged. "I sent word, but it's been rough all day on 11 East. Likely he's hung up in all that."

"We must receive his testimony today," Mr. Fuller insisted.

"Well, let's start with who we have," Mr. Bundini said reasonably. "Homer will be here as soon as he can, I'm sure." He looked around the room until his eyes lit on me. I looked away. I didn't want to get the assignment to go after Dad. I wanted to stay right where I was, hear every word. "Floretta," Mr. Bundini said finally, "would you call up to the mine, see what's holding Homer up?"

Floretta looked proud of the assignment. "I'll do what I can, Mr. Martin," she clucked, and off she went.

Mr. Fuller looked doubtful, cleared his throat a couple of times, and then said, "All right, Martin. Bill Nordman, you're up first."

Mr. Nordman was sworn in on the Bible. He was a fastidious man who wore old-fashioned wire-rimmed glasses. He polished them with a clean white handkerchief and then settled back in the chair that I had placed beside Mr. Fuller's table. After some initial questions as to Mr. Nordman's bona fides as the safety man of Coalwood and Caretta, Mr. Fuller asked, "Now, Bill, is it your opinion that Olga Coal operates a safe mine?"

I noted Mr. Mutman, the state inspector, lounging back in his chair while Mr. Amsteader, the federal man, was leaning forward. There was a feral look about him.

Mr. Nordman held forth. "In my opinion, Olga Coal operates one of the safest mines in West Virginia," he said. "That is borne out by its record."

Mr. Fuller leafed through a notebook on his table. "But there have been accidents, have there not?"

"Yes, of course. Mining coal is inherently a difficult and dangerous proposition."

Mr. Fuller frowned over his notebook. Without looking up, he said, "Would you be so kind as to describe the Olga Coal Company operations?"

Mr. Nordman raised his eyes to the ceiling, pondering a bit before proceeding. Then he said, "Olga operates two mines in the Pocahontas Number Four seam in the extreme southern portion of West Virginia. That is to say, McDowell County. One of our operations is in Coalwood, the other in Caretta. They're connected underground, and the coal from both mines is taken out at Caretta for processing and shipment."

"Approximately how many tons of coal are mined per day?"

"The last figure I saw was eleven thousand five hundred tons."

"Beats the hell out of any other mine in this county!" Troy called in from the open window, to the general merriment of all. I laughed as loud as anybody.

Mr. Fuller glowered at the man in the window and then consulted his notes again. "Is it a difficult mine to operate, in your opinion?"

"Yes. Very. The coal is soft and friable and the ribs classified as hard fireclay. That means it may heave badly during pillaring operations. Over most of the property is what is known locally as draw slate. Draw slate is inherently weak and has to be supported immediately after exposure. Typically, we use either timber or roof bolts for that support. There is also a tendency for bumps caused by a variety of factors, including the irregularity of the overburden."

"Overburden?"

"The mountains. Their peaks and valleys stress the coal pillars in sometimes unpredictable ways. Bumps refer to when those pillars fail—blow out, as it were. But that's not the worst of what we have to contend with down there."

Nearly everybody was leaning forward. No one in town had ever heard such a description of the dangers of the mine beneath us. Mr. Nordman looked around, his mouth open to continue, but then he clapped it shut, as if suddenly becoming aware of who was listening.

"Tell us what the worst of it is," Mr. Fuller prompted.

Mr. Bundini nodded to Mr. Nordman, who tugged at his collar, even though it was already open, and continued. "Gas, sir, and buckets of it. Methane is liberated freely from the faces as well as the ribs. This has influenced the layout of both our operations with multiple entries being driven for maximum airflow, and the provision for separate bleeder airways. We like to say if hell had the ventilation of Olga, it would be a cooler place than heaven." Mr. Nordman looked around, perhaps for one of Coalwood's preachers, to see if he'd strayed into blasphemy. I saw no preachers in evidence.

"And should all this ventilation fail, what would happen?" Mr. Fuller asked.

"A rapid buildup of methane."

"And that would mean what?"

Mr. Nordman frowned. "Mr. Fuller, you know as well as I do. Every person in this room knows it, too. One spark and wherever methane is, there will be rapid combustion."

"It will explode?"

"Yes."

"And that is your worst fear?"

"It is the worst fear of every man who works in the Coalwood and Caretta mines."

Mr. Fuller was back to his notes. "Now, on the night of May the third, 1961, did you not in fact lose ventilation in a section of the Coalwood mine?"

"Yes. Nearly every section, in fact. We had a powerful electrical storm in the area and it knocked out parts of the power grid. There were some direct lightning hits on several fans as well. All the sections were brought back to standards rather quickly except for the section designated

10 West. Two surface ventilating fans that support it were down for most of the night."

"Were you notified?"

"Yes, the mine superintendent called me and told me about what had happened and said that steps were being taken to rectify the problems."

"The mine superintendent being Homer Hickam."

"Yes. I gave Homer my recommendations and asked him to keep me apprised. My recommendations included not sending any men into 10 West until it was fire-bossed."

"Firebossed? You mean checked for methane?"

"Yes."

"And what did Mr. Hickam say in response?"

"He said he would see to it, that he would go with Tuck Dillon to fireboss 10 West. Tuck was foreman of that section."

A light murmur arose in the audience at the mention of Tuck's name. I felt a chill go up my spine. It seemed the heart of the matter was near. Mr. Fuller consulted his little notebook again and frowned deeply. "Mr. Hickam said he would go with Mr. Dillon. Is that correct?"

Mr. Nordman nodded. "He did."

For the first time, Jake spoke up. He was sitting on a wooden chair in the corner nearest the window that faced the post office. "After a ventilation failure, is it standard procedure for two management personnel to fireboss a section?"

Mr. Nordman shook his head. "No. I've preached it for years but it's never been put into our safety directives."

"And why is that?"

Mr. Nordman shifted uneasily. "Homer has stated numerous times that he doesn't want to be restricted by safety rules that might make sense at one time but not in another."

Mr. Fuller asked: "Did you speak to Mr. Hickam again that night?"

"Yes. At approximately four forty-five A.M., Homer called and said there had been a possible explosion in the mine. He told me to meet him at the man-lift of Olga Number One right away. I did. Doc Lassiter was with him and the three of us proceeded inside."

"What is your assessment of Mr. Hickam's state of mind when you met him at the man-lift?"

Mr. Nordman displayed a deep frown. "I would say . . . grim."

"Grim." Mr. Fuller made a note. I mentally spelled out the word for him: *g-r-i-m*. What else did Fuller expect? That my dad would be happy? His line of questioning was idiotic. I would have said so if anyone had asked me, which they didn't. Instead, Mr. Fuller asked, "And where did you go?"

"We went to 10 West," Mr. Nordman said. "There we found evidence of an explosion. We first found an overturned motor—that's what we call an electrical tram. Then we found the body of Tuck Dillon. Soon afterward, the mine rescue team arrived and work began to shore up the section and begin the cleanup."

"What was the physical condition of Mr. Dillon's body?"

Mr. Nordman squirmed. "There are ladies present, sir."

"Just a general condition, that's all I'm asking."

"Answer the man, Bill," Mr. Bundini said after Mr. Nordman dithered.

Mr. Nordman looked sharply at Mr. Bundini. "Well, he was on his back. He had some light burns and it looked as if his legs were broken. Doc Lassiter saw to him. It's in his report."

"I've seen it and it will be placed on record," Mr. Fuller said. "Unfortunately, the good doctor is attending a state convention of mine company physicians. What else did you observe?"

Mr. Nordman shrugged. "I patted Tuck down, just to make sure he wasn't carrying any matches or a cigarette lighter or anything. I wanted to be able to testify that it was without a doubt the motor—the electrical tram, that is—that provided the spark that set off the methane. All I found was his wallet in his hip pocket, his tag in his front pocket, and his glasses in his shirt pocket. His glasses were broken, not surprising considering the impact of the blast."

"Did you note anything else?"

"No, sir."

Mr. Fuller nodded. "Mr. Nordman, you depend on your foremen and supervisors to assure that safe conditions exist throughout the mine, is that correct?"

"Yes, sir. We hold weekly safety meetings with all our foremen."

Mr. Fuller consulted his notebook again. "Is it not true that on September 12, 1958, you showed up in Homer Hickam's office to brief the foremen and he canceled that meeting?"

Mr. Nordman seemed startled. He swept his eyes over the audience, rested them briefly on Mr. Bundini, then cleared his throat. "I'm not certain of the date but I do recall having one of my meetings canceled, yes, sir."

"And were you upset?"

"Upset? I wouldn't say I was upset, but I did suggest to Homer that he shouldn't cancel a foreman safety meeting without good cause."

"And what did he say?"

Mr. Nordman pursed his lips. "Well . . ."

A sinking feeling crept over me. Mr. Fuller, I suspected, had finally gotten to where he wanted to go. My father was in peril.

"What did he say, Bill?"

Mr. Nordman relented in a burst. "He said that he couldn't spare his foremen for a damn-fool safety meeting that just repeated what everybody knew, anyway." Then he added, "Homer apologized to me the next day."

"Did he?"

"Yes, sir, he did."

"And did he say why he canceled the safety meeting?"

"He didn't have to. I knew already. All the sections were down for one reason or another and Homer felt his foremen weren't doing their jobs. He wanted them to get to work."

"Did you think that was reason enough to cancel a safety meeting?"

"No, sir, I didn't, and I told Homer that. I held another meeting a week later, this one on timbering standards and general housekeeping of the gob. I remember it specifically because those were the topics Homer asked me to teach."

"So he thought he should choose the topics of your safety meetings?"

"In this case, yes. It was timbering and housekeeping that apparently had caused most of the sections to be down."

Mr. Fuller went back to his notebook. I didn't know where he was going with the testimony, but I could sense it was headed exactly where he wanted it to go. His next question confirmed it.

"So would it be fair to say that Homer Hickam's first priority in the mine is production of tonnage with safety a distant second? Is that what you're telling us, sir?"

In a courtroom, I would have expected a defense lawyer to jump to his feet and yell, "I object!" Nothing like that happened in these proceedings. There was only the rumble of the assembly while Mr. Nordman considered his answer. I discovered I was squeezing my hands into tight balls. My knuckles even cracked.

"Homer is a fine mine superintendent, maybe the best—"

"Please answer the question, sir!" Mr. Fuller said, raising his voice above the muttering in the audience. "In your opinion, does Homer Hickam believe the production of coal is more important than the safety of his miners? It is a simple question."

"Well, sometimes—" Mr. Nordman seemed to haul himself back. "No, sir, I don't believe that."

I puffed out a breath of relief. Mr. Fuller, however, wasn't through. "Homer Hickam canceled your safety meeting?"

"Yes."

"Homer Hickam canceled it because the sections weren't producing to his standards?"

"Yes."

Mr. Fuller glanced at the mine inspectors. "When he allowed you to have another meeting, it concerned items of his own choosing, those that specifically supported increased production?"

"Yes, but—"

"That will be all, Mr. Nordman."

"Now, look, Amos—"

"Step down, Bill."

Mr. Nordman walked away from the chair. Mr. Bundini nodded to him, but he shook his head. I looked around. Dad still hadn't arrived. I thought he'd better get here soon to defend himself or it was all going to be over. Then I thought—don't ask me why—maybe that was what he wanted. Maybe that was why he didn't seem worried. He'd already given up.

Mr. Fuller called Jack Caulder, the hoot-owl shift man-lift operator. "You were operating the man-lift at Olga Number One on the night of May third? You were also working the lamphouse? Did Tuck Dillon and Homer Hickam arrive around four A.M. to enter the mine?"

Mr. Caulder, a loose-limbed man in a pair of bib coveralls, gave an affirmative answer to each question. He nervously tapped a booted foot on the floor.

Mr. Fuller stood, walked around the table, and made a long study of Mr. Caulder. Then he went over to one of the windows that looked out onto the common green in front of the post office building. "Jack, did you see who went into the mine that night?"

"I was inside the hoisthouse. You can't see who's on the man-lift from there."

"But both Tuck Dillon and Homer Hickam were dressed to go inside."

"Yes. I gave them their lamps and saw that their tags were on the board."

"And after you let down the man-lift, what happened then?"

"Well, I went back to checking lamps, getting them ready for the day shift. Then, about forty-five minutes later, I felt what I took to be a bump. Only come to find out it warn't no bump."

"It was an explosion, as Mr. Nordman has related," Mr. Fuller interjected. "Now, Jack, after what you took to be a bump, who showed up next?"

"Mr. Hickam, along with Mr. Nordman and Doc Lassiter. I was surprised to see Mr. Hickam. I thought he was inside with Tuck."

"And how would you describe Mr. Hickam's emotional state?"

Mr. Caulder slid his big hands up the legs of his coverall. "He was . . . unhappy."

"Unhappy? Is that all he was? Unhappy?"

Mr. Caulder slowly shook his head. "Upset, maybe," he said.

"Upset like maybe Big Creek High lost a football game? Is that what you mean, Jack? Or was Homer Hickam more emotional than that?"

Mr. Caulder looked around the assembly for help, but there was none. He fiddled with a button on his shirt pocket, then shrugged. "He was . . . well, like I never seen him before. He was white as a sheet."

"Like he was scared or had a guilty conscience?"

"Amos . . . ," Mr. Bundini said in a warning tone.

Mr. Fuller drummed his fingers on the table. "You're right, Martin." He nodded to Carol. "Strike that. You can step down, Jack."

Mr. Fuller made a brief survey of the parlor and then said, "I still don't see Homer Hickam."

"I'm sure there must be something at the mine that required his attention," Mr. Bundini said.

"More important than this?" Mr. Mutman, the state inspector, asked. "I have trouble with that."

Floretta came into the room. She was carrying a three-by-five card. "I have a message from Mr. Homer for all ya'll," she said nervously. She looked at Mr. Bundini. "Sir, he said that the mine's gone all to heck and he's got to see to it."

Just about everybody in the room laughed at Floretta's announcement except the officials up front. Floretta put on the half glasses that hung from a chain around her neck and perused the card. "He also told me to tell you the only thing he's got to say to this testimony is this: He doesn't know why Tuck Dillon went into 10 West without fire-bossing it first. He only knows he was a man who had never made that kind of mistake before."

Mr. Fuller leaned back in his chair. "None of that will go into the record," he said. "But the record will show that Homer Hickam was unwilling to come before this assembly and make a sworn statement."

"Sir, Mr. Homer never told a lie in all his born days!" Floretta blurted. "He don't need no Bible to coach him to do it, neither!"

Mr. Fuller pointed the soup ladle at Floretta. "I'll thank you to be quiet, woman!"

"Well, I'll thank you to stop puttin' dents in my good oak table with that soup ladle!"

The audience laughed and then they clapped, clearly in

the belief that Floretta had gotten the better of the steel company man.

"I'd like to call someone to testify," Jake said, his voice piercing the tumult. After everyone quieted down, he nodded toward me. "Sonny Hickam."

I thought surely I hadn't heard right. Me? My face flushed hot and I turned around to make a run for it, but Tag barred my way. He pointed, and I turned around and trudged to the chair. Mr. Fuller gave me a surprised look when I stepped up to it. I guess he'd remembered his conversation with me when he thought I was a junior engineer.

I raised my hand, swore on the Bible, and sat down. My heart was beating so hard I thought it was going to leap right out of my chest. I couldn't imagine what Jake had in mind except to see to the further ridicule of my family.

"Sonny, the first time your father took you in the mine, you told me he made a little speech to you about something. Would you relate that speech to us now?"

"That was personal," I said, bristling. "Just between Dad and me. And I'm sorry I ever told you anything!"

"I think it relates to this investigation," he said, his face coloring.

Mr. Bundini said, "Sonny, you have to tell."

Since I'd sworn on the Bible and didn't have much choice, I gave in. "Dad was trying to convince me to become a mining engineer," I said. "That's why he took me inside."

"When was that?"

"I was a sophomore in high school. Spring 1958. I'd just started launching rockets. I was also making good grades in math, for the first time. I think he thought maybe I had some potential."

"What did he tell you?"

"He said he knew the mine like he knew a man, could

sense things about it that weren't right even when everything on paper said it was. He said every day there was something that needed to be done—because men would be hurt if it wasn't done, or the coal the company had promised to load wouldn't get loaded. He said coal was the lifeblood of the country, that if it failed, steel failed, and then the country failed. That's what he said."

Jake paced. "He said something about miners, too, didn't he?"

I took a ragged breath. "He said there were no men in the world like miners, that they were good and strong men, the best there was. He said I would never know such good and strong men, didn't matter where I went or what I did. He said I was his boy and since he was born to lead men in the profession of mining coal, maybe I was, too."

"And what did you tell him?"

"I said I wanted to go work for Wernher von Braun."

Jake waited until a rumble of voices, accompanied by a few titters, went through the crowd.

"One thing more, Sonny. What happened when you and your dad came outside that day?"

"My mom was waiting for us."

"Was she unhappy that your dad had taken you into the mine?"

"Mom has always said neither of her boys would ever work in a coal mine."

"But she was also unhappy for another reason, wasn't she?"

"I don't see what—"

"Answer the man, Sonny," Mr. Bundini snapped.

"A spot on Dad's lung had just been found," I said. "Mom was looking for Dad to quit the mine."

"That was how many years ago?"

I counted it up. "Three years."

"Three years. Yet your father continues to go inside the

mine nearly every day. Why do you think he does that, Sonny?"

I considered his question carefully. Then I said, "It's his job."

"Is that all it is?"

I'd had enough. It was late. I was tired and so was everybody else. I knew where Jake wanted me to go, and I knew he was going to get me there, so I saved him and me and everybody else the time and trouble. "My dad loves that mine more than anything in the world," I said, "more than me, more than my mom, more than his own health." I gave Jake my best dirty look.

Jake looked away and then down at the floor. "I just wanted that on the record," he said softly.

And with me glaring at Jake, and Jake looking as shamefaced as he deserved, the first testimony in the "trial" of Homer Hickam was done.

26

RITA'S CHANCE

I PUSHED through the sweating crowd. I didn't hear Jake calling, but he caught me on the first landing. "I'm sorry, Sonny," he said. "Since you wouldn't talk to me otherwise, you gave me no choice."

"I don't care, Jake," I lied. "Whatever you want to do, you just go ahead and do it, the big steel company man."

He looked at me with eyes filled with disappointment, as if I were at fault for what had just happened. "I have another question," he said quietly. "When was it that you lost your intellectual curiosity?"

I didn't know what he was talking about and said so. "You told the truth down there, Sonny," he replied. "Your dad loves that mine more than anything in the world. So don't you think it's kind of strange that he let Tuck go inside alone?"

"Maybe he was tired," I said, but even as I said it, I knew Jake was right. As long as the mine was in danger, my father wouldn't rest—or, at least, he never had before.

"Something very peculiar happened that night," Jake

said as he put his hand on my arm, "and I'm going to find out what it was."

I shook him off and continued my journey to my room. Jake had once taught me about the stars, and I'd admired him for the joy he took from life. Some people had called him a drunk and ne'er-do-well back then, but I hadn't cared. He was my *friend,* that's all I knew. Now he was a sober and respected steel company man, and even drove a Nash. But he wasn't my friend, not anymore, and there was nothing I could do about it.

I went inside my room and sat down at my bare table. The hurt was like a nail in my side. I hated Jake, hated him with all my heart and soul. How could he betray what I'd once told him, friend to friend, in utter confidence?

I willed calm. I was no high school rocket boy. I was a partially college-educated track-laying *man.* Why, I asked myself, did I really hate Jake? Was it because he had forced me to think in a direction I'd so far ignored? *What had happened the night Tuck Dillon died?*

I went over it. Dad had been ready to go into the mine, had his helmet lamp on, his tag hung, everything. Then he'd turned away and let Tuck go inside by himself. Jake's question about my intellectual curiosity had struck bone. He was right. It didn't make sense. And why had Tuck Dillon, a man known for his caution and judgment, committed the gross mistake of an utter novice—*he'd driven an electric motor into a section filled with explosive gas!*—an error that even a junior engineer would not commit?

I kept considering the situation until I had nearly worn myself out. *Sometimes,* I thought, *maybe things just happen.*

But not in Coalwood. *Not in Coalwood.* Here things did not just happen. There was always more. You just had to know where to look.

The passage from Proverbs that the Reverend Richard had quoted came back to me now: *It is the glory of God to conceal a thing; but the honor of kings to search it out.*

God might be in his glory here, I thought gloomily, but kings were nearly always in short supply in Coalwood.

I HEARD a rattle of little raps on my door, bringing me out of a shallow, dreamless sleep. I had to hear it a second time before I believed it. My first thought was that it was Floretta, that maybe Mom had called me on the phone in the parlor. If that was so, it wasn't going to be good news. The telephone never brought good news in the middle of the night. That much I knew for sure.

I grabbed my pants, drew them on, and fumbled my way to the door. When I opened it, I was astonished to see Rita in full junior engineer regalia, including her white helmet. An olive-drab dispatch bag was strapped over her shoulder. "Sonny, it's time," she said.

I just stood there, trying to sort out what was happening.

Rita was excited, that much I could see. "Get dressed in your work clothes, meet me downstairs." She looked up and down the hall, then whispered, "Bring your helmet."

While I dressed, I kept trying to figure out what was happening. Maybe, I thought, Rita just wanted to get me off alone with her in the dark. It's amazing how hope cheers the ever-faithful, foolish heart.

In the foyer, she put her finger to her lips and led me outside to her T-bird. I climbed inside and off we went. I was still in sort of a sleepy daze. There was a bank of low fog that hugged the road. It was as if we were driving through a cloud. I could smell her, a perfume of apple blossoms and peppermint. When we reached the vacant lot below the Todds' house on Tipple Row, she pulled in. "We'll walk the rest of the way," she said, tucking her hair beneath her helmet.

"What are we doing, Rita?" I asked.

"I helped you," she said. "Now it's time for you to help me."

I stopped. "What are you talking about?"

"I'll explain it while we go. Hurry."

We walked, passing my house, crossing the road to the path that led up to the tipple. I felt more reluctant with each step.

"I did a work order with Victor last week," she said as we worked our way along the dark path. "It was for a stopping. Do you know what that is?"

I did. It was a barrier, usually made of brick or iron plate, used to direct ventilation in the mine.

"Stopper work is done on the hoot-owl shift," she said.

I knew that, too. Rock dusting and nearly all the maintenance tasks were done on the hoot-owl shift.

"An engineer has to be thorough," she said. "Do you know why that is, Sonny? I'll tell you. Because usually the job we design is actually done when we're not around. That means everything has to be in the engineering package— every supply item, every step in the procedure, all the drawings. That's something you'll want to remember when you get to be an engineer."

"Okay," I said uncertainly.

"The stopper project I did with Victor depended on him to do just one thing," she said. "He's such a *putz*. I did all the work on the damn thing and all he had to do was put the package together. Tonight, the foreman on East Main D got the work order, but the engineering package didn't have the drawings. Victor screwed up."

"How do you know that?"

"Because when the foreman phoned Victor, Floretta went after him and found he wasn't in his room—probably over at Keystone or up at John Eye's, if I know that idiot— so Benson, that's the foreman on East Main D, sent Floretta after me. I guess he just wanted somebody to yell at and my name was on the package, too. Benson was really yelling, said if junior engineers couldn't do their work any better than that, then they should just stop trying." Then she lowered her voice. "'By gaw, girl, you better get me those drawings or there'll be hell to pay.'" She laughed. "That's what he said."

"So you have the drawings?"

She patted the bag over her shoulder. "Sure do," she said. "Along with my verbal orders."

"Verbal orders?"

She lowered her voice again. "'By gaw, girl, you better get me those drawings or there'll be hell to pay.'" She went back to her normal voice. "Well, we'd just hate for hell to get paid, wouldn't we?"

At the main gate of the tipple grounds, I said, "Rita, I don't think Mr. Benson meant for you to bring those drawings."

"He gave me an order, Sonny."

"And you want me to do what?"

"Get me a lamp and turn in my tag." She produced a brass tag from the front pocket of her tight jeans. It was polished as smooth and bright as any I'd ever seen. It glinted in the spotlights on the wire fence that went around the grounds. It was number 982.

I stared at the tag, trying to think. "Rita, I can't do this," I finally managed to say. "You go inside, the men will say the mine's not safe anymore. They'll go out on strike."

Her face clouded. "I've yet to run across a single miner who believes in that silly old superstition."

"Maybe not to your face, but trust me, they believe."

"You promised you'd help me."

"I also told you I didn't know how."

"Well, now you know."

"How will you get to East Main D?"

"I can drive a motor."

Her whole scheme became clear. Rita expected me to help her get on the man-lift, and then she was going to drive a tram all the way to East Main D. That was doubly illegal. Not only was a trip ticket required, but I would have bet money she didn't have the necessary certification to drive one of the little electric locomotives. "I can't do this, Rita."

"Can't?" Her eyes flashed. "Sonny, this is my chance. You promised to help me. We had a bargain. I've helped you. You must have noticed what I did yesterday."

I didn't know what she meant and said so. She shook her head. "Don't be silly. I did . . . things."

It hit me between the eyes like a thunderbolt—the wrong spikes, the late deliveries of ties to the Caretta section. Rita had caused that to happen. "I didn't know!" I gasped.

"Well, what did you think was going to happen when we agreed to help each other?" she demanded.

My head spun. "I thought you were talking about the stopwatch!"

She put her hand on my shoulder. "I knew you needed more help than that! Now it's your turn to help me. Please. You and I, fellow engineers against the world."

Every molecule in my body screamed at me to stop what was happening, but I just stood there.

"You told me about Mr. Bykovski," she said, "how he knew he could lose his job if he helped you with your rockets. But he did it, Sonny, and you told me why. Because it was the right thing to do. You know this is right, too. I should be able to go down in the mine."

She was right, at least about Mr. Bykovski. And, no matter how much trouble I knew it would get me into, I knew she was also right, that she needed and deserved to go into the mine. I thought of the grubby little place they'd given her in the hall of the engineering office, and how she had to go all the way up front just to go to the bathroom. The company had treated her like gob and it wasn't right, none of it. I started to get mad, for her sake.

"Come on," she said. "Please. For what's right, Sonny."

What man wouldn't want to do right for his woman?

That thought whipped across my mind. "Let's go," I said, and led the way through the gate and up to the remains of the old tipple.

RITA STOOD around the corner of the lamphouse and strapped on a battery and clipped a lamp to her helmet. I'd checked them out for her from Mr. Caulder, explaining the extra gear was for Victor, who'd be along any minute.

"He's puking in the bathhouse," I lied. "John Eye's whiskey didn't sit well with him."

Mr. Caulder gave me the eye. "He's not drunk, is he? I'd get in trouble if I let a drunk go in the mine."

"No. He's just sick."

"You vouch for him?"

"Yeah. I guess."

"Since when did you turn into a junior-engineer helper?" he wondered. "I thought you were a track-laying man."

"Somebody's got to hold their hands," I said, summoning a knowing laugh from him.

"Sorry about my testimony," he said.

"You had to tell the truth. So did I."

"I guess. Go get Victor ready. You going to be with him?"

"All the way."

"You got his tag?"

I handed him Rita's tag and my own. He glanced at them, then hung them on the board.

Mr. Caulder went inside the hoisthouse and I handed over the battery pack and lamp to Rita, who was standing in the shadow of the bathhouse. After a few seconds, she switched on her lamp. "Let's go."

At the man-lift, I put my finger to the bell to let Mr. Caulder know we were ready to go down. But I couldn't do it. All the doubts I had for the scheme came back in a rush.

Sweat appeared on my forehead. Rita pushed my finger out of the way and pushed the bell herself. "This is my chance, Sonny," she said harshly. "Don't ruin it." She opened the gate and stepped out on the man-lift. "You stay here," she said. "I can go the rest of the way by myself."

Then the bell rang three times, the signal from Mr. Caulder in the hoisthouse. "Here we go," she said, and started to pull the gate closed.

At the last possible second, I jumped aboard. Rita took a deep breath as the cage lurched once and then began a steady crawl down the shaft. "Thank you," she said. She touched my arm, but I pulled away. What madness had I signed up for? Then I thought of the testimony. My father was in the fight of his life, and now I was going to lay all this on top of him. There was going to be hell to pay, and a lot of it was going to come out of my pocket.

Frozen in fear for what I'd done, I silently watched as the eons of earth's progression passed before our eyes, layer upon layer. Rita's light swung around the shaft, then disappeared as she craned her eyes upward into the gloom. Her light came down and then I could feel it move across my face. "I'll never forget this, Sonny," she said.

I didn't know if she was thanking me or commenting on what she was seeing on the way down. I kept trying to think of something that would talk her out of what she was doing, but the words wouldn't come.

She walked around the man-lift. "The ride is a bit jerky," she commented. "Likely a need for more grease on the bullwheel or maybe the axle needs replacing. This open cage is dangerous, too. What if somebody accidentally knocked something into the shaft? Even a pebble could hit a miner hard enough to kill him."

She observed the slide rails. "Maintenance is the key to a good operation, Sonny. Look here. See those rust spots on the rails? They should be sanded and greased." She took the notebook from her shirt pocket and began to make notes. "New eyes see new things," she murmured to herself.

As we kept descending, I watched Rita. Even though my heart beat like a snare drum just at the sight of her, I realized that the Rita Walicki I had fallen tea over kettle completely in love with on Water Tank Mountain didn't really exist except in my imagination. I'd thought of Rita as beautiful and smart, which she surely was, but I'd also believed her to be soft and needy, too, a maiden in distress that I, Sonny the white knight, could rescue, even if it was from herself. But now I could see that Rita was tough, far tougher than I was, and didn't need or want rescue. Bobby had been right. He'd said Rita had experience in places I didn't even have, but those places, I now understood, were in her mind. I eyed her while she paced around the man-lift platform, scribbling in her notebook and muttering to herself, and remembered how close she'd been to tears during her pitch to rebuild the main line. At that moment, she had shown that she was vulnerable and my heart had gone out to her. But now I recalled she had fought back her tears and set her jaw against her hurt and hadn't asked for anybody to take up for her. I also remembered her comment that Coalwood had a history of mistreating its women. Maybe Rita was hurtling down the mine shaft this crazy night, with me dragged along behind her, because she was intent on righting all those wrongs she saw. It came to me in a flash, the way things so often did. Rita was not only out to prove false the superstition about women in a coal mine; she was also out to show she was as good as any man, and maybe better. It was such an alien concept it was nearly past my ability to grasp it, and as it was, I was only able to hang on to it for the briefest of moments.

Rita raised her face and took a deep, satisfied breath. "We're almost there. I can smell it!"

I could, too. The air billowing up from the mine below

was distinctive, the odor of wet gunpowder, cool and biting and dangerous. It gave me another attack of nerves. "Rita, we've got to go back up," I told her urgently. I fumbled for some way to reach her. "You said one time you wanted a good report from Dad, said it was the main reason you were in Coalwood. This isn't the way to get it. He'll cut you off at the neck."

She gave me a condescending smile. "Oh, Sonny, no he won't. Your dad will respect what I've done. In some ways, I think I understand him better than you do. He's a pure engineer. He'll know why I had to fight this superstition and put it to rest, once and for all."

"Trust me on this," I begged her. "You're not going to like what's about to happen. We've got to go up!"

She kept her confident smile. "What's the worst thing that can happen? We'll get yelled at, then people will laugh it off."

"You don't know Coalwood," I said miserably. "And you sure don't know my dad."

"I bet your mother would understand. From everything I know about her, she's been fighting the same battle for years."

I realized that arguing with her was hopeless. This was Rita's chance and she was taking it. But there was one thing I had to get straight with her. "If we still have jobs after tomorrow, Rita, I'm asking you now—please don't ever cheat for me again."

She frowned. "Those Caretta boys are experienced track layers. It wasn't a fair bet from the beginning. I didn't cheat for you. I just evened the score a bit."

"You *did* cheat, Rita. I knew the score before I took the bet. Anything you did to help me isn't right. Don't you see that?"

"But you'll lose, otherwise," she said. "Surely you don't want that!"

I gave up. "Just don't help me anymore, okay?"

Rita gave me a puzzled look, then shrugged as the man-lift platform dropped into the vast open room that housed the landing at the base of the shaft. Then the boards beneath our feet shuddered once and stopped twenty feet above the bottom gate. "What's wrong?" Rita demanded, squinting up the shaft at the frozen cables.

"I don't know." I looked up as condensed water came down the shaft, splattering on my glasses and misting them up. "This doesn't usually happen."

There was no one on the landing. A motor sat there, all ready to carry anyone who needed it back into the mine. Then the bell rang twice and the man-lift started back up the shaft. "Dammit!" Rita snapped.

Rita was silent all the way up, but I could feel her seething. As the cage rose past ground level, I saw the problem.

There stood Victor.

He had on a white shirt, one side of it hanging out, and there were very definite signs of lipstick on his collar. He was more sagging than standing. Wherever he'd been, he'd had a rough night of it, and apparently it had recently gotten rougher. Mr. Caulder came outside and opened the gate. "Sonny, this ain't right," he grumbled. "You could have cost me my job."

Rita stormed off the man-lift. "Victor, what the hell do you think you're doing?"

"When I got in, Floretta told me about the call," he said. "So I went over, saw the drawings gone. I figured out what you did, Rita. You're not going to get me fired, no way, lady."

Rita hit him on the chin with her fist so hard he turned around once before falling like a rag doll into the gob. He never even made a sound. I'd never seen a man collapse like that. She stepped over him. "You bastard. Why couldn't you stay in Keystone with your whore?"

"I guess because I ran out of money," Victor said, still facedown in the dirt. He made no move to get up.

Rita turned on Mr. Caulder. "Send me down!" she ordered. "Benson needs these drawings! I made them! I have a right to take them!"

"I can't do that, ma'am," he said, taking a step back from her.

She looked at me, then shook her head. I thought she was going to kick Victor, but he groaned and maybe she took pity on him, though I doubt it. She turned back to the man-lift. At first, I didn't realize what she was doing, and then I saw she was going for the steps.

I knew those steps. They scared the bejesus out of me. The first thirty feet of them were made of concrete and were covered with a wet slime. What followed was seven hundred feet of steel steps that went back and forth all the way down to the bottom of the shaft. In some places, there wasn't even a handrail. The steps were for emergency use only. I couldn't imagine a situation that would ever get me on those rickety old things.

"Don't, Rita!" I yelled, but it was too late. She started down the steps and then I heard her boots slip and a thumping sound, then the clatter of her helmet hitting the side of the shaft, then nothing.

I ran to the steps and looked down. To my everlasting relief, Rita was sitting at the bottom of the first landing. I carefully stepped down to her, pressing myself up against the stone wall as far away from the shaft as I could get. "Are you all right?"

"Do I look all right to you?" She got to her feet and looked down the steps.

"Don't try it," I told her. "You'll fall."

I watched as her shoulders sagged. Then she turned around and climbed past me. I followed, my heart rattling my chest. I saw that Victor had crawled to his feet.

"Give me the drawings, Rita," he said, holding out his hand.

She turned and tossed the bag into the shaft. "You want them, go get them." She took off her helmet, threw it down, then unbuckled her belt and dropped it into the dirt. Then she walked away, down the hill to the road.

2 7

A QUESTION FOR MOM

MR. CAULDER, Victor, and I watched Rita go. Mr. Caulder's jaw was unhinged from all that he'd seen, and Victor was rubbing his chin from Rita's blow. I was the first one to speak, mainly because I could. "I hope you boys will keep all this to yourself," I said.

Mr. Caulder closed his mouth, chewed a bit on his tobacco cud, then spat. "I wouldn't even know what to say," he allowed. "Craziest thing I ever seen. Naw, I'm not telling nobody."

"Same here," Victor said, tucking in his shirt. "I'd never live it down. But you'd better talk to Floretta. She fielded the phone calls."

Victor was right, one of the few times I'd ever known a junior engineer to figure something out pretty much on his own. Strapping on his battery, he headed for the man-lift while Mr. Caulder went back into the hoisthouse to lower him down. Victor would have to scramble around in the mud under the man-lift, but I thought he'd find Rita's bag without too much problem.

I looked around the grounds in the darkness and then at my watch, illuminated by the tipple lights. It was nearly three A.M., about the same time Dad and Tuck had gathered in front of the man-lift on the night Tuck had been killed. I took a moment to imagine what it must have been like that night. Low clouds and spitting rain were surely left over from the great storm that had just swept through the county. The tipple would have been dripping water, a constant staccato of drops plopping onto the packed gob below, and there would have been steam caused by the warm air rising from the shaft, curling into the sky. In the distance, there must have been the low rumble of thunder and flashes of far-off lightning as the storm pounded up through Mingo and Logan counties. It would have been eerie, a place filled with shadows, and frightening.

But then I thought—no, neither Dad nor Tuck would have thought that way. They were professional mining supervisors. Shadows wouldn't bother them, and there would have been no foreboding, just a job to do.

I turned and saw the glow of the Tipple Row streetlights that illuminated our house. It was then I thought— *Mom was home that night!* It was the first time that had occurred to me. It was nothing new to her to have the black phone ring in the middle of the night. That was, after all, the reason she had a separate bedroom. But I'd never believed she could sleep through Dad getting up at all hours. Often, when we'd lived under the same roof, I would hear her pull her blinds up in her bedroom to watch Dad heading in the dark to the mine. Now I wondered what Mom had seen or heard that night, or what Dad might have told her. Had anybody even asked her?

When Mr. Caulder came out of the hoisthouse, he walked over to stand beside me. I was still studying the Captain's house, the house where my dad now slept. Or was he lying awake, wondering what was coming at him down the track?

my dreams have all returned the same,
swinging along the homebound track
—just emptys cuming back.

Maybe, I thought, they aren't going to be empty this time, but filled with broken dreams, *his* dreams. I found myself troubled, more than I might have believed, over that concept. I had always spent so much time worrying about *my* dreams. But what about Dad's dreams? Weren't they as important as mine? What right did I have to think otherwise?

"Crazy times, Sonny," Mr. Caulder said, interrupting my churning mind.

A question came, nearly unbidden. "Mr. Caulder, when you gave your testimony, did you leave anything out?"

"Not that I can think of," he said. "God knows I been asked enough about that night. Now, don't *you* start!"

I ignored his protest. I'd always known Mr. Caulder to be a man who liked to talk. "Tell me what happened again."

Mr. Caulder hemmed and hawed a bit, but I could tell he was going to get to it, so I waited him out. "Tuck and your dad came up and I issued them their lamps," he said finally. "Then I saw them put their tags on the board. It warn't nothing unusual."

"Did they say anything?"

"Just that they were going to go down to 10 West and check for methane before the day shift arrived."

"Nothing else?"

"Well, I heard your dad talk about where they were going to park the motor and then walk in. I guess Tuck wasn't listening. That's what got him, driving that locomotive into the fire damp."

"Do you have any idea why he would do that?"

Mr. Caulder shook his head. "I don't know, Sonny. I'm not an inside man. Most men say Tuck probably figured the gas buildup was near the face, rather than back in the drift. That's usually the case. He just probably wanted to get a little closer so he didn't have to walk so far. He bet his life on it and lost."

"You believe that?"

Mr. Caulder pursed his lips, then slowly shook his head. "Not really."

"What happened after you heard Dad and Tuck talking?"

He shrugged. "I went in the hoisthouse, waited for the bell, and then let them down." He paused, squinting into the darkness. "Or I thought I had. When I came out, they were both gone, so I figured they were down there. Your dad's tag was on the board, so I was sure of it."

"Dad didn't go in the mine, but he left his tag on the board?"

Mr. Caulder nodded. "Yep. I noticed it when he arrived with Mr. Nordman and Doc Lassiter a couple of hours later. His tag was still hanging there—number thirteen, who could forget it?"

"Did you say anything to him about it?"

"I started to but then I thought I'd better not. Your daddy ain't one to mess around with. I figured he'd just forgot it after he'd decided not to go down in the mine."

"How about his helmet lamp?"

Mr. Caulder thought it over. "Nobody ever asked me that. He didn't leave it on the counter that night. I guess he took it with him when he left."

"He took mine property with him? Doesn't sound like my dad."

"Naw, it don't," he said, thoughtfully munching on his chaw. "It surely don't."

My mind was clicking along. I could sense I was close to something even though I didn't have a clue what it was. "How long were you in the hoisthouse before you heard the man-lift bell?"

Mr. Caulder ran his hand up under his helmet and gave his

head a good scratch. He spat a stream of tobacco juice. "It was a good, long time. I was about to come out and ask what was going on. Then I heard the bell. Maybe ten minutes."

There was nothing else Mr. Caulder could think to tell me and I had run out of questions, so I thanked him kindly, asked him again to keep what Rita and I had done to himself, and then walked back to the Club House. Along the way, I tried to let all the night's events sink in. It had been a peculiar and eventful one, that much was for certain.

In the foyer, I halfway considered going up and knocking on Rita's door and seeing if maybe she'd want to talk. But good sense somehow got the upper hand, and I went inside the parlor instead. I couldn't sleep, not after all that had happened, and anyway, I wanted to chew a bit more on what Mr. Caulder had told me. I sat on the couch, and that's where Floretta found me, fast asleep, a couple of hours later.

"Miss Rita done told me all what happened when she came back," she said when I told her where I'd been. "If I'd only known, I'd of never told Victor about that call. And no, I won't be telling a soul. It's too sad, breaks my heart, for that woman. She tries so hard and all she gets is the back of the company's hand. Now get on upstairs and get yourself ready to work. You got some track to lay, young man, and I got ten dollars on you to do it faster than those boys from Caretta."

"You put a bet down?"

She looked proud. "Walked up to John Eye's myself and handed him a ten-dollar bill, said put it on my boy! Did you know Mr. Alexander Hamilton himself is on that bill?"

I didn't, which surprised me. It was a rare gap in my Coalwood education. "I haven't seen many ten-dollar bills in my life, now that I think on it."

Satisfaction crossed her face. She was going to get to teach me something. "The reason for that is because the coal companies like to pay in two-dollar bills. That way all the businessmen over in Welch know where the power comes from in this county when they see old Tom Jefferson staring back at them. I heard tell there's more two-dollar bills in McDowell County than anywhere in the whole country. But a ten-dollar bill? Rare as a grin on a blue jay."

I absorbed her history, sociology, and ornithology lesson and then said, "I hope you don't lose your money, Floretta."

She waved my concern away. "I already won more from John Eye Blevins than he'll ever win from me. I bet him twenty dollars Cecil Underwood would be governor back in 1956. Just because Cecil was a Republican, the odds were about a hundred to one. I still ain't got around to spending all the cash money I made!"

AFTER BREAKFAST, I tried to call Mom but got no answer. In the evening I tried again, still with no luck. Finally, I called her contractor's office and was lucky to get the secretary just as she was locking up. I had one question I needed answered and begged that the work crew might carry it to Mom. The secretary agreed and wrote it down:

When did Dad come home the night Tuck got killed?

Rita didn't come to supper the next night, nor the next. I finally got up the nerve to go into the kitchen and ask Floretta about her. "She asked if she could have her supper in her room for a while, Sonny," she told me. "She's had it with all you men right now."

Even though I'd come to a new understanding of Rita, I still found my heart wasn't satisfied. I wanted her to know how much I cared but I also sensed it wasn't the time to do anything but wait. That night, I put aside my worrying about Rita, and Dad's trial, and worked on the time study instead. One thing I could see right off the bat was that Johnny was taking a lot of time measuring levels and making adjustments. Bobby and I were too often idle waiting for him to finish. I doubted the Caretta crew was doing as much measuring, but I also doubted if I could talk Johnny into doing less. He was a stickler for it.

But I spotted some other things that would help us go faster. We could position the new ties so they'd be ready to go while Johnny was measuring and we could also put the spikes where they were needed in advance, saving us time going back and forth to the kegs. I worked out a few more things—combining work, prepositioning our supplies— all designed to keep us fully occupied with as little slack time as possible. I presented my work to Bobby and Johnny on the man-trip as we rode in to work.

"First-rate work, Sonny," Bobby said. He got a stubby pencil out of his shirt pocket and worked on the sheets some more. "How about we get ahead by taking off the fishplates from three tracks at once? That way instead of needing the wrench about twelve times a day, we'd only need it maybe a half dozen."

I considered his suggestion. "Yes," I said, and Bobby lit up like a thousand-watt bulb.

I handed over my work to Johnny. He studied it. "You college boys," he said, but the way he said it was almost proud.

All day, we tried our new efficiencies. They appeared to be working. I sensed we were coming together even more as a team, too. When Bobby was on a pee break, Johnny said, "Your dad would be proud of your work."

"I doubt it," I replied sadly.

"Why do you say such a thing?"

I shrugged. "How many times have you ever heard him

brag on me, Johnny? But how about Jim?" I mimicked Dad. "*My boy is the best football player in this state!* I bet a lot of people who know Dad would be surprised to learn he has two sons."

Johnny swung his hammer, knocked in a spike with three solid blows. "Bragging don't measure the way your father feels about you," he said, flipping the hammer over in his hand with the ease of a majorette tossing a baton.

"Then what does?"

Johnny pounded another spike home. "That he gave you to me."

"Because he thought you'd run me off!"

"Is that what you think?"

"That's what *you* said."

"I know better now." The beam of light from his helmet filled my eyes. "He gave you to me because he knew I'd make you work harder than you'd ever worked in your life. He gave you to me, not because he thought you'd quit." His light flashed away. "But because he knew you wouldn't." His hammer fell, driving the spike deep into the tie. "Praise God!"

After our shift, aboard the man-trip, I kept thinking about what Johnny had said: *Because he knew you wouldn't.* I savored those words. And I hoped they were true.

When we stepped off the man-lift, we looked on the chalkboard and saw the Caretta team had laid eight sections of track that day. Johnny got the chalk, paused dramatically while the other miners pressed around us, then wrote our number down—nine.

For the first time, we'd beaten Garrett and his football boys.

"We're on our way," Bobby said.

"Johnny's team," I said.

Johnny grinned, then ducked his head. "Glory be," he offered while those men who'd bet on us slapped us on our backs.

When I got back to the Club House, I found a message tacked to my door. It was written down by Floretta but it was from my mom. At first I didn't understand it, but then I remembered my question to her. When had Dad come home the night Tuck was killed?

It was a typical Elsie Hickam answer, short and to the point. In its entirety, it read:

He didn't.

PAYDAY

MY FIRST payday finally came. Floretta received my pay voucher in the Club House mail and slid it under my door. I eagerly ripped open the envelope and beheld an astonishing number. After subtracting taxes and surcharges for Doc Lassiter and Doc Hale and what I owed the Big Store for clothes and mine equipment and the Club House for rent, laundry, and meals, it read, gloriously, $268.52! *I was rich!*

Then I remembered the amount I owed for the repair of the Buick—$135.78. I made a quick mental calculation. After paying it, I would still have $132.74 left over. Then I remembered I hardly had a shirt that I could button, and my pants were getting tight. All my clothes had shrunk. I would soon have to visit Mrs. Anastopoulos at the Big Store and buy some more. It was a lesson in economics, but not one I much appreciated.

I cashed my check at the Big Store, took out the Buick money, and stowed the rest of my roll in my sock drawer. I didn't worry about hiding it. Nobody was going to steal it, not in Coalwood. Then I thought of the junior engineers and decided maybe I ought to at least stuff it inside a sock. Then I thought of the junior engineers some more and put the sock in a pillowcase. Then, when I thought of the junior engineers one more time, I found a loose board in the back of my closet and hid the pillowcase behind it, went downstairs to Floretta's tool closet, and came back with a hammer and nails and nailed the board down.

After supper, I decided to walk up to the house to pay Dad for the Buick. I had a question for him, too, and I was bound and determined to get it answered.

As I came outside, I saw Jake and Rita walk out of the engineering office. Jake was talking animatedly, and Rita was listening with her arms crossed and her head down. My face flushed hot. Jealousy is a cruel thing. The green-eyed monster, as Floretta called it. I knew Jake and Rita had been friends when they were children, and it was natural they would have something to talk about. But I still didn't like it.

Rita looked up and caught sight of me. I couldn't turn away. They came up on the porch. "Hello," I said to her, trying to sound a lot more cheerful than I felt.

"Hello, Sonny," she said, and then her head went back down as if she was pondering something pretty hard.

Jake nodded. "Sonny," he said formally.

They kept going, into the Club House. They were just friends, or had been. They were just talking, too. I kept repeating that mantra and also reminding myself of the real Rita I'd observed the night she'd tried to get into the mine. I was still infatuated with her, but now more guardedly so.

Dad wasn't home, so I petted Dandy and Poteet, then made my way up to the mine. Dad's office door was closed, so I handed over the money to Wally, who took it and stuck it in his desk. He wore a little grin that gave him the appearance of a happy toad. "Your dad will be pleased, Sonny," he said.

"I'm glad. When's he going to be through in there?"

"Your guess is as good as mine. He's talking to some of the day shift foremen."

"I need to talk to him, too."

"I'll tell him," he said, shrugging. "Maybe he'll have some time tomorrow."

"I'll wait." I sat down in one of the filthy plastic chairs along the far wall of the tiny alcove.

Wally eyed me. "It could be a while."

"I don't have any appointments."

"When he finishes, he may have somewhere else he needs to go."

"I'll take that chance."

Wally hummed a tuneless tune. Then he said, "Sonny, here's some advice for you. Your dad will be happy that you came up here and paid off the Buick. Leave well enough alone."

"I'll wait," I said stubbornly.

Wally shook his head and went back to shuffling his papers. I wondered if those papers ever changed or if they were the same ones he'd been shuffling at the beginning of the summer. They were dirty enough to make me suspicious.

The electric clock on the wall hummed the minutes past. Outside, men clumped by, evening shift stragglers. There were always a few on any shift. They'd get their pay docked unless they had a good reason. Doc Lassiter could sign their chits if their delay was caused by an illness in the family. Not much else counted. Even the union wouldn't back them up. Late work meant less pay.

An hour passed and the clock hummed on. Wally had shuffled the papers on his desk at least four times. I just sat there, musing and occasionally resting my eyes on the Mining Machine Parts, Inc., calendar with a sketch of a bathing beauty on it. Wally turned to see where I was looking and frowned as if I were admiring his personal girlfriend. For some reason, I was happy to irritate him. Wally considered himself the gatekeeper of the most important man at the mine, and that, at least as far as he was concerned, gave him the right to occasionally give everybody who tried to see Dad a hard time, including me. Wally was close to getting above himself.

Finally, the office door opened and I heard a rumble of voices and laughter, too. That surprised me. I always figured Dad's meetings with his foremen were grim affairs.

Mr. Marshall greeted me as he came out. "There's that track-laying man!" He punched me so hard in the shoulder that he nearly knocked me off my feet. Such a blow was tantamount to a hug in Coalwood, so I gratefully accepted it. He kept going.

Other foremen came out and did the same. My shoulder got sore in a hurry. "Got twenty bucks on you," Mr. Nick Paul said. He was a Caretta foreman, and the fact he'd bet on me made me proud.

Dad ushered the last of his men out of his office. "Sonny, come on in," he said when he spotted me. I advanced cautiously, closing the door behind me while Dad settled in behind his huge desk. "So what brings you here?" he asked.

"To pay off the Buick. Wally has the money."

"Thank you." He looked amused.

"And I have a question."

"Let's hear it."

"Where did you go the night Tuck got killed?"

His chair squawked like a mad crow as he leaned forward. "What do you mean?"

"Mr. Caulder said both you and Tuck were gone when he came out of the hoisthouse, so he assumed you had gone down in the mine. But Mom said you didn't come home at all that night. I was just wondering where you went."

Dad shook his head. "This is Coalwood business, Sonny."

"I was raised in Coalwood," I pointed out. "I'm a product of the Coalwood School, I'm a Coalwood miner, and I'm a member of the Coalwood union. I think I'm eligible to know Coalwood business, too."

"Then let's say it's *my* business. You're not eligible for that."

I persisted. "There had to be a good reason why you didn't go inside with Tuck."

"There was a very good reason," he said. "Tuck was a competent foreman. It's not against the regulations for a foreman to fireboss his section alone. I let him do it."

"Dad, I was there at the testimony. Mr. Fuller made a good case. Maybe you didn't break the law or even a regulation, but you put Tuck in danger by not going inside with him. Mr. Fuller is going to say it fits a pattern. What are you going to say to that?"

Dad sat back, a startled look on his face. "You have no right to come up here and badger me like this," he said. "Who do you think you are?"

My answer crackled out of my mouth like lightning. "I'm your second son."

Dad's good eye blazed, then seemed to subside. I could feel him gathering control. He waved a hand in dismissal. "Sonny, I'm done talking about this with you. Thank you for paying for the Buick. Good night."

I stood my ground. "Why won't you defend yourself?"

"Good night!"

As I went by his desk on my way out, Wally sang, "I tried to tell you."

I thought about saying something smart-alecky back, but decided to keep my peace. For one thing, he was right.

29

DOC HALE

ON THE walk back to the Club House, one part of my mind kept asking where Dad had gone the night of Tuck's death. The other part wondered why nearly every time we talked, it turned into an argument. I might have thought some more about it, but I found Doc Hale, Coalwood's dentist, sitting on the porch, enjoying a cigar and the evening. He seemed delighted to see me. "You're keeping late hours, aren't you, Sonny? I've bet a hundred dollars on you. If you want to catch up with those Caretta boys, you need your rest."

"I'm heading to bed right now, sir," I reported.

Doc Hale dropped his cigar in the coffee can that had been left on the porch for that purpose and walked me into the foyer. He was always a snappy dresser and tonight was no exception. He was wearing white slacks and a long-sleeved light blue shirt, a pale yellow sweater draped over his shoulders, its arms tied around his neck. Sporting brown leather shoes with white trim, he walked with an athletic grace. In fact, he resembled Fred Astaire so much, he could have broken out into a tap dance and I wouldn't have been much surprised.

"So, how are you, my boy?" he asked. "I've been remiss. I should have dropped by your room, told you hello, and welcomed you back to Coalwood." His voice was soft and mellow. Mom had always said there was no one smoother in Coalwood than Eddie Hale.

"It's okay, Doc. I know you keep pretty busy."

He cocked his head. "Floretta tells me you're turning into quite the coal miner."

"I'm learning a lot."

"Your capacity to learn is something I've always admired about you," he said. "And how are your parents?"

"Mom's pretty much on top of the world, I guess," I said. "You know about Dad."

"Yes." He contemplated me. "Does it worry you? About your dad, I mean? I only caught the tail end of the testimony but it sounded pretty rough."

Sometimes I can be a blurter. It's as if everything builds up inside me, and then somebody asks me a question, and it all comes bubbling out. This was one of those times. "They're going to get him, Doc, and it's going to be awful."

Doc Hale raised his eyebrows at my torrent of misery. "Tell you what," he said. "Why don't you stop by my apartment for a nightcap?"

"Sir?"

"A drink and a talk. Maybe I can help you."

I followed Doc Hale down the hall, past the staircase, to his apartment. "If you don't mind," he said, pointing at some sandals beside the door, "I'd appreciate if you wore those. I believe the Japanese are correct in never wearing street shoes into their homes. The home should be considered distinctly sacred, unsullied by the dirt of the outside world."

That made sense to me. I pulled off my boots and put

on the sandals. Just inside the door was a zebra-skin rug. I hesitated before walking across it. "It's okay, Sonny," Doc Hale said. "It's dead."

Doc Hale's apartment resembled a Hollywood movie set. Potted plants bloomed everywhere, including a huge fern that looked like it belonged in a prehistoric forest. Here and there were marble sculptures, busts of what appeared to be ancient warriors—Greeks and Romans, I thought. Framed paintings on the walls didn't look like ones a person would buy in the company store.

A big elephant tusk leaning against one of the bookcases got my attention. I ran my hand over it. It felt like a huge piano key. "He was a rogue, that one," Doc Hale said, nodding at the tusk. "It came down to him or me."

A lion-skin rug, its mouth open and fangs bared, lay beside a white baby grand piano. The lion had a surprised look on its face. "A long shot," he said. "She never knew what hit her."

I looked at the diplomas and testimonials he'd packed on one wall. Doc Hale was a member of the Pittsburgh Masonic Blue Lodge, the International Brotherhood of Magicians, and the Episcopal Church. The latter membership, I supposed, explained why he was usually playing tennis on the court opposite the Community Church while the Methodists were singing Sunday-morning hymns.

"What'll it be, Sonny?" Doc Hale asked from behind the bar. "Coca-Cola, Pepsi, Royal Crown, Dr Pepper, or something stronger?"

"Do you have a Canada Dry?"

For some reason, my answer made him laugh. "Oh, yes, we have plenty of that," he said, and produced a bottle from a little refrigerator.

My eyes strayed to an ink drawing of several nearly naked ladies. "Do you like it?" he asked, noting my gaze. "It's a print of an etching by William Hogarth titled *Strolling*

Actresses Dressing in a Barn. If you look close, I think you'll see Hogarth was quite expressive utilizing the comedy and eroticism that was prevalent during the rococo period."

The women in the print seemed kind of plump to me, but nearly naked ladies were nearly naked ladies, so I admired them a little longer. "Very nice," I said, but I would have called it the rotundo period if anyone had asked me.

Doc Hale hauled out a bottle of clear liquid. It could have been some of John Eye's best, but the little V-shaped glass he poured it in was entirely too delicate for that rough stuff. "I'll be drinking a martini," he reported as he plopped in an olive.

I looked at his glass. I'd heard of martinis on television and the movies, of course, but it was the first time I'd ever seen one for real. "What's in it?" I asked.

He put away the bottles, licked his fingers, and replied, "Gin, vermouth, and attitude."

"What about the olive?"

"That's the attitude."

He handed over my tumbler of Canada Dry and pointed toward a leather couch, its throw pillows covered with what looked to be leopard skin. I sat down carefully, afraid to bruise the fancy material, and eyed the glass coffee table. It had curved horns for legs. The magazines on the table were *National Geographic, Look, Field & Stream,* and *Argosy.* I felt uncomfortable, like a coal miner wearing a tuxedo.

Doc Hale settled into a chair that squished as he sat. "Buffalo hide," he said, patting the armrest. "Most dangerous creature in Africa, next to the hippo. This one was in a terrible temper when I took him down."

"What's it like to be in Africa?" I asked.

He sipped his martini delicately. "Marvelous. A grand place of adventure. I loved it all—the animals, the people, the lawlessness of nature. It's so vastly different from Coalwood." He thought a little. "Then again, there are some similarities."

"You shot all these animals?"

He nodded. "I bagged the big five."

"Big five?"

"Lion, leopard, rhino, elephant, and buffalo."

"How about the hippo?"

"Too ugly. Ernest Hemingway told me once he'd just as soon shoot a dog as a hippopotamus."

My eyebrows rose at that one. "You know Ernest Hemingway?"

He sipped his martini again and gave me a distant smile. I knew I was in for a story.

"I joined him on his 1953 safari. I had traveled down from Mombasa to the Percival farm and found him there with his entire retinue. He was a rookie in the bush, though he was averse to admitting it. In comparison, I was an old Africa hand, having spent some time in the Belgian Congo the year before. I thought Kenya was pretty tame in comparison. Papa didn't like it when I started telling my tales of the wild Congo. He always had to tell a bigger story. He claimed one time he jumped in the water off Key West and wrestled a swordfish until he drowned it. I knew enough about pelagic fish to be certain that such a thing was impossible."

"You thought he was lying?"

"I thought he was being colorful."

"Do you like him?"

Doc Hale gave my question some thought. "I do. But I think he lives his life as if he's watching his own movie. He has to do everything in bold strokes." He mused into his glass. "But at bottom he's a shy man who never feels comfortable in his own skin." Then he laughed. "Oh, the times we had when we split off from the women! Papa fancied this Akamba girl. I recall her name was Debba. I myself liked a girl named Nobba." His face took on a wistful cheeriness. "It was on Christmas Day. The ladies in our party had become bored with the bush and had journeyed back to the Percival farm for the holiday festivities. Ernest and I had our own brand of festivities in mind, so we stayed in camp. He had a difficult time explaining his collapsed cot later to his wife. In fact, he broke poor Debba's wrist when it happened. Luckily, my medical training included setting fractures. Darling girls. He wrote me later to speculate that he now had a child in Africa."

I stared at the dentist, sorting through his story, and lit on the part that intrigued me the most. "You were with an African tribal woman?"

He chuckled. "Is that so hard to believe? Women the world over are much the same, Sonny. Although I must say the women in the bush had a certain . . . shall we say, abandon?"

"Wow," I said, meaning it.

"How old are you, Sonny?" he asked.

"Eighteen," I said. "How about you?"

He laughed at my audacity. "I'm sixty-five years old. The dinosaurs had just died out when I was born."

"I heard you were from New York."

He nodded. "Indeed. I am from the heartland of the Yankees, I'm afraid. My family was quite prosperous. The fence-line gossip is correct on that score. I was born with the proverbial silver spoon in my mouth. Or perhaps the golden teat, if you will." He laughed at his own joke. "How do you like working in the mine?"

I set my glass on the coaster he'd provided. It said *Famous New York Explorer's Club* around its rim. "It's different than I thought it would be," I said. "It's hard, but for some reason, it makes me proud to do it."

"Maybe you're a living example of the maxim that work is as good for the soul as it is for the body," he said.

"I hope so," I replied.

Doc Hale looked at me out of the tops of his eyes. "So, Sonny. Down to cases. About your dad."

"Yes, sir."

He cleared his throat, pursed his lips. "I was here when Homer first came to Coalwood. He was shy, a bit withdrawn, but essentially just another boy out of Gary, desperate for a job. The Captain saw something in him, though, and took him under his wing, taught him everything he knew about mining. I watched your father change over the years until he became the man he is today, as near like the Captain as he could possibly be. But deep down, I sometimes wonder if that boy from Gary is still inside him. If he is, I'll bet you he's scared. Your mother knows this better than I do. Maybe that's why you're here this summer. Your mother wants that boy from Gary inside your father to have at least one friend in this town. Do you understand?"

Although I knew I would need to mull over everything he was saying, I said, "Yes, sir, I think so."

"This thing with Tuck Dillon. It's caused by the history of Coalwood. Do you understand that, too?"

"No, sir."

He let out a long, slow breath. "Have you studied evolution?"

I thought back. "A little, in the tenth grade. Mr. Mams went over what Darwin had to say about it."

"So you understand how animals change over time? It's pretty simple and part of God's miracle, all in all. An animal is always reacting to its environment in order to survive. It has a need to hear better and its ears grow longer. A need to run faster and its legs grow stronger. A need to think logically and its brains grow bigger." He leaned forward, looking into my eyes for a glimmer of understanding. "Your father and your mother—all of us, really—have changed, been modified by this town and what we do here and how we have to live."

"But how does that have anything to do with Tuck Dillon?" I asked.

He pressed his hands together and rocked them against his chin for a few seconds. "It was evolution that killed Tuck. An accumulation of events. Cause and effect. History." He searched my eyes again. "That's all I can tell you, Sonny. That's all I *will* tell you. But it is the answer to everything."

"If that's the answer to everything," I said, shaking my head, "then I don't know the answer to anything."

Doc Hale picked up his martini glass and finished it off, including the olive. "I'm sorry I can't make myself any clearer. You'll just have to allow things to unfold."

I could tell he was finished. "Thanks for the Canada Dry, Doc," I said.

Doc Hale walked me back through his fancy digs. At the door, he said, "Good luck with all this. I'll see you in a few weeks."

"Where are you going?"

"The Sunshine State. Florida. Driving down first thing in the morning. I'll be there through miners' vacation. I'm ready for a little surf, sand, and golf."

"I'm ready for some of that, too," I said, thinking once again how close I'd come to spending the summer in Myrtle Beach. "Of course, I don't know how to play golf."

"Come on along with me, then," he said brightly. "I'll teach you. And there are some very pretty girls to be found in Florida."

I smiled at the offer, but, because I knew it was impossible, I couldn't put much joy in it. "I wish I could. Good night, Doc."

"Good night, my boy. And don't worry. Everything will . . . evolve."

THAT NIGHT, as I lay in bed, I thought about all the things Doc Hale had said. I kept trying to ferret out his meaning, but in the end, I couldn't penetrate it. I skipped to what I did understand, Doc Hale's safari with Ernest Hemingway. I chuckled when I thought of Hemingway breaking his bunk while on top of his girl. Then I thought of something else Doc Hale had said: *Luckily, my medical training included setting fractures.*

Staring up into the darkness, I kept thinking. An answer to the truth I sought was so close I could almost smell it. Then fatigue took over and I fell asleep. When I woke the next morning, I sat bolt upright in my bed. Like an airmail letter through the night, an answer had arrived. Doc Lassiter had refused to say anything about setting Nate's wrist, had said he hadn't done it. But maybe that was because he really hadn't. Maybe, for some reason, Mrs. Dooley had taken Nate to Doc Hale. But, if so, why?

I tugged on my clothes and raced downstairs to Doc Hale's apartment. I knocked on it once, then again. Floretta came out in the hall. "I gave him a bag of breakfast biscuits for his trip an hour ago," she said, frowning at my raised fist over the door. "He's probably halfway to Florida already."

"Damn!" I blurted.

"Don't cuss in front of me, young man," Floretta snapped.

"I'm sorry."

She inspected me. "You going to put your boots on or are you going to lay track in your bare feet?"

I rushed back upstairs to collect my boots. Along the way, I reflected I had always been taught that to discover a truth was an end in itself, that only goodness and virtue could result. But now, for the first time in the entire history of my life, I had discovered a truth, or thought I had, and even though I knew it was probably an important one, I didn't have a clue as to what it meant.

Was it possible, I wondered, *that there were truths that meant nothing?*

Questions, answers, lies, truth: In Coalwood, it was sometimes hard to tell one from the other.

30

COALWOOD BUSINESS

ON MY march up the road to the mine that morning, I saw Mrs. Dooley at the fence and went over to have a word. "Did Doc Hale set Mr. Dooley's arm?" I asked.

She took a drag on her cigarette and regarded me with tight eyes. "Yes," she said, blowing smoke above my head.

"Why?"

"Doc Lassiter was busy."

"Doing what?"

"What difference does it make?"

"I don't know."

"Then why ask?"

I voiced the suspicions that had been slowly forming in my mind. "Did somebody deliberately hurt Mr. Dooley? Is that why you went to Doc Hale? Because he would keep it quiet, where Doc Lassiter would make a report?"

"All this is Coalwood business, Sonny," she answered. "Let the adults handle it."

"Did somebody hurt Nate?"

"Coalwood business."

"Are you afraid of the man who hurt him?"

"Coalwood business."

"My dad told me the same thing yesterday about his trial."

"Then you should listen to him," she said, and left the fence and went inside.

On one of our runs to pick up a tie, I told Bobby of my suspicions. "Coalwood people have always looked at Doc Hale as the emergency backup to Doc Lassiter," he said. "He was probably out on a call and Mrs. Dooley just naturally went where she could."

"Then why didn't she just tell me that?" I said, picking up one end of the tie.

"Ask Doc Hale," Bobby said, picking up the other end.

"He's gone to Florida," I said as we raced back, ducking the low roof.

"Okay. Ask Doc Lassiter," Bobby said, grunting as he nearly tripped in the gob. "I'm sure he knows what happened."

"I did the night we got sworn into the union," I answered, wincing as a splinter from the tie jabbed through my glove. "He said he didn't do it, then walked away. Anyway, he's out of town until after miners' vacation."

We threw the tie down and stood for a moment, panting. "Then I'd say you're out of luck," Bobby observed succinctly.

"I guess I am," I agreed, taking my glove off and sucking on my wounded finger. The splinter was still in it. I nipped it with my teeth and drew it out. "But I don't like it," I said, then spat the bloody splinter out. "God bless it, that hurt!"

"Don't take the Lord's name in vain in the mine!" Johnny yelled from down the track where he was working to level the new ties. "Stop jawing and get to work!"

We picked up our pry bars and starting popping out spikes. "You're lucky I'm around this summer to help you through all your problems," Bobby said amid the squawk of the spikes being drawn.

"It's kind of funny," I said, "but I'm trying to figure out how you've helped me, and I'm blamed if I can come up with anything."

We pushed a rail off the old ties into the gob. "How about we work on your softball skills this weekend?" Bobby asked.

"Maybe."

"Come on. It'll be fun."

"Fun?" I asked. "What's that? I'm not allowed to have any fun this summer."

Johnny came over. "You boys going to talk or work?"

"Johnny, what do you know about Nate Dooley's broken wrist?"

"I haven't heard anything about it, one way or the other."

"Are you sure? Nothing at all? With all the gossip—"

"I don't listen to no gossip," Johnny snapped. "Goldie tries to tell it to me and I just say, Woman, that ain't none of our affair. Me and my college boys got a bet to win!"

Bobby and I caught each other's eye and burst out laughing. We were so tired, we'd turned giddy. It didn't have to make sense. Johnny threw his head back and laughed, too. "Keep going, boys! We'll lick those rascals yet!"

When we came outside that day, we looked on the board and found the Caretta boys had beaten us again by one rail. Bobby saw fit to blame it on me. "I saw you slack off once or twice," he said.

"When was that?"

"You took too long to pee."

"I took the time I needed. Was I supposed to pee in my pants?"

"No, but you could stop being so shy. You must go halfway to Bradshaw. Just go behind a crib or something and pee."

Our argument had gathered a little crowd. When I looked up, I was surprised to see Dad among them. "We Hickams have always had bashful bladders," he said before a foreman grabbed him for a word.

I watched him go. "*We* Hickams?" At least Dad still saw me as a member of the family, even though the family trait he'd recognized wasn't one I was particularly proud of. When I focused back on Bobby and the miners around the board, I found they were still debating my urological situation. "I'll pee closer in," I promised. Anything to make them stop talking about it.

THAT NIGHT, I sat at my table and tried to concentrate on the results of my time study. I'd worked it as far as I knew how to do. If there were any more efficiencies that could be squeezed out, I couldn't see them. The Caretta team was just bigger, better, and stronger. We were going to lose the bet. It was one of those inevitable mathematical certainties.

But then, I thought, there was nothing about Coalwood that was mathematical or certain. When I'd been a rocket boy, Quentin, the brains of the outfit, had come up with something he called a body of knowledge. It was a crude form of the scientific method where everything we did determined our next steps. Remembering how we'd approached problems back then, I tapped my pencil on the paper, making a number of tiny dots. I looked at the dots, then drew lines connecting them. The resulting jagged formation didn't make any sense, but neither did some of the things I knew and didn't know.

My intellectual curiosity, the one Jake had challenged me to rediscover, was taking hold about Dad's trial, about Nate Dooley, about the secrets in Coalwood. I'd always been curious about things. Mom said more than once my tendency toward it was one of my major problems. She had often reminded me that curiosity killed the cat, and I had just as often reminded her that satisfaction had brought it back. It was curiosity that had gotten me stranded in the attic of the old Community Building when it was being torn down. I was eight years old. Jackie Likens, Bobby's younger brother, convinced me there was a treasure of navy silver up there that had been hidden by Harry Truman's sailors when they'd moved out. We built ourselves a pyramid of boards and boxes and climbed up it into the attic. There we discovered not silver but about a million startled bats, most of which did a dance in our hair before flinging themselves out through a broken window. Then our rickety pyramid collapsed and we were trapped. It took the entire mine rescue team plus my dad to rescue us. When Mom finally gathered me in her arms, she said, "Sonny, you keep this kind of thing up and you're going to get yourself killed someday."

Dad had suggested, since he'd almost been hit in the head by a collapsing wall of bricks during the rescue, that maybe the proper time for my death was more or less immediate. What was scary was that Mom actually seemed to consider the wisdom of his suggestion.

Curious Sonny, however, was still alive and well. I contemplated my dots and jagged lines. *What doesn't make sense?*

I turned the time study over and wrote my questions down on its back. Maybe by looking at them, I could see something I'd missed. I wrote:

Why didn't Dad go inside with Tuck?
Where did Dad go instead?

Then I wrote down the other thing I was curious about:

Who broke Nate's wrist?

Then I added into the equation my other major mystery:

What should I do about Rita?

I hadn't caught sight of Rita since the night I'd seen her talking to Jake. She was still taking all her meals in her room, as far as I knew, and working long into the night at the engineering office. Jake had left town. Floretta said he'd gone back to Ohio. "He told me he didn't want to go but he had a meeting he needed to attend."

"Did he say what kind?"

"Something that's supposed to help him keep from drinking is what he said."

Jake had always been a drinker. In fact, the first time I'd seen him, I had to wake him up to get him off the floor since he was sloshed from John Eye's stuff. I was delivering the morning *Bluefield Daily Telegraph* at the time, and there I'd found him, lying halfway in and halfway out of his room, his outstretched hand still holding an empty moonshine jar. Jake had kept himself in trouble his entire stay as a junior engineer in Coalwood because of his drinking. He'd even dated Miss Riley for a while, but the story I heard was she said it was the drink or her and he had apparently decided the wrong way. It was welcome news that Jake had decided to do something about it. I was glad for him, but I was still angry for what it looked like he was trying to do to Dad. Mixed emotions were the only kind I got to have, so it seemed.

I went back to my list and stared at it, my eyes flicking from one question to the next. I kept looking and thinking until I couldn't stand to look and think anymore. Finally, I decided to take a chance. I looked up at the ceiling and mumbled a prayer.

Dear Lord, help me see what can't be seen. Dear Lord, let me know . . .

"Coalwood business," I said out loud to the ceiling and everything above it.

It was done, the request made. I sat back and waited, trying not to worry, while the angel that caught it got in the long queue to heaven's throne.

3 1

KITCHEN TALK

I PACKED a duffel bag, left a note on Floretta's door to let her know where I'd be, and walked up to the Likens's house for my weekend of softball training camp. Mr. and Mrs. Likens greeted me enthusiastically. "It's going to be so much fun having you, Sonny," Mrs. Likens said. "I've been looking forward to spending some time with you," Mr. Likens added. I think they actually meant it. They were just nice people.

Bobby and his brother, Jackie, came to the breakfast table still bleary-eyed and in their pajamas. Jackie and I were nearly the same age, although I'd started school a year earlier. He had always been one of my favorite kids in Coalwood, even though he'd almost gotten us killed in our navy silver-hunting caper. He had an easygoing attitude about nearly everything, and was always quick with a joke. He was also the only boy I knew who could sing "The Witch Doctor" song from end to end without missing a word, which wasn't easy considering you had to know the whole *Ooo-eee-ooo-ahh-ahh-ting-tang-walla-walla-bing-bang* chorus.

Jackie was tall and slim, whereas his older brother was built like a fireplug. Despite their age and physical differences, though, it was easy to tell the brothers were friends. They came to the table hitting each other on the shoulder, trying to trip each other, and arguing about this and that. I envied them. Jim and I did all those things, but when we did them, we were serious, and sometimes somebody, usually me, got hurt.

"Jackie's been standing on his head all morning," Bobby reported.

"How come?" I asked.

He looked at his brother admiringly. "Just because he can, I guess."

Jackie demonstrated his prowess and proceeded to walk on his hands all around the kitchen. "Jackie, come to eat, dear," Mrs. Likens said.

Mrs. Likens dished up scrambled eggs and bacon. She was a pretty woman with high cheekbones, a set jaw, and an intelligent gleam in her eye. Many a girl had felt her wrath in home ec class for inattention or burnt apple pie. She acted more or less like the assistant principal at the school. I liked her mostly because one time she'd shown me how to slide down the playground slide using a sheet of wax paper. I'd slid so fast I'd sailed six feet past the end of the slide right into a mud puddle.

Mr. Likens sat at the head of the table, looking like a benevolent bulldog. He was a wide-shouldered man with twinkling blue eyes and a quick smile. "Well, Sonny," he said, "been swimming much this summer?"

I had to confess I hadn't. Mr. Likens had taught me how to swim, along with nearly all the other boys and girls in Coalwood. Every summer, during his vacation from Coalwood school principal duties, he drove a company-provided bus and twice a week reconnoitered the town, stopping to pick up any kid standing alongside the road with a rolled-up towel. Then he took us across Welch Mountain to the Linkous Park pool. I'd even gotten my Red Cross Junior Lifesaver's certificate from Mr. Likens, a prized possession.

"You're a good swimmer, Sonny," he said, "one of the best I ever taught. I hope you don't give up on it. Maybe you can be a scuba diver, too. You liked being underwater a lot, I remember."

"*Sea Hunt* is my favorite program," I said.

"There you go. I predict you will someday be a wonderful scuba diver."

"So I understand you've decided to be an engineer *and* a writer," Mrs. Likens said, sitting down at the table. Jackie had jumped up and helped her with her chair. "Thank you, dear," she said.

"Yes, ma'am," I said.

"Well, I'm sure you'll be a good one, writer or engineer," she said formally. "After all, you did receive the bulk of your education from our school." She smiled lovingly at her husband, and I thought again how much I envied her family. They all just seemed to *like* each other. It was a remarkable thing to see.

After breakfast, I stowed my duffel bag in the Likens's spare bedroom. Bobby came in behind me. "I'm sure glad you came, Sonny."

"I decided eight hours a day with you Monday through Friday just wasn't enough," I replied. It was an attempt at humor, which failed even with me.

He nodded as if he really believed me, which he probably did. "If you like, we can talk over all your problems while we practice."

"Let's just concentrate on softball. If you and your dad can get me up a notch from awful, maybe I won't embarrass myself too much."

"You're going to do fine."

A limerick I'd just made up popped into my head. "There was a young man named Sonny. Everybody in Coalwood thought he was funny. Bobby Likens said, Hey, I'll teach you to play, and then we lost all of our money."

"Very amusing," he said. "Have you decided to become a poet, too? Be careful. Poets commit suicide."

"No, they don't," I said. "They just don't get published. But they get to live in New York City in garrets and wear black and drink lots of coffee and make out with lots of girls who also wear black, don't ask me why."

"You don't even know what a garret is," he said. "You read that in some book."

It was true, although I couldn't remember which one. "You hate it when I take up for myself, don't you?" I parried.

"No, I hate it when you kid yourself," he replied, and then left me to make up my own bed in more ways than one.

All weekend, I practiced softball with Bobby, Jackie, and Mr. Likens on the ball field in front of Little Richard's church. The Reverend came out once to watch us and, of course, applauded me even though I was terrible. I couldn't catch the ball and I couldn't hit the broad side of a barn with my bat, either.

During a break, Mr. Likens and I sat down with the Reverend on the stoop of his church while Bobby and Jackie kept tossing the ball back and forth. Little said he had been asked to give the invocation at the Fourth of July celebration. "You'll do a grand job," Mr. Likens told the Reverend.

"It is very important that I do, sir," he replied.

"What are you going to talk about, Reverend?" I asked politely.

"Well, Sonny, that's been hard to figure," he said. "At first, I thought I'd talk a bit about Coalwood, ponder a bit on all the goodness we have here. It is my belief that God just likes Coalwood, and the life we've built for ourselves here, and our mountains and hollows, too. But then I thought that sounded puffed up, and now I'm down a different track. As a matter of fact, Mr. Likens, I must confess my prayer has something to do with your profession."

Mr. Likens took off his hat and used a bandanna to wipe the sweat from his nearly bald pate. "Would you like to talk about it?"

"I would, indeed, sir."

I left them to their conversation and went back to dropping balls and swinging at air with my bat. Every so often, though, I was catching one, and hitting one, too. *Keep your eye on the ball, Sonny.* That's what Bobby, Jackie, and Mr. Likens kept saying, over and over. *Keep your eye on the ball.* That seemed to be the main thing to remember. Everything else was just details.

On Sunday evening, Floretta met me in the parlor of the Club House when I came back from my training. "Mrs. Likens called me to say you were on your way back here. Did you have a good time? I've been worried about you all weekend."

"The Likens house is only two hundred yards up the road," I pointed out. "Why didn't you just walk up to see me?"

"Even a mother eagle has to let her babies fly."

"I didn't fly very much, just practiced softball."

"Your mama called."

"Oh?"

Floretta gave me a look. "I hate to tell you."

I shrugged. "Go on. I can take it."

"She said she didn't know if you were planning on coming to Myrtle Beach for miners' vacation, but if you were, not to do it. She said for you to stay right here. Your dad's coming to see her and your mama said she'd like some time with him by herself."

My feelings were a bit wounded, but I could see why Mom would want it that way. "Fine," I said. "I'll stick around town, help the Dooleys, play with the dogs, help you, too, if you need it."

Floretta startled me with a hug, nearly squeezing the air out of me. "Sometimes I'm so proud of you, Sonny Hickam! How about some blackberry pie? I picked the berries myself."

"Yes, ma'am!"

Floretta led the way into her kitchen, where I proceeded to chow down on her wonderful pie, hot out of the oven. I was working on my third slice when Tag Farmer strolled in. He nodded to me, then said, "Got some bad news for you, Floretta. No fireworks on the Fourth of July."

"Why not?"

"Because it hasn't rained in about a month," he said, shoveling pie onto a saucer. "I just got the paperwork. State forestry department says no fireworks this year. I know you've got a closet full of Roman candles so thought I'd come tell you, before I have to arrest you."

"Well, shoot," she said. Then she squinted at him. "You came all the way down here to warn me off my Roman candles? My pies wouldn't have had anything to do with that, hmmm?"

Tag chuckled and Floretta got busy elsewhere, leaving me and the constable together. It occurred to me that maybe Tag would know the answer to at least one of my questions. I laid it on him. "Tag, how did Nate Dooley break his wrist?"

Tag looked around. "Wonder if Floretta's got any ice cream?"

"About a hundred gallons in the freezer there," I said, pointing at the big chest along the kitchen wall.

Tag dug into it and lifted out a big carton of French vanilla. "You want some?"

"Sure."

He ladled it on, one scoop, then two, then three. "Enough?"

"Doc Lassiter didn't set Nate's bone," I said.

"Do tell."

"I think it was Doc Hale."

Tag put the ice cream away. "Doc Hale's been known to set a few bones when Doc Lassiter's out somewhere."

"So where was Doc Lassiter?"

Tag shrugged. "Probably up Snakeroot Hollow or Mudhole or somewhere. What's all this, anyhow?"

I didn't see any harm in telling him my suspicions. "I think somebody broke Mr. Dooley's wrist and Mrs. Dooley's scared to tell who it was."

Tag stopped eating, raised his eyebrows. "What makes you think that?"

"I don't know. A hunch, maybe."

"What difference would it make if Doc Lassiter or Doc Hale set the bone?"

"I'm not sure," I had to admit.

Tag wiped his mouth on his sleeve. "Well, Sonny, I'm sure not going to ignore a hunch by a college boy. I'll swing by and have a talk with Mrs. Dooley right away."

I peered at him. His broad face was open and sincere. That's how I knew he was lying. "Thank you," I said.

"You can count on me," he said, setting his empty dish in the sink and running some water over it. "Floretta," he called, "you still make the best blackberry pie in McDowell County!"

Floretta's distant voice (it was a big kitchen) answered, "Thank you, Tag, honey. Go on now and catch yourself some delinquents."

He laughed. "God knows there's a bunch of 'em in this town."

Tag clapped me on my shoulder and left. I watched the kitchen door flap shut behind him. It went back and forth on its spring, back and forth again, then closed tight. It was, I reflected, just like the conversation I'd had with the constable.

3 2

THE FOURTH OF JULY

THE SUN bobbed up over the mountains and splashed Coalwood with such glory that when I looked out my window, I had to squint from the mirrored brilliance of the snowy-white Community Church and the reflected emerald glow of the enfolding mountains. Everywhere I looked, Coalwood seemed to shimmer in the hot blast furnace of the deep West Virginia summer. If I was going to make a fool of myself on the softball field, at least I was going to do it on a grand and glorious day.

My joy in the beauty of the sunny morning was tempered by what Tag had said about the drought. I studied the deep woods behind the church. The trees, vibrantly green, waved and rustled in the gentle breeze. In a drought, I knew it wasn't the trees that were the problem. It was the dense brush and leaves beneath them that could turn into a flood of fire suddenly washing through the woods. If the woods started burning, it wouldn't be long before Coalwood's houses caught on fire, and then we would all be in a fix. Coalwood had no fire department. The Welch and

War fire departments might come to help us providing they didn't have any other calls, but they were a long way away.

I dressed and went down to breakfast. Victor and Ned were there and a few contractors too far from home to leave for the holiday. I surprised the junior engineers by sitting with them. I guess I needed the company. "You boys ready for the game?" I asked.

Victor looked up. "Is it true you're a terrible player?" he asked.

"It's true," I confessed, "but I've been practicing."

"How much?"

"All weekend."

"Did you learn anything?"

"Yes. That I'm still a terrible player."

Victor looked relieved. He probably had some money down on his side.

Floretta brought out breakfast. "My, just look at my little ballplayers," she said fondly. "All you boys do good, now, you hear? Make Floretta proud of you."

We mumbled agreeable answers and then dived in.

After breakfast, I joined the stream of people heading for New Camp. Bobby fell in beside me, tossing me a glove. "It's Jackie's," he said. "He said maybe it would give you some confidence."

I admired the glove. It was a well-worn beauty. I smacked my fist into it a couple of times, getting the feel of it. Bobby trotted on ahead, turned around, and threw a ball to me. "Catch."

I flubbed his pitch, then ran after the ball rolling down the road. "Got my money on the right team, sure enough," I heard a man say to the laughter of others.

I flung the ball back to Bobby and missed him by a mile. He went running after it, fielded it smoothly, and then turned in one fluid movement and fired a hot one back at me. I put my glove out in front of me and it smacked home. I clutched it to my chest.

"Attaboy!" Bobby called.

I pitched back to him, missing again. He came trotting back, frowning. "Look where you're throwing the ball," he admonished. "That's the whole secret of playing, keeping your eye on whatever you're doing and following through. Didn't anybody ever play catch with you?"

Nobody ever had, of course. Dad was always at the mine, Jim was playing catch with his pals, and I was off somewhere usually reading a book. That was how it had all worked out.

"Come on, throw it to me again," Bobby said, running ahead. "And pay attention to what you're doing."

I kept my eye on him as best I could and followed through. The ball sailed to him, although a bit high.

"You see? You have it in you to be a great player."

Although I appreciated Bobby's opinion, I had, in fact, only two hopes: one, that I wouldn't hit myself with the bat, and the other, that nobody would hit a ball in my direction. They were forlorn and little hopes, but they were all my own.

THE COMPANY had built the park above New Camp mainly to create a playing field for the Coalwood Junior High School football team, but every spring, it was converted into a baseball and softball field, complete with a high screen behind the batter's box, limed baselines, cloth bases, and a pitcher's mound. It was all pretty fancy. Farther up the hollow, the company had also installed heavy-duty steel swings, seesaws, and merry-go-rounds fabricated in the company machine shops. They were there for anybody who wanted to make use of them. People from Davy and Welch even came over and used them from time to time.

Mr. Bundini, dressed in his usual snappy splendor, including a bright red vest, was the master of ceremonies for the Fourth of July ceremonies. A stage, decorated with red, white, and blue bunting, had been built for the occasion. My dad, dressed in his khaki mine uniform, joined Mr. Bundini on the stage, as did Reverend Richard, who wore a black suit. Mr. Bundini called for quiet and then introduced Reverend Richard to give the invocation. Everybody crowded around the stage. The Reverend walked up to the podium, and this, pretty much, is what he said:

Dear Lord, we are gathered here to celebrate not just the independence of our great land, but also the document on which it stands. There is much to admire in that document but what we best remember is this: We hold these truths to be self-evident; that all men are created equal; that they are endowed by their Creator with certain unalienable rights; that among these are life, liberty, and the pursuit of happiness.

To prepare for this invocation today, I have pondered long and hard these words. Most of you know that I rarely go anywhere without my Bible. It is an old Bible. It belonged to my grandfather. What you don't know is that inside this book, I have always kept a copy of the Declaration of Independence. It also belonged to my grandfather. He believed it to be as holy as his Bible.

When I was a boy, somebody once asked me if my grandfather had been a slave. I couldn't imagine that could be true so I went to him and asked him: 'Grandfather, were you a slave?' He said, 'Child, there was a man called me that but I was never a slave and you know why? Because I could read. My mama, she taught me when that man wasn't looking, just as her mama taught her.'

When he became officially a free man, my grandfather purchased this Bible and a copy of the Declaration of Independence. He kept them both until the day he died. He left them to me.

I have come to understand my grandfather was right. No man is a slave if he can read. Especially if he can read the Bible and the American Declaration of Independence.

But that means there are still slaves in this land. There are

*slaves who do not know that they have unalienable rights given
to them by God, and that they also have, by the grace of the
Lord, life, liberty, and the right to pursue their happiness and
the happiness of their families.*

*They are slaves to their own ignorance. Ignorance is the
ultimate slaveowner.*

So on this Fourth of July, I pray a special prayer.

*I pray for the day when the tyranny of ignorance will be
banished all across this great land and every man, woman, and
child can read and understand what they read.*

I pray for that day.

I pray every day for that day.

The Reverend sat down, and for the first time ever, as
far as I knew, the Fourth of July invocation got a big round
of applause.

I pitied the speaker who had to follow.

It turned out to be my dad.

Dad stood up, nodded to Reverend Richard, and said, "I
am here to represent Olga Coal Company on this our celebration of Independence Day. I would remind one and all
that it was the coal company that built Coalwood and it will
be the coal company that will keep it going forever. If I believe in anything, it is this: Support this town and the town
will support you. That's what Captain Laird taught me.
That's what I believe. Now let's eat, then play ball!"

Dad got an ovation, too. There was nothing Coalwood
people liked better than a speech, especially if it was short.

THE UNION softball team gathered in a huddle along the
third-base line. Mr. Dubonnet called out our roster. "I'm
pitching," he said, then looked up sharply from his clip-
board. Nobody argued with him, so he kept going.
"Catcher, Hub Alger. First base, Bobby Likens. Second
base, Gordo Franklin. Shortstop, Sam Fragile. Third base,

Billy Cooke. Left field, Jabbo Terrell. Center field, Billy Joe Blevins. Right field, Sonny Hickam. Third-base coach is Leo Mallett. Any questions?"

"Who's their pitcher?" Jabbo asked, nodding toward the management team, which was having their own little huddle, along the first-base line.

"Not a clue," Mr. Dubonnet said. "Some ringer, I'm guessing."

"If he's not a company employee, I say we put in a protest," Sam said. Sam had been a classmate of mine at Big Creek. It was good to see him. He was a big, strong guy, and one of the best basketball players the high school had ever produced. I hoped he could play softball, too.

"Hold your horses, Sam," Mr. Dubonnet counseled.

Mr. Dubonnet handed out our team shirts. They were a dark blue with white letters on back that said COALWOOD UMWA LOCAL #768. I was proud to wear the union colors.

I studied the management team as they took the field. They were wearing red jerseys that said OLGA COAL COMPANY on the back.

Jake walked behind home plate. His pads and face mask showed him to be the catcher. Then I saw their pitcher. Mr. Dubonnet saw who it was, too. We both stared, but he spoke first: "What the Sam Hill?"

All of the UMWA team, and the crowd as well, grew silent as Rita, holding a softball in her left hand and tapping it on her hip, walked to the pitcher's mound. "They can't play a girl!" Mr. Dubonnet protested.

"That's no girl," Guy Cox, the management player-coach called back with a grin. "It's but a junior engineer."

Jake settled down into a crouch and held up his catcher's mitt. Rita stepped up on the mound, whipped her arm, and threw. The softball streaked along what seemed a grooved path until it hit Jake's mitt with a sharp *crack*. Dust erupted from his glove.

"Holy Mother of God," Mr. Dubonnet said, his jaw dropping.

"Don't wear your arm out!" Jake yelled to Rita.

She frowned, and yelled back, "I know what I'm doing!"

Jake walked out to the mound and leaned in close. Rita's frown deepened and she shook her head. Jake stalked back and crouched. Once more, Rita wound up. When her pitch came, the ball seemed to turn invisible the second it left her hand. It didn't become whole again until it appeared in Jake's glove. He took off his face mask and his glove, shook his hand, and threw the ball back to her. "Easy!" he yelled.

She turned away from him, rubbing the ball and kicking at the dirt.

Bobby was first in our lineup. He knocked the dust off his cleats and stepped into the batter's box.

That's when I saw who the umpire was. It was a day for surprises. It was Dad.

"Both sides agreed," Mr. Dubonnet said when he saw where I was looking. "Everybody figured he'd be honest."

"But he doesn't know anything about softball," I said.

Mr. Dubonnet gave me a piercing look. "Don't you know your daddy was one of the best ballplayers, softball or hardball, to ever come out of Gary Hollow? I was about the only one who could ever fan him. Man, he could hit that ball hard!"

That was news to me. And then I thought—if he was so good, why hadn't he ever taught me a blamed thing about playing? Of course, I knew the answer. The coal mine and his job there. His almighty, holy job! How much of his life had it stolen from our family?

Rita fanned Bobby, though he swung hard, and also our next two at-bats, *zip, zow, zup!* It was an amazing thing to watch. Dad's job was easy. He just watched the balls go straight down the middle like runaway trains. The women in the stands, management and union alike, started to cheer each time she threw. The men, management and union alike, fell into silence. A woman beating men, especially miners? Nothing like that had ever been seen in Coalwood, or imagined!

With our side retired, we took the field. I went out to right field and started praying nobody would hit anything my way. Mr. Dubonnet was a pretty fair pitcher. Mr. Wotring, the first management man up, flied out to Bobby. Next up was Mr. Cox. I'd always heard that he could have been a professional baseball player if he'd been scouted right. He knocked a couple of long fouls and then got a solid double. Then Jake came up next and managed to hit a line drive. Fortunately, it was right into Sam Fragile's glove. Sam almost tagged Mr. Cox out, but he was able to scramble back to base.

Then Rita came to bat.

Jabbo had started us chanting in the outfield. I joined him. *Swing batter, swing batter.* She did as we suggested and connected with a hard fastball. It went sailing up, up, and then away. A shrill cry came from the stands. Oh, the women of Coalwood were having a fine time. Rita's ball landed on the bank just beneath Highway 16. It was a home run!

Rita trotted around the bases. The women began chanting:

Go Rita Go! Go Rita Go!

Mr. Cox, followed by Rita waving at her admirers, sailed home, and we were behind two to nothing. The men in the stands spat in their cups without joy. The women kept cheering.

After Rita, Victor came to bat. Mr. Dubonnet drilled one in and he hit it and it went high and to the right.

To me.

I squinted up at the ball, a nearly invisible little dot in the sky. I'd never caught a ball hit so high. Victor was chugging up the first-base line and Bobby was yelling at me, "Keep your eye on it, Sonny!"

Victor rounded first base and headed for second. I moved up on the ball, then saw I'd overestimated and moved back. The ball looped on. "Get under it!" I heard Bobby cry.

Time seemed to slow to a crawl. I kept my eye on the ball. Then, to the amazement of everybody at the New Camp field including myself, I put up my glove and caught it over my shoulder!

I didn't hear the cheers, although I was told later there were a lot of them. I just kept looking at the ball in disbelief. *I had actually caught it!*

Bobby waited for me in the infield as I trotted in. "Pretty good," he said. "Now smile. That's it. Show off a little."

"Attaboy," Mr. Dubonnet said as I came trotting in.

Mr. Likens took me aside. "Let me see your batting stance," he said. I showed him what I remembered from our weekend of practice, and he adjusted me. "Hold the bat up a little higher, feet apart, that's it, knees bent a little." He clapped me on the shoulder. "Just keep your eye on the ball, then let instinct take over. You'll be fine."

I went back to sit on the bench with the team. Rita didn't let up a bit. The audience was starting to fall silent at her every pitch. It was like watching an artist at work. Our next two batters went down swinging. Then it was my turn. She turned her back to me.

"Ease up a little," Jake yelled at her, then sighed heavily, threw off his face mask, and trotted out to the mound. She kicked the dirt and he did, too. Then Mr. Cox trotted out to the mound and sent Jake back in. "She's wearing her arm out," he griped to Dad. "I'm nearly sorry I talked her into doing this."

"Looks like she's doing fine, Jake," he said.

I turned to look at them. How could Dad talk so friendly to Jake? Jake caught me looking at him. "What?" he asked.

"Is this what you had to talk to Rita about? Playing softball?"

"Sure. What else would I talk to her about?" He peered at me. "Did I make you jealous?"

"You make me jealous?" I laughed. "A drunk like you?"

I didn't know where that had come from. I colored, and Dad called a time-out. He pointed at me, then took me aside. Jake stayed in his squat, looking down at the ground.

"I'm sorry," I said before Dad could say anything.

"That's your answer for just about everything, isn't it?" he demanded. "You figure if you say it, then everything will be all right. Look, Sonny, Jake is your friend. He took up for you in this town when everybody got down on you about your rockets. Have you forgotten that?"

"No, sir. But he's here now to destroy you. He's not my friend anymore."

Dad put his face nearer to mine. "I'm not going to tell you this another time. That's my business. If Jake and me have a problem, I'll deal with it."

"You always said he was a drunk," I replied, looking to defend myself. "If you can do it, why can't I?"

"Because it isn't right for you to do it. I was his boss. He was your friend, but more to the point, you were his. Or doesn't friendship mean anything to you?"

"Play ball!" somebody in the stands yelled.

"Come on," Dad said.

I tried to shrug away Dad's indictment, even though I knew he was completely right. I reentered the batter's box and dug in, but I was having trouble concentrating. Rita wound up, gave me a look, then—*zoop!* I only had a fraction of a second to look at the ball, and then it was in Jake's mitt.

"Strike one!" Dad called.

Jake threw the ball back to Rita. I had to get my focus. "I apologize, Jake," I said. "I was way out of line."

"No, you weren't," he said. "You were right on target."

I felt a small dose of absolution and planted my feet, just as Mr. Likens had said, and raised my bat. The next pitch came flying. You could almost hear it sizzle. Jake yelled, "Swing batter!"

I did, swatting nothing but air. "Strike two!" Dad called.

"Neat trick," I said. I heard Jake slap his catcher's mitt with his fist. Now I was mad at him again.

The next pitch seemed slower. I watched it hum in, mesmerized by its flight. I thought it was high and let it go. "Swing batter!" Jake yelled.

"Ball one!" Dad called.

I looked back at Dad, but, in the way of all umpires, he ignored me, keeping a studied nonchalance.

I dug in, unlocked my knees, waved the bat, and Rita let go. It was another hummer, straight on. Then, just as happened when I'd caught the fly ball, time seemed to slow down. I tracked the ball, noted its stitched seams turning as it roared toward me. I uncocked my bat and started my swing. The ball and the bat had their own trajectory. I was just applying the muscle power. I felt the collision, a sharp *snap*. Then I unleashed and kept swinging.

Then time sped back up. I heard people cheering. The ball was accelerating over Rita's head, moving out, almost like one of my rockets. Victor watched it soar over him. Out in center field, Mr. Nordman reached up under his cap and scratched his head.

I'd hit the blame thing clean up on the highway!

"I knew it!" Jake griped. "Threw her arm out!"

I just stood there and gaped. I couldn't believe it. Jake finally broke my reverie. "Go on, Sonny. Take a lap. You've earned it."

I looked at Jake, then at Dad behind him. Dad looked back, eye to eye. "Take your lap, son," he said.

"Yes, sir!"

I trotted around the bases, then touched home plate. Floretta broke from the cheering crowd and hugged my neck. Little Richard came out, too. "Good boy!" he said, patting me on my shoulder.

As all such moments tend to do, my personal glory passed and we kept playing. It was a hard-fought contest, but in the end, Rita murdered us, 10 to 3. Despite Jake's concern, her arm stayed strong all the way through the last inning. On that Fourth of July in the summer of 1961, there was no beating Rita Walicki.

3 3

DANDY

MINERS' VACATION began with the rumbling sounds of a general evacuation as cars and trucks loaded with people and supplies headed out of town toward destinations in every direction. Some folks were headed for Myrtle Beach, others for the Smoky Mountains. Another favorite was Hungry Mother State Park just across the Virginia state line. I rose from my bunk, savored for a moment my home run in the Fourth of July softball game, then remembered that we'd lost the game and that I was stuck in Coalwood with nothing to do for nearly two whole weeks. My spirits sank, then rose again. I would at least get plenty of sleep and not have to lay track.

The first thing I did was to see if there was anything I could do for Mrs. Dooley. I found her sitting on her porch swing with the mister. He was watching a cardinal singing on a limb and took no note of me. "Heard you almost pulled it out for the union yesterday," she said. "But your girlfriend was too tough for you."

"She's not my girlfriend, but I guess Coalwood's never

seen a better pitcher," I replied. "Mrs. Dooley, anything I can do for you?"

"Tomorrow, I'd like to give Nate another bath," she said. "The grass needs mowing. I'd appreciate it if you gave the garden another good weeding. Otherwise, things are going along good."

"I'll come up in the morning for the bath," I said. "Looks like the grass could wait a day or two for the mowing. I'll go take care of the garden right now." Then I tried again. "Mrs. Dooley, how did Nate bust his wrist?"

She rocked in the swing. "He did it to himself," she said.

"How?"

"He fell," she said.

"What made him fall? Did someone push him?"

"He fell, that's all," she said, and by the set of her jaw, I knew she was through answering that particular question to me forever.

I HELPED with Mr. Dooley's bath the next day and mowed the grass a few days later. The Dooleys were about the only people I saw. Floretta was gone off to visit relatives in Kentucky, the junior engineers to Panama City, Florida. The tick-tock of the grandfather clock in the Club House parlor sounded like it was in an echo chamber.

Since the Sharitzes were also on vacation, it was my job to feed the dogs. After a stop at the Dooleys each day, I walked on up to the house. Dandy seemed to have adjusted to his blindness. When Poteet made her daily excursion of the yard, he trotted behind her, sniffing her air, stopping when she stopped, then lumbering on. He even managed a few weak barks in the direction of a passing car or two. Poteet seemed to pace herself to let him keep up.

Dad had left the house unlocked, and I wandered through its rooms. I admired once more Mom's beach painting in the kitchen. It was really a work of art, better, in my opinion, than anything hanging on Doc Hale's apartment walls. I had nearly forgotten Mom's addition to her mural, her pet fox, Parkyacarcass. I examined it anew, wondering what Dad thought of it.

The dining-room table was still stacked with mail. I poked through it, finding unpaid bills and unopened letters. My grades were exactly where Dad had tossed them when we'd had our argument. I walked into the foyer, looked at my old piano. I even sat down and played from some sheet music: "All I Have to Do Is Dream" by the Everly Brothers. It was what we rocket boys had called the song of the Cape, an anthem to the power of dreams. I had also sat down to a duet with Ginger Dantzler two Christmases past and we'd played that same song. My eyes became a bit damp at both memories.

I peered into the living room. The family Bible sat on the coffee table. I took note of its well-chewed pages. Chipper had shredded generations of Hickams inscribed on the family-tree pages. Mom had forgiven him for it, of course. I walked out on the enclosed porch. It was called the Captain's porch. Captain Laird had directed its original construction so that he could sit on it and rock in a rocking chair and contemplate the tipple he'd designed.

Upstairs, I naturally gravitated to my room. I looked at it from the hall, but I couldn't go inside. I didn't feel like I belonged in it anymore. I was no longer that boy of hope and passion and dreams. I wasn't certain who I was anymore, but I sure wasn't that boy.

Back in the yard, I saw that Poteet had finished her excursions and Dandy had drifted off to sleep, a golden curl on the green grass. I picked him up and held him while I sat on the back steps. I thought of the day I'd first seen Dandy. He'd come into Coalwood aboard a freight train all the way from a kennel in Pennsylvania. As far as I knew, he was the first purebred dog to ever arrive in town. I had been distressed the instant I saw him because somebody had cut off his tail. Mom said that was what Yankees did to cocker spaniels to make them win dog contests. I couldn't fathom such a thing. I told her thank goodness human beings weren't so foolish to do that to themselves. Mom said yes they were. Up north, she claimed, women punched holes in their earlobes to hang their earrings rather than clamp them on like the women in Coalwood did. And over in some countries, she said, people stuck bones and sticks through their noses, their lips, and even their tongues. It made me sick just to think about it, and I was sure glad Americans, even the ones up north, were smarter than that.

On the fifth day of miners' vacation, I found Poteet sitting regally on the picnic table in the backyard. She looked like she was standing guard. When I approached her, she whined but kept her position. I went down in the basement to check on Dandy, but he wasn't there. I looked all around the yard and still couldn't find him. "Where is he, girl?" I asked, and, with a snort, Poteet jumped off the table and led me to a place along the fence behind the garage where there was a hole. She slithered through it.

I climbed over the fence and followed Poteet into the alley behind the house. I called Dandy's name, then listened, hoping to hear him blundering through the brush up on the mountain. All I heard was the cawing of some crows and the insistent chirp of a cardinal. Poteet stopped and looked over her shoulder. I kept following her until we went between the garages that lined the alley and then down to the narrow little gurgling creek.

It was there I found Dandy, lying on his side, his snout near the water. By the lay of his fur and the way his legs were splayed, I knew he was dead. Poteet sat down beside him and cocked her head. I reached down and closed his great brown liquid eyes, then picked him up.

When I got back to the alley, I saw Jim's car, a blue-and-white Ford Fairlane, parked behind our house. Jim stood by the gate. He didn't say anything, just looked at me and Dandy. Poteet trotted up to him and he patted her on her head. When I got closer, Jim put out his arms. "I'll take him," he said. "There's a place up on Water Tank Mountain I have in mind."

"What are you doing here?" I asked my brother.

"I got up this morning and knew I needed to go home. Now I know why."

I gave Dandy to my big brother and went into the basement and got a shovel and a cardboard box. "I can't get over how big you are," Jim said as he placed Dandy in the box. "And look at your arms. You been lifting weights?"

"I'd say I have," I answered, thinking of the hundreds of ties and posts I'd hefted over the past month.

Jim carried Dandy and I followed with the shovel. We crossed the road and climbed up Water Tank Mountain. Jim kept going until we reached a stand of pine trees. "You can see the house from here," Jim said. "Dandy would like that."

I started digging. I had become an expert at using a shovel. Jim sat down beside Dandy's box and let me have at it. "I wish I'd paid more attention to Dandy," he admitted, his hand on the box. "Seems like I was always too busy to give him much more than a pat in passing."

"Dandy surely loved you," I said. "He loved all of us. I hope we gave him a good life."

"Did he suffer, do you think? At the end?"

"I saw him yesterday. He seemed pretty spry."

Jim smiled a sad smile. "I wonder how I knew to come home. I hadn't thought a thing about Coalwood all summer. Just trying to get through summer school."

I climbed out of the hole I'd dug. "Jim, I've come to believe there are things in life we'll never figure out. I mean, just being alive is a miracle when you stop to think about it. Lately, I've tried not to think about it. I'm afraid if I figure everything out, it'll drive me crazy."

He laughed. "You don't have far to go, boy. You never have."

"You're still an idiot," I said, happy to trade insults with my older brother.

"You're still a little sister," he said. "But, dammit, you're a big little sister these days. I'd hate to arm-wrestle you."

" 'One fist of iron, the other one of steel,' " I said, quoting Tennessee Ernie Ford, " 'if the left one don't get you, then the right one will.' "

He laughed. We sat together, not too close. "Why did we always fight so much growing up?" I asked.

He tossed a rock, watched it roll downhill. "You did things to aggravate me."

"Oh, I see. It was my fault. Like what kind of things?"

"You'd take my coloring books and color them all the wrong colors before I got to them," he said. "And you'd take my puzzles and solve them before I'd halfway figured out what they were even about. I never could spell a hoot and you could spell everything even before you started to school. That really bugged me. Mom would go around spelling things like 'Let's give Jimmie his m-e-d-i-c-i-n,' and I wouldn't have a clue what they were talking about, but you'd go, 'His medicine! Ewwww!' I mean you weren't even in the first grade and you could already spell big words!"

I could have pointed out that he still couldn't spell medicine, at least not out loud, but I held my tongue. Instead, I considered his accusations, and then gave him one of my own. "I hated that you gave me every disease in the world. You'd catch the measles and Mom would make me go in and hang around your bed until I got it, too. Same thing for the mumps and nearly everything else."

"That wasn't my fault," he said. "That was Mom's. It made it easier on her if we both got sick at the same time. That way she'd only have to deal one time with that particular disease."

"I didn't like wearing your hand-me-down clothes, either. They were always too big."

"Still not my fault," he said. "Boy, you were just resentful, that's all. I ought to knock you upside the head right now for it, straighten you out."

I laughed. Then I looked at the forlorn cardboard box. "Guess we need to see to our little boy here," I said.

Jim nodded, and together we lowered Dandy into the place I'd made for him. The dirt smelled fresh and clean like the good turned West Virginia loam that it was. I shoveled until the box was covered, and then Jim and I hunted around the mountain for loose rocks to make a border. Jim fashioned a cross from two limbs using birch bark to tie them together, then stuck it at the head of the grave. We stood over it. "Do you remember how we got Dandy?"

"Mom bought him, didn't she?"

Jim shook his head. "It was you and me. I came up with the idea to have a cocker spaniel and Mom showed me where we could buy a puppy through some magazine. I got you excited about it and we saved up, you and me together. We begged and borrowed pennies from everybody we knew. We made ourselves true nuisances all up and down the row. Every time we got a hundred pennies, we traded them in for a silver dollar at the Little Store. When we had enough dollars, Mom mailed our order in and when the railroad man called, said we had a C.O.D. that was barking, we walked down to the station at Coalwood Main and handed over our bag of coins. Dandy was about dead in that old wooden crate he came in, not even any water to drink, and he was covered with fleas. But I knew I loved him with all my heart the first time I saw him."

I remembered now. It was the only thing that my brother and I had ever done together, but it was a good thing. Dandy had become the one link between us during all those years whether I realized it or not. Tears started to leak down my face, and when I looked over, I saw Jim was brushing something from his eyes, too. "Got to get back to school," he said.

"Stay, Jim," I told him.

He shook his head. "Can't," he said, and then gave Dandy's grave a final pat and led the way back down to the house. He climbed into his Fairlane. "This place seems so strange now," he said of Coalwood. "I remember everything about it, but it's like I wasn't ever really here. It's hard to put into words."

I knew what he felt. I felt the same way. We'd always been aimed out of Coalwood. High school was supposed to be the end of it. When we came back, we didn't fit, somehow.

He closed the car door, rolled down his window. "You want me to call the folks, tell them about Dandy?"

"Yes."

He nodded. "What's going to happen to Dad?"

"I don't know. He doesn't seem to care if they fire him or not. He just keeps going like there's no problem, one way or the other. It's really strange."

"I think Mom's up to something," he said.

"What makes you think that?"

"Because she's always up to something." He stuck out his hand. I took it and we both squeezed hard before letting go. He looked up on Water Tank Mountain. "Dandy was sure a good old dog."

"He sure was."

Jim drove his Fairlane out of the back alley, then turned left onto Highway 16, heading back to the outside world. I stood quietly for a while, listening to the trees on the mountains whispering to themselves, then went through the gate to feed Poteet. She greeted me, her tennis ball in her mouth.

34

THE CABIN

A FEW days passed. I walked a lot, there being hardly anyone to pick me up and give me a ride. I even walked all the
way down to Cape Coalwood. The ancient slack dump
stretched out before me, waves of heat coming off it.
There wasn't a single board left of the Big Creek Missile
Agency's old blockhouse. Some concrete chunks were all
that remained of our launchpad. I searched around and
found some metal fragments, the remnants of abor-
tive launches. I could still smell the burnt propellant on the
slivers of steel and aluminum. I put them back where I'd
found them. They seemed almost like holy icons from another page. I felt like an intruder.

I walked back up the road until I got to Frog Level. A
truck rumbled up next to me. It was Red Carroll. "Where
you going, Sonny?"

"Nowhere," I said.

"How about a ride there?"

"Why not?"

We rode along, neither of us saying anything until we

got to Coalwood Main. He stopped at the Club House. "You want off here?"

I shrugged. "I guess so. Any word from O'Dell?"

"Off to Germany soon. I'm so proud of him I could bust."

I nodded and started to get out, but Red stopped me. "Why don't you volunteer for fire watch up at the Cabin?"

"Fire watch?"

"Tag's been asking around for somebody to go spend miners' vacation at the Cabin and watch the mountains in case there's a wildfire. You got a lot of time on your hands. Why not?"

The Cabin Red was talking about was officially titled the Coalwood Conservation Club. It was a rustic lodge on top of Coalwood Mountain that was mostly used for poker parties by the company managers. Schools used it every so often for day outings, too. "Can't do it, Red," I said. "I have to feed Poteet every day."

"I'll take care of her," he said. "You want me to tell Tag you're interested?"

I sure did. It sounded like an adventure, and I was ready for one.

That night I heard a yell from the foyer. "Hey, Sonny boy!" It was Tag.

I came downstairs. The constable gave me a big grin. "I got your sleeping bag, your food, everything you need in the trunk of my car except a change of clothes. Go get packed and come on."

"Am I really needed up there?" I asked. I had been having second thoughts. After all, who would walk aimlessly around town if I wasn't around to do it?

"We need every set of eyes we can get," Tag said.

"Then I'm your man." I ran inside to pack my few pitiful clothes and a couple of books. I was working on a new book I'd bought at the company store titled *To Kill a Mockingbird*. I was enjoying it quite a lot. It was narrated by a little girl, and I especially enjoyed reading about her father. Atticus Finch wasn't much like my dad, at least not outwardly, but I thought they shared at their core a certain decency, and honesty, too.

On the way up Coalwood Mountain, I asked, "Did you talk to Mrs. Dooley?"

"Must have slipped my mind," he remarked. "What was that about again?"

"Never mind."

At the crest of the mountain, Tag turned left and we started climbing a steep dirt road. The dust boiled out behind Tag's patrol car. "Driest I've ever seen it," he worried. "Usually, there's some dew in the morning to keep things wetted down a bit, but even the air's dried out."

"How am I supposed to let anybody know if I see a fire?"

He reached in his shirt pocket and produced a key. "This is to the Cabin. There's a black phone in there."

"What do I look for?"

"Smoke. Make sure it's not coming from a coal tipple or something. I've included some topo maps in your stuff so you can tell where you're looking."

At the Cabin, Tag helped me unload the gear, which included a little gas stove. He had my food in a cardboard box. Nearly every can was beef stew, which was good. I knew how to heat up a can of stew.

Tag walked me around the Cabin grounds. The view was wonderful. As far as I could see, mountains were stacked behind each other like the pages of a book. A fire tower sat on one side of a grassy meadow. "That's the best place to keep your eyes on things," he said. "But just about anywhere up here will do."

We climbed the tower and I stashed the topographical maps in a metal box on the top platform. Inside it, I found a compass. I practiced with it, finding north right off. Then I spotted a plume of smoke and determined that it was coming from the east. "I see it," Tag said. "It's a long way off, though. No threat to Coalwood. But I'll call it in, just to be on the safe side."

When it looked like he was about to leave, I decided to get something off my chest. "Tag, why did you lie to me?"

He gave me a surprised look. "What do you mean?"

"You didn't have to ask Mrs. Dooley about what happened to Nate, did you? You already know what happened to him. Isn't that right?"

Tag pushed his hat to the back of his head. "You know, Sonny, I'm not a real policeman. I'm just a company stiff dressed up to look like one. I do what the company tells me to do, which isn't very much. They just keep me around so folks will have somebody to call if they've got a problem like somebody stealing somebody else's tomatoes. If a real law gets broken, I call in the county."

"Okay," I said, and waited.

"There's not been any real laws broken here," he said after a bit. "It's just Coalwood business."

"You mean nobody hurt Nate Dooley?"

"Not on purpose."

"What does that mean?"

Tag looked off to the east. "I better go call in that smoke."

"Tag . . ."

He spat over the railing. "For God's sake, Sonny, let it go! Your dad doesn't want any of this to come out. That's all you need to know."

"What does Dad have to do with Nate Dooley?"

Tag shook his head and headed down the steps of the fire tower. I followed him all the way to his car. "Forget I said anything," he said.

I couldn't oblige him. "Tag, what does Dad have to do with Nate Dooley getting hurt?"

"I didn't say he did."

"But you said—"

"You got my number?"

"Yes, sir, but—"

"Call me if you need anything. And thanks, Sonny. You're doing a real service here."

"Do me one favor," I said. "Swing by the Dooleys and tell Mrs. Dooley where I am."

"Sure. It's nice of you to try to help her out."

"She picked me, not the other way around."

"Some folks say you owe her," he said. "I don't happen to believe that. You were just a baby when all that happened. Don't worry. She can always call me if she needs anything."

"Why didn't she call you when Mr. Dooley broke his wrist?"

Tag stared at me, then shook his head. He climbed into his patrol car and sped down the dirt road. I watched the cloud of dust rising from his tracks for a little while and then trudged back up the hill to do my duty.

I SPENT the next five days alone at the Cabin. I called in three plumes of smoke, both far away. I also got a pile of thinking done. I didn't figure everything out, but by the time my work at the Cabin was done, I was somewhere close, of that I was certain.

Nate Dooley.

Tuck Dillon.

Dad.

Where there was Dad, wasn't there always Mom? Just a little more information, I believed, and all would be clear, the mysteries solved.

But then, as usual, Coalwood threw me a curve.

Red Carroll came to get me in his garbage truck. "Did you have fun?" Red asked as he drove down Coalwood Mountain.

"I sure did."

"Good, good," he said, a bit distracted. He drove us through Six, then along the straight stretch that went past the mine. "Look at all those fancy cars, Sonny," he said.

I looked. There were a bunch of them—Cadillacs, Chryslers, some big trucks, too. Then I saw a lot of men dressed in suits walking over the grounds. "What's happening?"

"Inventory teams," he said. "From about a dozen holding outfits."

"Why are they here?"

He looked at me carefully with his sad eyes. "I forgot. You don't know, do you?"

"Know what?"

"The company's going to be sold, Sonny. Lock, stock, and tipple."

35

BOBBY'S PLAN

MONDAY, JULY 17, 1961, was the first day back to work after miners' vacation. At the mine, the foremen were all crowded into Dad's office while common miners, such as myself, milled around uncertainly in front of the man-lift.

Johnny, just back from Myrtle Beach, was listening to Bobby tell about his vacation in Lebanon, Tennessee, where his grandmother had a farm. He'd also spent some time on Holston Lake. "Fishing was great," he said. "I caught about a hundred crappie."

"Did you cook them up?" Johnny asked hungrily.

"Sure did. Never a better eating fish in the world."

I was startled that they both seemed so calm. "How can you talk about fish when the mine's being sold?" I demanded.

"It don't change our job, Sonny," Johnny said. "We still got to lay that track down."

"I'm not so sure of that," I said. "What if they sell the mine and fire us all?"

"There you go again," Bobby said. "Ever the pessimist."

"Sonny, you got to get your tail unwrapped this morning," Johnny said. "It's always this way after miners' vacation. Your dad's got to tell his foremen his plan to get production up and running. We won't do much today except inspect and repair. Most likely, Dwight Strong will have us walk the track, just to check out the job."

"No track laying today?"

"Nope. But tomorrow we'll hit it as hard as we can."

"Can't wait," I said, thinking how sore my muscles were going to get all over again.

Bobby shook his head at my sorry attempt at sarcasm. "Your mother gave me an impossible job."

I heard the thumping of boots on wooden steps and saw the foremen coming out of Dad's office. They raised their hands as they did. "Gather around," each of them called their men in turn.

We gathered around Mr. Strong. "Boys, we're going to spend the day pulling maintenance on the equipment and inspecting the face." He looked at Johnny. "Johnny, you take Bobby and Sonny and walk the line, see what you got to do yet."

Johnny nodded compliantly, but I piped up. "What about the Caretta team? Are they going to lay track today?"

Mr. Strong smiled. "Worried about your bet? No, they'll walk their end of the line, too."

"What about the mine getting sold, boss?" one of the continuous miner operators asked.

"It's not a done deal," Mr. Strong answered. "There's still a few *i*'s to be dotted, *t*'s to be crossed."

"But it's going to happen, ain't it?"

Mr. Strong shuffled his boots in the gob. "Most likely."

"I hear the company that's going to buy us is Southern United. They been known to shut a mine down, pull out all its equipment, and sell it for scrap."

"I don't know, Jarrow," Mr. Strong said. "I've heard the same thing, but as far as I know, it's a rumor. There's no sense worrying about it. We'll know when we know."

We descended the shaft once more, caught the man-trip, and got off where we'd laid our last rail. It felt a bit like a homecoming. I breathed in the air whistling down the main line. It smelled of electric motors, coal dust, and gob, the perfume of the mine.

Johnny pointed his light down the track. "If the Caretta team's walking their end, we'll walk until we meet them."

It was some hours later when we saw a trio of lights approaching us—the Caretta boys.

Garrett Brown greeted us. "Hey, Johnny. Hey, boys."

"Garrett," Johnny growled. His light crawled across Delmar and Chinky. "Boys."

"Sonny," Delmar said. His cheek bulged with a big chaw. "Got my three hundred dollars ready?"

"I wouldn't spend it just yet," I said. I tucked my tongue in my cheek to make me look tough. He laughed, don't ask me why.

"Bobby," Chinky Pinns said, and spat.

"Chinky," Bobby said, and spat, too.

We stood crouched under the roof, just contemplating each other's air. "Well, ain't this something?" Garrett finally chuckled. "I wondered when we'd run into you boys. The lime mark's about a half mile back that way." He tossed his thumb over his shoulder.

"How many rails you got to go?" Johnny asked.

"Two hundred and twenty-two," Garrett said. "How about you?"

"I forgot to count," Johnny said.

Garrett laughed. "You're ashamed to say. Maybe you ought to go ahead and give up."

"Why should we give up?" Bobby snapped. "We're going to kick your butts!"

326 || SKY OF STONE

"You pissant," Chinky hissed. "You want to try to kick my butt right here and now?" He raised his fists.

Bobby scuttled in, rolling up his sleeves, but Johnny put his fingers to his mouth and whistled. "There ain't going to be no fighting," he said. "It's against union rules."

Bobby and Chinky gave each other the evil eye, then backed off. Garrett laughed, then turned and waved his hand. "Come on, boys. I'm tired of smelling Coalwood. Let's get back to Caretta."

We watched them go, their flashing lights gradually growing dim until they disappeared around a curve. "Come on," Johnny said.

"Where are we going?" I demanded.

"Let's see how far away the lime mark really is."

We walked on. When we got to the mark, Johnny said, "I counted two hundred and ninety-eight rails from where we left off at miners' vacation to this mark. We're averaging eight a day." He looked at me.

I did a quick mental calculation. "About thirty-eight man-days to go," I said.

Johnny squatted, took off his helmet, and ran his hand through his hair. "How many rails did Garrett say they had to go?"

"Two hundred and twenty-two," I said. "They're averaging about the same we are. That means they'll be to the lime mark in about twenty-eight shifts. They're going to beat us by ten full days. My God, we're going to be embarrassed all over this mine."

"What if we laid ten rails a day?" Bobby asked. "Two hundred and ninety-eight rails divided by ten is equal to twenty-nine point eight. We'd have a fighting chance if we did that."

"Ten rails a day?" I shook my head. "Eight is almost killing us as it is."

"But I've got a plan," he said. "I came up with it while I

was fishing. All we have to do is approach this job from a different direction—backward."

I rolled my eyes. "Right. Sure."

"Let the man talk, Sonny," Johnny said.

"What keeps us from doing ten rails a day?" Bobby asked.

I was really in a prickly mood. "Time, energy, and you talking all the time?" I suggested.

"No," he said, ignoring my jape. "It's because all the rails have to be in place before the man-trips can go out at the end of the shift. I've noticed we start to pace ourselves toward the end of the day to make sure we don't have a rail out when the shift is over. But what if we pulled out the spikes on ten sections first thing in the morning, rolled off the rails, then started working backward to the first one? We'd have to do it. We'd have no choice. We'll also be moving toward our supplies, not away from them."

I laughed. "And what happens if we don't make it? Excuse me, Mr. Bossman. I guess we kind of let your man-trips wreck."

"Hold on, Sonny," Johnny said. "Maybe Bobby's on to something. If we work backward, and move toward where the hoot-owl shift stacks our supplies, the job will get easier as the day wears on, not harder."

"That's right," Bobby said. "The way we do it now, we start off fast because the new ties are right where we need them. We're also fresher. But we slow down toward the end of the shift because we have to haul the ties farther and farther when we're the tiredest. We also slow down because we're afraid to knock out another rail and not get it laid back in time."

"That's my whole point!" I cried. "We'll end up wrecking the man-trips!"

Bobby was unruffled by my outburst. "Pessimism is just your middle name, isn't it?"

"It's Hadley, actually."

"What did your parents have against you?"

"That I got born, far as I can tell."

"Now you're being melancholy."

"More cynical, I thought."

"No, melancholy is the adverb, I'm pretty certain."

"Actually, it's an adjective."

"Who cares? We're seven hundred feet down in a coal mine with a slab of sandstone that weighs a billion tons hanging an inch over our heads!"

Bobby had a point. Even I could see that.

"We'll try going backward tomorrow," Johnny said, interrupting our banter. "Eight rails, just to see if it works."

"It'll work," Bobby said. "All we have to do is get lucky. If something, anything at all, slows the Caretta boys down, we've got them."

I was astonished at my two crewmates. We were headed for disaster, that's all I knew. I had never been so certain of anything in the entire history of my life and I said so, just to make sure they knew it.

"Maybe so, but it's worth a try," Johnny said.

"Then it's agreed?" Bobby asked.

Johnny flashed his light in my eyes. "Sonny, are you with us or not?"

"Do I have a choice?"

"No!" they chorused.

The next day we laid eight rails going backward, then stood around with time on our hands at the end of the shift. We could have easily laid at least one more. "What did I tell you?" Bobby bragged.

"We need to send you fishing more often," Johnny said.

"How about the rest of the summer?" I suggested.

Bobby laughed. "Thank you, Sonny. I appreciate your willingness to admit when you're wrong."

I had indeed been wrong, and I knew it would make me a better man to confess it, but I still didn't. There was no use giving Bobby more of a swelled head. The way I saw it, I was doing him a favor.

When I got back to the Club House that evening, I was startled to see the chairs set up again in the parlor. Floretta's look told me all I needed to know.

It was time for the second testimony, and this time, I was certain, Dad was going to have to sit in the dock.

THE SECOND TESTIMONY

FLORETTA RUSHED me off to take my shower, order-ing me to return to help her finish preparing the parlor. When I got back, I found Tag in the kitchen with her. "Just got back from John Eye's," he said. "Hate to tell it, but he says most of the bets are for the Caretta boys."

"He doesn't know what I know," I said, smugness personified.

"Sonny ain't going to lose my Alexander Hamilton," Floretta said.

"I hope you're right," Tag said. "I've got five bucks down myself."

"The last of the big-time spenders," Floretta laughed. Then she said, "Get on with you, Sonny. Finish putting up the chairs. The C.O.W. ladies will be here soon, mooing for their iced tea and cookies. I got to get Miss Rita's sup-per to her, too."

"Rita's back?" I asked nonchalantly.

"Yes, she's back." She gave me a look. "Leave her be, Sonny."

I ignored her. "How about Doc Hale? Is he back?"

"I don't expect him till the weekend."

"Doc Lassiter?"

"I ain't seen him. Why, you sick?"

"Sonny thinks he's a detective, Floretta," Tag said.

"You mean like in a Mickey Spillane book?"

"I'm trying to find out who broke Nate Dooley's wrist," I said.

"I'm sure he broke it all by himself," Floretta said entirely too quickly.

Floretta knew more than she was saying. I could see it in her face. But who didn't know more in Coalwood than me? "Mickey Spillane would go nuts in this town," I said.

She contemplated me. "I do believe you growed some more over miners' vacation."

"I had to buy new work clothes again yesterday," I said, trying not to sound too proud about it.

"Your mama is not going to know you, uh-uh, not at all."

"She'll know me," I said confidently. "I'll be the one she's yelling at."

THE ARRANGEMENT in the Club House parlor was the same as it had been for the first testimony. Mr. Fuller glowered at his table up front. Jake sat off to the side in a straight-back chair. Mr. Amsteader, the federal inspector with the wooden leg, and Mr. Mutman, the state inspector with the fat belly, sat up front, surrounded by the C.O.W. ladies. Mrs. Mallett chattered in Mr. Amsteader's ear like she was sure he wanted to hear everything she had to say. She even put her hand on his leg once, although I don't think he noticed it since it was his wooden one.

By dusk, people were gathering, and it didn't take long before all the seats were filled and the extra people gathered on the porch. Somebody opened the parlor windows so they could hear.

I found myself a position at the arched portal between the foyer and the parlor where I could keep good watch on the proceedings. Beside me, Tag leaned in his most nonchalant manner against the wall. Then Mr. Bundini and Dad came inside. In his yellow sport coat, Mr. Bundini looked for all the world like he was going to a party. Dad was wearing his khaki work uniform. He carried his old canvas snap-brim hat. Mr. Bundini gave me a big grin. "There's that track layer," he said heartily, and moved on to press some hands.

Dad edged past me. "Good luck," I said.

He gave me the eye. "You and Jim dug a fine grave for Dandy. I went up and looked at it. He was a good old dog."

"Yes, sir. I hope you had a good time at the beach."

"I did. Your mother says hello."

Dad moved to an empty chair that had been reserved for him on the front row. He and Mr. Fuller traded nods, then he sat down. Mr. Bundini sat beside him but continued to converse with folks over his shoulder. Somebody must have told him a joke, because he burst out laughing. He even slapped his knee, which made me a little angry. My father was about to get crucified. I couldn't imagine how anybody could laugh at a time like that. For his part, Dad didn't seem much concerned, either. He took his daily log from his shirt pocket and started reading it.

Then I watched Mr. Fuller watching Dad. His expression was one of benign patience, like a cat that had already caught his mouse but hadn't killed it yet. He tapped on the table with the soup ladle Floretta had once more provided him. "Shall we begin?" he asked silkily. When nobody paid attention to him, he banged the ladle a little harder. "Shall we begin?"

The conversational noise slowly subsided. Mr. Bundini was the last one to stop jabbering. "Thank you, Martin," Mr. Fuller said with a smile that would make milk curdle.

"I'd like to slap that man silly," Floretta muttered. She was standing behind me.

Mr. Fuller's head jerked in her direction. "I'll have quiet here," he demanded.

Floretta grumbled under her breath, then fell silent. Mr. Fuller frowned at us as if we were criminals, then went back to his business. There were two books on his table, one a loose-leaf notebook with a green binder and the other the Bible. He touched the notebook. "I have a transcription of the last testimony," he said. "If anyone needs a review before we begin, I shall be happy to read any part requested."

Nobody said anything except Mr. Bundini. "Get on with it, Amos," he said.

"Thank you, Martin. I call Homer Hickam to the chair."

Dad stood, put his hat on his chair, and walked to the table. He put his hand on the Bible. Jake stood up. "Homer, do you swear to tell the truth, so help you God?"

Dad glanced at Jake. Jake blinked but held Dad's eyes.

"I do," my father said, and sat down.

Mr. Fuller leaned back, regarded Dad as if he had never seen him before, then stood up and walked around the table. He looked out over the audience. In my estimation, he was clearly puffed up. He asked a few quick questions of Dad, establishing who he was. Dad survived them. If there was one thing Dad knew, it was who he was.

"Now, Homer," Mr. Fuller said, "let me take you back to the night of May the third, 1961." He spoke carefully, with a pause between each word. It was clear he was winding himself up for something important.

"Amos," Dad interrupted, "you don't have to take me back anywhere. Just ask me what you're going to ask me."

"I think we should establish the scene," Mr. Fuller said.

Dad's good eye radiated confidence. "Let me do it for you. It was early in the morning, it was dark, it had just stopped storming, the fans had come on after being down all night, and Tuck Dillon and I were at the man-lift, getting ready to inspect his section for a buildup of methane."

Mr. Fuller rocked in his black leather shoes, which squeaked sharply in the hushed room. "Why just Tuck's section?" Mr. Fuller asked. "What about the rest of the mine?"

Dad leaned forward, clearly eager to answer the question. "Because I was afraid his section wouldn't be properly ventilated in time for the day shift."

"And why was that?"

Dad clasped his hands, interlacing his fingers. "When the storm hit and we lost power, I sent men to every fan to find out their status. When power was restored, I found out that only one fan, the one that provided most of the ventilation to Tuck's section, was still not operating. That was the number three fan up Snakeroot Hollow. I got an electrician—Fred Hardin—and we started troubleshooting. It turned out a company power line had been knocked down. It took us a while to find it and fix it."

"When did you call Tuck?"

"After power to the fan was restored. About three-thirty in the morning."

"What did you tell him?"

For the first time, Dad hesitated. He seemed to go over something in his mind, then said, "I told him to go inside and check his section for methane."

"But first you wanted him to meet you at the number one tipple, isn't that right?"

"Yes. That's right."

"Why didn't you just wait until the day shift and inspect Tuck's section then?"

"I needed to clear Tuck's section before I could get production going."

"So after this huge storm and all the fans were down for hours, you figured to start production on the shift immediately after it was over?"

"Yes. That's my job."

Mr. Fuller rocked in his shoes again and they squeaked

again. He looked down at them, rocked some more, and they squeaked some more. "When was Tuck supposed to meet you at the mine?"

"As soon as he could. I met him around four o'clock or so. We dressed out and prepared to go inside to do the inspection."

"But *you* didn't go," Mr. Fuller said.

"No."

"Why not?"

"Tuck Dillon was a competent foreman," Dad replied in a reasonable tone of voice. "He knew perfectly well how to inspect for methane. I trusted him to do it by himself."

"Then why did you get your lamp and your tag if you weren't going in with him?"

Dad sat back and cleared his throat. "I meant to go, but after I was sure Tuck had all the facts, I decided it wasn't necessary."

"And what facts might those be?"

"The probability of high concentrations of gas in his section."

"Is that dangerous?"

"You know it is, Amos."

"I do, indeed. Did you warn Tuck about the gas? Tell him to be cautious?"

"I—yes, we discussed all that."

"And what was he supposed to do if he found gas?"

"He was to let me know. If there were major buildups, I'd have to arrange for ventilating curtains or maybe even some stoppers before the regular shift went inside."

Mr. Fuller rocked and squeaked. I longed to take an oil can to his shoes. "So even though you were all prepared, had your work clothes on, your hard-toe boots, your belt, your lamp, your tag hung on the board—after all that, you decided not to go inside. Is that what you're telling me?"

"Yes."

"Why? Were you sleepy?"

There were a few titters from the C.O.W. ladies. They covered their mouths. Floretta grumbled something behind me.

"Sure, I was tired," Dad admitted, casting his gaze at the audience. "It had been a long night."

"So you were tired."

"I said I was. Yes."

Mr. Fuller frowned, as if in deep thought. "Let me make certain I understand you. Is it your testimony that because you were tired, you decided to let Tuck Dillon go inside alone to fireboss his section?"

Dad's cheeks reddened. I could tell Fuller's question had touched a nerve. "Tuck didn't need me," he said.

"Homer," Mr. Fuller said, "is Tuck Dillon dead?"

"You know he is."

"How did he die?"

"There was an explosion."

"Why was there an explosion?"

"A spark from his motor."

"From his electric locomotive?"

"Yes."

Mr. Fuller put his hands behind his back, then paced over by the window that looked out on the town green in front of the post office. He stared through it. "Tuck Dillon drove his electric locomotive into a section that you told him was probably filled with pockets of explosive methane?"

"Yes."

Mr. Fuller turned about. "And you still testify that he was *competent*?"

Dad's lips hardened into a straight line. "Tuck Dillon was one of the best foremen who ever worked in the Pocahontas coalfields."

"Yes," Mr. Fuller said, "and I'm sure he was also a fine father and a regular churchgoer. But that doesn't change what he did. He killed himself by doing something stupid."

"Tuck Dillon was not stupid," Dad said. His right hand clutched the armrest of the chair.

Mr. Fuller nodded, then walked back to the table. He put his hand on it, as if he needed it to keep him upright because he was in such deep thought. Then he straightened and walked until he was standing behind Dad. His hands went up as if he was going to put them on Dad's shoulders, but then he seemed to have second thoughts. He dropped them along his sides. "I believe you, Homer," he said in a soft voice. "In fact, I have inspected Tuck's employment record. It is very impressive. Highest marks on his foreman's exam, a member of the West Virginia Mine Rescue Association. He even contributed several articles on safety to its quarterly. Tuck Dillon was not stupid. He was well educated in mine safety. In fact, you trained him yourself, didn't you?"

"Yes," Dad said. His hand on the armrest twitched.

"What else did you teach him?"

"I don't know what you mean."

"Have you not given lectures to all your foremen from time to time about a variety of subjects?"

"I suppose."

Mr. Fuller opened up the notebook and withdrew two sheets of yellow legal paper. "I found these remarks in the company file. You gave them last year to the new Olga Coal Company foremen. Do you recall what you said?"

Dad shifted in the chair but remained silent.

"Tell you what," Mr. Fuller said. "Let's not tax your memory. Why don't you just read what you said?"

Dad frowned and looked at Mr. Bundini. Mr. Bundini nodded, and Dad took the yellow sheets from Mr. Fuller. He withdrew a pair of reading glasses from his shirt pocket, squinted at the paper, then closed one eye. He squirmed until finally he seemed to be in the posture he needed to read. "The qualities of a foreman," he read aloud.

"That's the name of your talk, correct?"

"Yes."

"The *qualities* of a foreman. Read on, please."

Dad eyed Mr. Fuller, then cleared his throat and read:

If you are going to be an Olga Coal Company foreman, you must make a decision. Are you for the company or are you for the union?

At this, Dad looked up. I followed his eyes as they landed on Mr. Dubonnet. Mr. Dubonnet's face was grim. Dad went back to reading:

I am not saying to be anti-union, but certainly you must be pro-company. John L. Lewis said to his union officers that if you eat my bread, you sing my tune. The same is true for the management side. You may not agree with management but as long as you are a foreman, you must side with the company.

Dad put the papers down on his lap and said, "The rest is just a list of attributes I think a foreman should have." Then he coughed the deep, phlegmy hack of a miner, a rasp, as familiar as it was, that made me cringe. He reached in his back pocket and drew out a blue bandanna and pushed his mouth into it.

"Keep reading, please," Mr. Fuller said softly.

Dad wiped his lips but held on to the bandanna. He read:

The attributes of an Olga foreman:

We are proud of who we are. We were chosen to be Olga men. We are morally straight. We don't lie, cheat, steal, or tolerate those who do. That not only goes for work, but everywhere.

We never stop learning.

We give orders and take orders like a man.

We don't make deals. We tell our men what to do and then stick to it.

We don't watch the clock. We get to work early and leave only when the job is finished.

We don't make decisions on what somebody else said. We go and see things for ourselves.

When things go wrong, we don't hunt for someone else to blame. We fix it.

We don't buddy with our crews.

We're not afraid to tell a man he's no good. A man can't get good if he doesn't know he's bad.

We're the boss. We never tell the men to do something because somebody else said so. We say so and we make sure they do it.

We know production is the key. Without it, all the good things we have in Coalwood and Caretta, our homes, our schools, and all that we hold dear, all will be lost.

Dad took off his glasses, tucked them in his shirt pocket, and put the papers on the table. He looked straight ahead, his face expressionless.

"'Production is the key,'" Mr. Fuller quoted. "'Without it . . . all that we hold dear, all will be lost.'" He paced a bit. "Odd. I never heard you mention the word *safety* a single time in your little lecture."

"Safety is inherent to a foreman's job," Dad said. "They all know that."

"But you never mentioned it. Interesting."

Dad kept his peace.

"Tuck Dillon made a mistake that even a common miner wouldn't make," Mr. Fuller pressed. "But you say you don't know why. Is that right?"

Dad didn't say anything, so Mr. Fuller paced some

more. "Here's what I think happened," he said after taking a slow lap around the table.

Perhaps in a court of law, a defense lawyer would have jumped up and cried, "Speculation, your honor!" or somesuch, but this wasn't a court of law, not by a long shot. Mr. Fuller got his say.

"Homer, I think at the last minute you decided not to go in with Tuck because you wanted to be around when the day shift arrived. And why was that? You said it yourself. *We're the boss.* You personally wanted to kick the tails of your foremen, get them inside as fast as you could so production wouldn't suffer any more than it already had. That's why Tuck Dillon died, isn't it? You wanted production!"

Dad stayed silent, his eyes held rigidly straight ahead.

The federal inspector, Mr. Amsteader, leaned forward. "I have a question for you, Homer." His reedy voice sounded strangely calm after Mr. Fuller's outburst. "If Tuck Dillon had all the information he needed, would he have entered a gas-filled section in an electric locomotive?"

Dad glanced at the federal man, then mulled the question over. "I can't imagine that he would."

"You were his supervisor, responsible for providing him with all the information he needed?"

"Yes."

Mr. Amsteader sat back and patted his wooden leg. A smile formed on Mr. Fuller's face. "I think we've heard all that we need to hear," he said.

"Are you done with me?" Dad asked bitterly.

Mr. Fuller waved his hand in airy dismissal. "We've heard enough. You may stand down."

Dad struggled to his feet. His face was red and he was having trouble getting his breath. I started to go and help him, but Tag held me back. "You'll shame him," Tag said, and I knew he was right. Dad walked unsteadily to the door, his bandanna still pressed to his face. The crowd in the foyer parted before him.

Jake and Mr. Fuller huddled at the table while a conversational buzz began to grow in the parlor. When I thought I'd waited long enough, I followed Dad but was surprised to find him on the Club House sidewalk in deep conversation with Mr. Dubonnet. As I came up to them, I heard Dad say, "Don't worry, John. I would sooner be fired."

"Thank you," Mr. Dubonnet said, and put his hand on Dad's shoulder.

Dad shrugged his hand away and walked toward the Buick, which was parked in front of the Big Store.

"Sonny," Mr. Dubonnet greeted me when I came up beside him.

We watched Dad climb in the Buick and pull out, heading up Main Street. "Why did you thank Dad?" I asked.

After a moment of obvious deliberation, he said, "Because he protected one of my men in there tonight."

"But Mr. Dillon wasn't a union man," I said.

"I didn't say he was," Mr. Dubonnet answered, then trudged away.

— — — — — —

3 7

THE HONOR OF KINGS

THE SECOND testimony finished and people poured out of the Club House while I wandered around in the dark, lost inside my own head. I figured I had most of the story now, including a working theory as to why Tuck Dillon had gone in the mine by himself. But why he had blown himself up—that remained a puzzle. God, in His sly way, was still concealing things from me and everybody else.

More walking and thinking didn't help. By the time I climbed the steps and went back inside the Club House, the place was empty and Floretta had closed herself up in her apartment. Breakfast found me entirely by myself in the dining room. Even the junior engineers didn't turn up. The second testimony had worn everyone out, I supposed. A note in the kitchen from Floretta told me she was sleeping in, and I could fix my own breakfast. She'd at least packed my lunch.

The day on the track found me sluggish, off center, and prone to error. I kept missing spikes with my hammer and dropping my pry bar, tripping over rails and slamming my head into the roof. Bobby and Johnny let me go my sloppy way without comment. At the end of the shift, we were one rail short of finishing.

"If we have to flag down the first man-trip, what happens, Johnny?" Bobby worried.

"We lose the bet, that's what happens," Johnny said grimly. "Garrett would hear about it, for sure, and say we'd cheated by working past our shift."

"Full-court press," Bobby said. He came over to me, squeezed my arm until it hurt. "Full-court press, Sonny!"

I pulled away from him. "What are you talking about?"

"Like in basketball. We've got to run, throw away caution, go as fast as we can!"

"Full-court press," Johnny said. "Yeah!"

It had been my fault we were behind. "Let's do it!" I yelled.

We pressed. Spikes flew, hammers pounded, shovels shoveled, ties were flung to the side. We ran like bandits, oblivious to the roof. I slammed into a roof bolt, was knocked on my back, and my glasses went flying. Even though all I could see was a blur, I got up and charged ahead anyway. I went by feel alone. We drove in the last spike just as the first man-trip rounded a curve and its glaring white spotlight was flung down the track at us. We backed off, watching it roar past. Its wind buffeted us. "Can somebody help me find my glasses?" I begged.

"I'll look," Bobby said. He wandered up the track, his light going from side to side. I peered into the shadowy gloom. I couldn't even read the yellow sign with black letters that marked the main line. My light reflecting off it just made it smudgier, and even squinting didn't help.

Bobby returned and handed me my glasses. "Here. Maybe you ought to tie a string to them or something."

After we got out, we walked down Coalwood Main in silence. I was mulling everything, a mix of Dad and Tuck, Mr. Dooley, even Rita. Bobby was polite enough to let me do it in peace. Inside the Club House, I found Floretta sitting in the parlor on one of the folding chairs. She'd cleaned up but left the chairs and everything else in place. The room seemed to still reverberate with Mr. Fuller's accusations and Dad's lonely words of futile defense.

"Floretta, last night Mr. Dubonnet thanked Dad for protecting somebody, a union member. I've been thinking and thinking about who that might be. Do you know?"

"Yes, Sonny," she said tiredly. "And so do you, if you'd give it two seconds of thought."

I gave it three. I opened my mouth to name who I thought it was but she shook her head. "Just keep it to yourself. It was never supposed to go this far, see? It was all supposed to be swept under the rug. That's what we do here, hide what we need to hide because it's *our* business, *our* way. But the steel company's got its business, too. Nobody's ever seen them come after a man like they're coming after your daddy. The only way he can save himself is by telling Coalwood business—what you've guessed now—and he ain't going to do that."

"But *why* are they after Dad? That's what I can't figure."

She raised her hands toward the ceiling. "I don't know about any of that. Mr. Fuller took off this morning, heading up to Ohio to report the dirty work's about done, I imagine."

"Jake didn't go?"

She shook her head. "Judging by the empty whiskey bottle outside his room this morning, I think he decided to get himself drunk."

"Oh, no," I said sadly.

"I guess all this got him pretty rattled." She looked up at the ceiling. "Poor boy. It's enough to make anybody fall off the wagon, I guess. Jake's between the old rock and the hard place. I didn't used to see that, but I do now. Steel company gave him a job—what was he to do but to do it as best he could? Fuller told me before he left that the last testimony is to be next Friday. Not a real testimony, just a report of findings. Pretty clear what it's going to say."

"That Dad was negligent."

"Yes, and Tuck Dillon was a fool."

"And then Dad will lose his job and Mr. Dillon will have his good name smeared."

"That's the long and the short of it, Sonny."

"What good will that do the steel company?"

She shook her head. "That's what nobody can figure."

I sat with Floretta, both of us thinking. There had to be something that could be done, not only for Dad, but Tuck, too. Tuck's whole life had been sullied by the way he'd died. I pushed my glasses back on my nose. They were still gritty with gob where I'd dropped them. I took my glasses off and looked at them. "It's the honor of kings . . . ," I murmured.

"What is?" Floretta asked.

"To find the truth." I stood up and walked to the stairs.

"Where are you going?" Floretta demanded.

"To talk to Jake."

"What can Jake do?"

"Maybe," I said, "deep down in his heart, Jake Mosby's but a king."

Floretta looked dubious. "He's a steel company man, Sonny. And now he's a drunk again. That's all he is."

Maybe so. Maybe not. I headed upstairs to find out.

38

THE THIRD TESTIMONY

A WEEK passed, Friday night came, and once more the town gathered at the Club House for what was to be the third and last testimony. In the previous testimonies, before things got going, the audience had gossiped and otherwise entertained one another. Now they sat quietly, even the C.O.W. ladies. It was as if they were gathering for an execution, which, in a way, I suppose they were. I took my place standing just inside the portal from the parlor. I'd already said a prayer. Mentally, I had my fingers crossed. Maybe, just maybe, something was about to happen that nobody expected.

Everybody knew where to plant themselves. Mr. Fuller took his place at the table. Jake came in late, pushing through the crowd. His hair was in disarray, and his work uniform looked like he'd been sleeping in it. He went to his chair in the corner. He glanced at me, gave me a nod and a wink. I nodded back. All I'd done was tell him what I knew, or at least suspected. He'd sobered up fast and headed out. Where he'd gone, what he'd done, I wasn't certain. All I knew was he'd been gone all week, doing what he needed to do. I had high hopes.

Mr. Amsteader and Mr. Mutman, the inspectors, came in and found their seats. Dad and Mr. Bundini came in last. Dad's expression was hard to judge. Grim but resigned, I thought.

Jake pulled up his chair and sat beside Mr. Fuller. Their heads moved together. Jake was doing all the talking, Mr. Fuller vigorously shaking his head. Jake got up and walked to the window and looked out on Coalwood Main. I studied his profile. He seemed composed. And he was definitely stone-cold sober.

Mr. Fuller banged the ladle on the table. "Let's have order," he said, which wasn't difficult since hardly anybody was talking.

"We are here to conclude this business," he said, "and make final recommendations. I've talked things over with the federal and state inspectors and I believe we are in agreement about the particulars."

"We don't know all the particulars," Jake interrupted, turning from the window. "Not yet. I'd like permission to call another witness."

Mr. Fuller banged the ladle down, although the room was as silent as a graveyard. "I told you the time for testimony is over, Jake," he said.

Dad spoke up. "He's right, Jake. You've got all you need."

"Just one more," he said, holding up his index finger. He ignored Dad and looked at Mr. Bundini.

Mr. Bundini nodded. "Go ahead, Jake," he said.

"I'd like to call Mrs. Nate Dooley."

Dad leaned forward, whispering furiously into Mr. Bundini's ear. Mr. Bundini raised his eyebrows, then shook his head and put a restraining hand on Dad's arm. I silently pleaded with Mr. Bundini to make my father be still.

Floretta was standing behind me. She poked me in the ribs with her finger. "This is your fault," she said.

Dad stood up, pulling away from Mr. Bundini's hand. "Jake, in a hearing on mine operations, you don't have the right to call somebody who doesn't work for the company."

Mr. Bundini tugged at Dad's sleeve. "Sit down, Homer," he said firmly.

"Martin, you don't know everything," he said.

"I know more than you think I do," Mr. Bundini snapped. "Now *sit down*. I'm your boss. Remember your own lecture: To give orders, you have to know how to take them."

Dad sat.

"Mrs. Nate Dooley," Jake said again, and Mrs. Dooley made her way in from the foyer. She wore a thin cotton dress with printed flowers on it and carried a lace handkerchief in her birdlike hands. She was wringing it like a dishcloth.

Floretta released a long sigh. "That poor woman." She poked me again.

"I had to do it," I hissed at her.

"God's going to get you for this, boy."

"I think He already has."

"Hand on the Bible, please," Jake said, pointing at the Good Book.

Mrs. Dooley was sworn in. She subsided in the chair and began to twist the hanky into knots.

Jake led Mrs. Dooley through the particulars of her identity. His voice was gentle but insistent, hers a mere whisper. Finally, he asked, "Mrs. Dooley, what does your husband do for Olga Coal Company?"

Her lips trembled. "He's responsible for cleaning the bathhouse at the number one tipple."

"How long has he had that job?"

"Since 1948."

"Who gave him that job?"

Her voice got stronger. "Captain Laird."

"Your husband has had that job for thirteen years.

How many times, during all those years, has he actually cleaned the bathhouse, would you say?"

Dad erupted. "Jake, *stop it.*"

Mr. Bundini clutched Dad's arm. Jake glanced at Dad, then continued. "How many times, Mrs. Dooley?"

"As often as he could, Mr. Mosby," she answered, a bitter edge creeping into her voice. Her back was straight as a ruler.

"What kept him from going every day?"

"My mister was hit by a tram in the mine, got his head bumped against a crib. It left him . . . different."

"So he can't actually do his job, can he?"

Mrs. Dooley lowered her eyes, and shook her head.

Mr. Fuller seemed to come out of a trance. His head jerked up. "A secret man? Is your husband a secret man?"

"Some call him that," she spat out. She looked into the silent audience, then down at her feet. "But mostly, he's a good man who gave everything to his company. The Captain said—"

"The Captain doesn't work here anymore!" Mr. Fuller growled.

"Amos," Jake said quietly, "this is my witness."

Mr. Fuller sat back after a sharp look from Mr. Bundini. Dad had dropped his chin into his cupped hands.

"Who would you say was your best friend in this town? Who helped you the most over the years?"

"Until he got killed, our next-door neighbor—Tuck Dillon," said Mrs. Dooley, without hesitation. "My mister—Nate—always liked Tuck. They were almost like brothers. Tuck never had a brother, so Nate was it for him."

"So Tuck helped Mr. Dooley—Nate—when he could?"

"Yes. He helped me give him his bath, and when Nate wandered, I'd call Tuck and he'd go after him."

"Wandered?"

Mrs. Dooley allowed herself a cautious smile. "Every so often, Nate would realize who he was. Doc Lassiter says it's like he's got a short circuit in his brain. Sometimes a spark will jump across it and he'll think he needs to go up to the tipple and go to work. Usually, the other miners would keep him safe. He wasn't able to hold his thoughts together for too long, you see. Tag would bring him home most times, and Tuck sometimes did, too."

"Mrs. Dooley, did Nate wander on the night of May the third of this year?"

I silently willed her to answer the question the way I was certain it had happened.

She nodded. "Yes. I thought he'd gone to bed. He does that sometimes when he gets scared. Thunder and lightning scares him, and there was enough of it that night. But when I checked on him, he was gone. Out the back door, I think. He's done that before, just run away because he got scared. I called Tag, but his mama said he was out patrolling. So then I called Tuck."

"About what time was that?"

"Eleven o'clock, thereabouts. Tuck said he'd go out and look for Nate. I told him to look up at the tipple first. Nate always felt safe there, for some reason. When I didn't hear from Tuck for a while, I got nervous and called Loren—Mrs. Dillon. She said Tuck wasn't back."

"What did you do then?"

"I waited. What else could I do? The rain was fierce." Mrs. Dooley raised her voice, as if she had to talk over the rain she was hearing in her mind. "Then Loren called—I don't know what time—said Mr. Hickam had called the house wanting Tuck to go in the mine with him. She said she told him Tuck was probably already up at the tipple looking for Nate. I thought I'd better get on up there and see what was going on. If Tuck needed to go inside the mine, somebody would need to bring Nate home. I called Tag and this time he was home."

I looked to my right, and there stood Tag at attention. He looked like he was made out of concrete. Not a muscle twitched.

"Tag came and got me," she said, "and off we went. We found Tuck standing by himself at the man-lift, ready to go inside. He said he'd found Nate at the tipple but then lightning had struck nearby and Nate had taken off. Tuck had to chase him up in the woods, then wrestle him back to the tipple. Tuck said he was sorry, but Nate had got hurt. Nothing too serious. Maybe a broken wrist or a bad sprain."

"You didn't see Mr. Hickam?"

I glanced at my father. His chin was still cupped in his hands, and his eyes were closed.

"No. Tuck said Mr. Hickam had taken Nate off to Doc Lassiter, that we'd just missed them. Mr. Hickam was supposed to call me as soon as he got to the doctor."

"Did Tuck say why *he* didn't take Nate to the doctor?"

"Yes, but he told me not to ever tell anybody the real reason."

I saw Dad rub his eyes, then lean his forehead against his hand.

"You have to tell us what Tuck said, Mrs. Dooley," Jake said gently.

Mrs. Dooley looked at Dad. Her lips quivered and her eyes went sad. "I'm sorry, Mr. Hickam."

"You have to tell us," Jake said again.

She nodded. "Tuck said Mr. Hickam was worn out, that he had gone into one of his coughing fits—you know, those spots on his lungs and all—so he convinced him that he could handle checking for the gas if Mr. Hickam would deal with Nate. I think Tag and I must have passed Mr. Hickam and Nate on the way. I remember a car going past us." She wiped her nose with her handkerchief. "Then Tuck rang the bell and got on the man-lift. It was the last time I ever saw him." Twin streams of tears ran down her cheeks.

"Then what happened?"

"Tag took me home and then later Doc Hale brought me Nate. Doc Hale told me there'd been some sort of accident at the mine and Doc Lassiter and Mr. Hickam had gone on up there. Doc Lassiter had called Doc Hale to finish working on Nate's wrist."

Mr. Fuller came alive again. "None of this means anything except a man has drawn pay from this company for thirteen years for doing nothing and Homer Hickam knew about it. That's a criminal offense, all by itself. It also doesn't explain how Tuck Dillon got killed, except due to negligence by his supervisor, and that is cause to relieve him"—he pointed at Dad—"Homer Hickam—from his duties."

"Amos," Jake said. "Do me a favor, would you? Take off your glasses, put them in your shirt pocket, and stand up."

"I don't see what good that—"

"Just indulge me."

To his credit, Mr. Fuller did as he was asked. Jake walked up to him and took the palm of his hand and thumped Mr. Fuller on the shirt pocket. Mr. Fuller was knocked back a step. "Hey!"

"Are your glasses broken, Amos?"

"They better not be!"

"But are they?"

"How can I be sure until I look?"

"Why don't you look, then?"

Mr. Fuller reached into his shirt pocket and brought out his glasses. One of the lenses had been knocked out, and they were badly bent at the nosepiece. "You'll buy me a new pair," he grouched.

"Gladly, Amos." Jake caught my eye and nodded a silent thank-you for the theory I'd given him. It was all because I'd lost my glasses that day in the mine, which had set me to thinking. "Tuck Dillon was nearsighted, although he hated to admit it. It was a gradual thing, his wife told me, and he tried to hide it most of the time. I think when Tuck got down to the landing and got in his motor, he found out that his glasses were broken, probably during his struggle with Mr. Dooley. That's why his glasses were found broken *inside* his shirt pocket, not on his face or off in the gob somewhere. Tuck couldn't see the signs to his section."

Jake turned to the audience, then leveled his gaze on the inspectors. I stared at them, too. What were they making of all this? I would have floated another prayer up to heaven, but I figured there was a backlog by now.

"What would you do in that case?" Jake asked the inspectors. "How would you figure out where you needed to go in a coal mine if you couldn't see?"

Floretta poked me. "I'm glad we got that boy on our side," she whispered proudly.

"We?"

"Hush!"

The inspectors looked thoughtful but had nothing to say. Jake continued. "I know what I'd do if I couldn't read the signs. I would count the turns. I think that's what Tuck did. But if Tuck counted them that night, there would have been a problem."

Jake went back to his chair, opened his notebook, and drew out a white form. "This is a completed Olga Coal Company engineering work order, signed off on the evening shift, May the second, 1961. This was the shift Homer ordered out of the mine when the storm hit. But before it left, this crew got its work finished. Their job was to put in a brick stopping and take out the turn leading into it. In other words, they sealed off a tunnel that led into an abandoned part of the mine. They also removed the sign for that turn."

Jake paused, waiting for all he'd said to soak in. Then he

continued. "If Tuck was counting signs to find where he needed to park his motor, he would have miscounted by one because of that stopper. Before the stopper was put in, there were nine signs on the way to his section. Ten West was the tenth one. I'm sure he had that memorized. He probably meant to turn into the ninth cut, the one he thought was just before his section. But because he miscounted, because one sign had been removed, he turned onto 10 West instead. He hit a gas pocket not fifty feet inside. That's how Tuck Dillon died. It was an accident, pure and simple, and that's all it was."

I felt a nudge at my shoulder. I thought it was Floretta, so I shrugged it off. There followed immediately another nudge, this one more insistent. "Sonny boy. You've grown."

I turned to stare at a woman as fresh and tan as if she'd just come off a sun-drenched beach. Her graying hair had a windblown look to it. Still, there was no mistaking who it was. "Yes, ma'am," I said to my mother. "I sure have."

"Pay attention," she said, nodding toward the proceedings.

I went back to watching. Mr. Fuller was still fingering his broken glasses. "Homer Hickam still deserves to be fired," he said. "He cheated this company out of thirteen years of false payments."

"No, he didn't," came a booming voice in the foyer, and then a huge, wide-shouldered man pushed through the assembly and walked to the table. He was dressed in an old-style wide-lapel navy-blue suit and wore a white shirt cinched at the neck by a black string tie. His wing-tip shoes were as big as boats, and he had a nose that looked like the hooked beak of an eagle. "Homer Hickam didn't do anything but what I told him to do," he said. He smiled at Dad. "He knows how to give orders because he learned how to take them. *From me.*"

Dad rose slowly from his chair. I had never seen him look so deferential in all my life. In fact, he looked positively worshipful. I kept looking at the big man until finally it registered in my brain exactly who he was. Although he was a good bit older than when I'd last seen him, I knew him perfectly well.

Everybody did. His mark was everywhere you looked.

A big grin spread across his vast face. "Let's talk turkey," he boomed.

Captain Laird had come back to Coalwood.

39

TALKING TURKEY

"CLEAR THE room," the Captain said. When most people hesitated, he put his head back and bellowed toward the ceiling—"*Now!*"

Such was the rush to obey him that a few chairs were knocked over by people scrambling out of the parlor. "Not you, Homer," the Captain said. "Sit yourself down."

My father sat and the Captain kept barking orders. "Mrs. Dooley, how do, ma'am, stay with us, won't you? Martin Bundini, stay. You two inspector gentlemen, I beg you to leave. This is company business. We'll be talking to you later. Elsie, come on in. You'll sit by Homer, of course. John Dubonnet? How do, John. You can stay—this involves the union, too. Tag, shut those windows and guard the door. Thankee. Floretta, how do, dear. You can stay."

The Captain's eyes landed on me and they sparkled. "Almost didn't recognize this young man. Sonny, I hear you've turned into a combination coal miner and rocket scientist. That's a mighty strange mix. Catherine figured you for a writer, as I recall."

Catherine Laird was my third-grade teacher, and the Captain's wife.

"Mrs. Laird used to mimeograph my stories and send them around the school, sir," I said, confirming that I was that boy, indeed.

"Hell, boy, she used to bring 'em home and make me read 'em, too!" He laughed his booming laugh. "I thought they were pretty good, but I always thought you wrote down more than you needed. A reader don't need a lot of descriptions, how somebody parts their hair, what color the flowers were on the other side of the creek, all that. Just give the reader a hint and he can figure out the rest. You know what I'm saying?"

"Just a hint. Yes, sir. I'll try to remember that."

"So what are you going to be? Rocket scientist, or author?"

Mom sat down beside Dad. "He's going to be both, Captain," she declared.

The Captain considered her answer and raised an eyebrow in my direction. "Well, that's fine. But remember, son, a cauliflower ain't nothing but a cabbage with a college education."

"Yes, sir. I don't think I'll have any trouble remembering that."

Tag opened the parlor doors, and I was astonished to see Rita come inside on the arm of an older gentleman. She was wearing a powder-blue suit, pillbox hat, and high-heeled shoes. I'd never seen her look so elegant—or so old. She even wore a strand of pearls around her neck. She might have passed for the First Lady herself, and I halfway expected John F. Kennedy to come in next, his head down, his hands behind his back, deep in thought about tax cuts or the Russians or the moon.

Rita led her gentleman over to me. He had a walrus mustache and twinkling blue eyes, and even though I didn't want to do it—since I figured he was her date—I liked him at first sight. "Father," she said, "I'd like you to meet Sonny Hickam. He's my friend."

I glanced at her, then looked at her father's out-stretched paw and took it. He nearly wrung my hand off. "I've heard a lot about you, young man."

I took back what remained of my hand and gave Mr. Walicki a smile and a nod, signifying nothing.

Her father moved on, shaking hands around the room. Rita held back with me. "How do you like the way I look?" she asked.

"You look beautiful. You always look beautiful."

She gave me a smile, but it didn't last. "Father always likes to see me in a dress. I can play the good daughter when I have to."

I was so happy to see her, and have her talking to me, I couldn't help but gush. "Rita, you would look good in a flour sack."

"I prefer my khakis. Listen, Sonny, I hope you know this isn't my idea."

"What are you talking about?"

"Your mother came up with it," she continued as if I hadn't opened my mouth.

"Came up with what?"

"She didn't tell you?"

"Rita, I haven't talked to my mom for a couple of weeks. I don't have a clue."

"You'll see," she said.

I started to demand an answer but before I could, Rita tottered along in her high heels to sit beside her father. When I looked, I saw Mom watching me from her chair beside Dad. Her face told a half-dozen stories at least, but one of them was *I'm in charge of this. Sit down, shut up, and listen.* I nodded to let her know I'd received her message and pulled up a chair near the door where I could watch everybody go through their paces, whatever they were about to be.

The Captain was still choreographing. "Amos? Sit yourself down over there. Yes, by yourself. You represent the steel company. What part of Ohio are you from, anyway?"

Mr. Fuller found himself a chair over by the fireplace. "I'm not from any part of it," he said. "I'm from California."

"Do tell. Northern or southern?"

"In the middle."

"Desert country?"

"Yep. Dry as the oil wells my daddy drilled there."

The Captain eyed Jake. "Mr. Mosby, I don't know you but I like the cut of your jib. You get up here and ask the questions. I'm too old to do all the talking. I'm going to sit down and hold Elsie's hand. She's the one who stirred me out of my cage, after all."

The Captain did as he'd threatened, sitting down in the chair beside Mom and taking her hand. "You are the prettiest girl to ever come out of Gary, West Virginia," he said to Mom. "Homer's a lucky man."

"You might want to remind him of that," she said.

Dad frowned, then resumed his respectful expression.

"Come on, Jake," the Captain said, raring back in his chair. "We don't have all night. Let's get this turkey talked and get on to more important things."

Jake was looking bewildered. "Well, Captain, what brings you here?" he asked.

"Coalwood business. Sometimes I just have to get in the middle of it."

"That's because you caused most of it, Captain, one way or another," Tag said from his guard post at the doors.

The Captain laughed. "You're right, Constable. Me and the Carters—Walter, the father, and James, the son—we thought up this town, put together its proposition, and made it the place it used to be and the place it is. But what's it going to be in the future? That's the question now. Elsie here"—he patted Mom's hand—"called to say it was time I got involved. Thankee, Elsie. You were right to do it. I've been moldering up in Elkins for too long."

"You were the only one who could get things settled and sorted, Captain," Mom said.

The Captain stroked Mom's hand. "And you were right, Elsie." He studied her. "But for more reasons than you know."

Dad grimaced, but held his peace.

"You don't have a part in this anymore, Captain," Mr. Fuller growled from his isolation chair. "You're retired."

The Captain smiled benignly. "Amos, you're a man who loves trouble and I respect that. A company needs a man like you who doesn't care how much pain he causes another man as long as he gets his job done. That's why they picked you to come down here and get rid of Homer. Bless me, I'm sorry, Jake. You're in charge here. Go ahead and ask Amos why you boys have been working so hard all summer to get Homer out of Coalwood."

Jake scratched his head. "Captain, Amos and I just came to make an investigation, not get Homer out of Coalwood."

"Maybe that's why you came, son," the Captain replied, "but Amos here knows better. He came with explicit instructions to make certain Homer Hickam was cut off as mine superintendent."

"I have nothing to say," Mr. Fuller responded, and leaned back and crossed his arms.

The Captain shrugged. "All right. Let's do it this way. Jake, ask me what happened when James Carter and I went up to visit Harry Truman back in 1947."

"All right, sir, consider it asked."

The Captain's eyes narrowed, and he let go of Mom's hand. He leaned forward. "It was after old Harry sent in the navy to force James—Jimmy was what I always called him—to unionize," the Captain said. "Jimmy said he needed to see Truman about it so off we went. The president himself opened the door to let us in the Oval Office. Then he served us tea. For a pinko sumbitch, he could be pretty near charming when he put his mind to it. We bantered about this and that for a while, and then Jimmy got down to cases. He said—'Mr. President, I guess you win. I'm going to give up, but before I do, I just wanted to tell you to your face that you're a rat bastard.'" The Captain looked around, and then broke into a devilish grin.

"I suppose that made the president pretty mad," Jake said.

The Captain slapped his knee. "Not a bit of it! President Truman thought it was the funniest thing he'd ever heard. 'Carter, you're right much of a rat bastard, too,' he said back. 'But I like you. You and me, we can do some business.'"

The Captain looked at Mom. "Elsie, you remember when Homer asked you to marry him and you said you'd do it if he had a plug of Brown Mule in his pocket?"

Mom nodded. "That's what you told me to say."

"I did, didn't I? Homer, you remember much about that week when you asked your bride here to marry you?"

Dad gave it some thought. "I remember you gave me a fresh plug of Brown Mule every time you saw me. I must've collected a dozen chaws. I had one in every pocket."

Captain Laird threw his head back and laughed. His eyes found mine. "My most successful campaign!" After he trailed off to a chuckle, he waved at Jake. "Keep going, son. You're doing good."

Jake walked around the table and sat on its edge. "So what kind of business did Mr. Carter and President Truman do?" he asked.

The Captain leaned forward. "Well, Jimmy said, 'Mr. President, my daddy built Coalwood from the ground up. Then my friend Captain Laird here and I came back from the war—the same war you fought in—and we made it into the nicest little town you ever seen. If I have to give Coalwood up just so you can show the country how much you love labor unions, I want a quid pro quo.' And President Truman said, 'If I can do it, I'll do it.' And Jimmy said, 'I want you to get hold of John L. Lewis and make him do something that'll be good for everybody across this great land, including you.' "

The Captain sat back, his huge hands grasping his bony knees.

"And what was that?" Jake asked.

The Captain squinted, as if it might help him see the memory better. "Jimmy said, 'Tell John L. Lewis he has to agree to let in full automation, not just in Coalwood but the whole of West Virginia. It's time to get away from the pick-and-shovel work. The union's all that's been holding our mining operations back from being the most productive in the world.' "

The Captain paused, maybe to let us all absorb what he'd just said. Then he started up again.

"Well, Mr. Truman chewed on Jimmy's quid pro quo a bit and then said, 'How can I ask for something like that? Coalwood—that's just a little, insignificant place. The UMWA would never go for it.' But Jimmy said, 'Oh, yes, it will, because John L. Lewis has always wanted Coalwood. It's his crown jewel. He's fought for thirty years to get it. He'll do what it takes to get it, even this.' "

Captain Laird looked over his shoulder at Mr. Dubonnet. "What do you think of that, John?"

Mr. Dubonnet allowed himself a hint of a smile. "I think Mr. Carter was correct."

Dad turned around, eyed Mr. Dubonnet. His face told me how astonished he was. I felt pretty astonished myself. I remembered all the arguments between Dad and Mr. Dubonnet over the years about automation. Mr. Dubonnet was always going on about how it would end up cutting men off, and how dangerous it was. But somehow, Dad had always won those debates and the contracts were signed, letting in the continuous mining machines, and even the long wall plows.

"As soon as we got back to Coalwood," the Captain continued, "somebody from the Truman administration had already left a message that it was a done deal. A week later, Jimmy sold out to you boys in Ohio." He nodded to Mr. Fuller and then to Rita's dad. "Then John L. Lewis rolled in here like he was Napoleon at Austerlitz, and within a few years, we all got automated. I never liked that pug-nosed bastard, but by God, if he gave you his word on something, he'd stick to it or die trying. That's why West Virginia mines are the most automated in the world today."

Jake got up from the table and walked over to the window. Maybe walking helped him think. In that case, I was ready to run a mile because I was thoroughly confused.

It turned out Jake was, too. "What does that have to do with why we're here today?"

"I think I know," Mr. Bundini said. "Steel's down all over the country, and our steel company owners need money. Selling us is a good way to get it. But they're having trouble with the sale."

"Very good, Marty. How about it, Amos? What's the problem with the sale?"

"We're working on it," Mr. Fuller said, grim as cold ashes.

The Captain's eyebrows went up. "Yes, indeed, you are. You have been since the day Tuck got killed. The Ohio boys saw their opening then, didn't they? Which brings us to why you came to Coalwood. Your buyer doesn't want everything you have to sell, and that, most of all, is Homer Hickam. Am I right? You need to get rid of him first, correct?"

Mr. Fuller tossed his hand, a resigned wave. "Those are your words, Captain. Not mine."

The Captain leaned over and looked at Dad. "Homer, the first day I laid eyes on you, I knew you'd take my place someday. Even though you didn't have a degree, you were the smartest man who ever worked underground."

Dad started to say something, but the Captain shook his head. "Let me go ahead and get this out. Martin here needs to hear it, too."

The Captain looked at Mr. Bundini. "Martin, when the steel mill boys came down here in 1947 to sign the sales paper with Jimmy, it turned out they not only wanted to buy the mine, they wanted to buy me, too. If I wasn't around to be mine superintendent, they said there'd be no sale. I guess I had a pretty good reputation as a mining engineer. But the truth was I was planning on quitting, going with Jimmy up to New York City and living a life of ease. But I thought about it and said I'd stay on here in Coalwood for at least five more years if they gave me the right to name my successor."

My mother caught my eye. Silently, she said, *Keep listening. We're all learning something tonight.*

The Captain asked for water and Floretta scurried off. "I figured that was the only way Homer would ever be able to take my place," he said. "Otherwise, I knew they'd hire an engineer with a college degree. Just to make sure they didn't renege, I also stipulated that when Homer took my place, he couldn't be terminated except for cause. The steel company agreed to my demands, and that's what we shook to. Sure enough, when I retired, Homer took over, and he's been here ever since. Funny thing is I didn't need to make my stipulation. Nobody was going to get rid of Homer Hickam. He was too valuable—until now. *Now* he's a problem."

"A handshake deal's not legal," Mr. Fuller grunted.

"You're right, Amos. It's *sacred*," the Captain retorted. Floretta came back with a tumbler of water. The Captain nodded his thanks and took a long sip. "Sweetest drinking water on the planet," he said.

Jake went back to the table. He shook his head. "I guess I'm dense. I still don't understand why a buyer wouldn't want Homer to stay. He's the best, most honest mine superintendent in the country."

"That's *precisely* why they want to be rid of him, Jake," the Captain replied. "These companies ready to snap up Olga Coal right now don't want the best mine superintendent in the country. And they sure don't want an honest one, either. They want their own man so he can run the mine into the ground. High profits and low overhead. That's the name of the game these days. These companies run around buying up other companies, then run full bore until everything wears out, and they sell the place for scrap. There's a pile of money to be made using that philosophy. Of course, nothing's left behind but jobless men and poor families."

"But Homer couldn't stop them from doing that," Jake pointed out.

"No, but he'd see what they were up to and raise holy hell with them about it. Knowing Homer, he might even go up and chew on Governor Underwood's ear about it. Or side with John Dubonnet over there, take up the union's cause as his own. These old boys in these buy-now-never-pay-later companies, they're in it for the buck, not for trouble. If somebody like Homer's on the job, they want no part of it."

Mr. Fuller was intently studying his hands. Jake was just as intently studying Mr. Fuller.

"So that's the whole shebang," the Captain announced. "Homer, Amos came down here to use poor Tuck Dillon as an excuse to see you fired—for cause, just the way my handshake agreement stipulated was the only way you could be let go. With you out of the way, Olga Coal could be sold, the steel company could get itself a pile of money without even making an ounce of steel, and the angels would play their trumpets in heaven. But that's not going to happen. That's why I'm here, and that's why Mr. Saul Walicki is here, too. Saul? I think it's your turn." The Captain harrumphed once, took another long sip of water, and settled back into his chair.

Mr. Walicki stood up, and all our eyes went to him. He twitched his mustache and said, "As most of you know, I own a seat on the steel company's board, which gives me a certain clout, although I confess I don't ordinarily get involved in day-to-day transactions. The Captain and I, however, have had a number of conversations during the past week, and, accordingly, I have decided to throw a monkey wrench into the proceedings."

"You're a good man for it, too, Saul," the Captain added.

"Thank you, Captain. I do, however, have one quid pro quo for my support." Then he smiled and I thought I knew why. "My daughter should be allowed to go inside the mine and do her job."

It was a naked abuse of Mr. Walicki's power, so, naturally, just about everybody in the room admired it, except Dad. "The men would walk out," he said.

"Oh, Homer," Mom said. "Nobody's going to walk anywhere because that girl goes inside your precious mine. I'll see to that."

"What can *you* do?" Dad demanded.

"*I* can talk to the women. If the men in this town want their meals cooked, their clothes washed, and a moment's peace, they won't say a word." She looked at Rita. "Honey, you go get your stuff right now. Homer's going to take you in his mine this very night and get it over with. Then you can keep going inside that filthy hole every day you want to, although I can't imagine why you would. Nobody in Coalwood will say a word, I swan."

The Captain stood and walked over to Mrs. Dooley. He took her hand and kissed it. "Ma'am? I do hate that you and

Nate have been run through the wringer on this. When I decided to keep Nate on, I set you up for trouble, I suppose. But a secret man's not unusual in this state. I'd like to see an Ohio company try to get after you about it in our state courts. It would be a rout. Isn't that right, Amos?"

"You've got all the cards today, Captain," he allowed. To my surprise, he didn't sound all that unhappy. I guess, in the end, he was just a man doing his job. He'd done his best and that, at least, was something West Virginians could appreciate.

Mom said, "Amos, if you'd like another excuse to fire Homer, I know plenty of other things he's done you won't like. Let's talk."

Mr. Fuller laughed and so did everybody else in the room except Mom.

The Captain looked benevolently at my parents. "I got one more thing to get straight," he said. "For this, I only need Elsie and Homer." He looked at me. "And I think you should also stay, Sonny. You need to hear this, too."

40

PARKYACARCASS

THE CAPTAIN stood beside the window that looked out on Coalwood Main, his brow furrowed against the darkness outside. "Elsie, ever since you came to my office and demanded I make Nate Dooley a secret man, I've been carrying around a heavy burden."

"You agreed with me right off," Mom said quickly. "It was the right thing to do."

"Was it?" the Captain asked quietly.

Mom glanced at me. "He saved my child."

"Yes, he did. And did you ever wonder," the Captain said, "why Nate was the one who took up for you, who made the navy doctor come to your house?"

Mom studied the Captain. "I guess he liked me. Or maybe Homer. Or maybe Sonny. I don't know. I didn't ask him. All I know is that he was a good man who did my family a good turn."

"Nate Dooley was a good man," the Captain allowed. "But that good turn he did you was owing to a guilty conscience."

Dad had his head bowed, shaking it slowly, but he held his silence. The Captain ran his hand through the shock of gray hair on his massive head. "I've watched you and Homer over the years, watched the resentment inside you grow and grow, until now you've upped and left him. He'd never tell you, but I know it's killing him inside. But resentment always has a starting place, and maybe tonight I can tell you where yours started. I'm praying it will make some difference. I think your resentment against Homer started with that damned fox! That's what kicked you off, made you so mad at Homer, after a while you didn't even know why. That damned fox."

"You're wrong, Captain," Mom said. "If I have any resentment against Homer, and I'm not saying I do, it's because he's always put this town and the mine before his family."

"Are you talking about Parkyacarcass, Captain?" I interrupted.

The Captain glanced at me, then locked his eyes on Mom. "Elsie, Homer didn't carry off your fox. And he sure didn't kill it. Nate Dooley and I did."

Dad sat back in his chair, touched his forehead, then brushed at his hair. He still didn't say anything. I looked from him to the Captain to Mom. She was standing very still. Then she went to a chair and sat down, and folded her hands in her lap. It was like she'd had the wind knocked out of her.

The Captain shrugged, a vast gesture for him. "Nate ran traps—coons mostly, and possums. He made a little money on the side selling the furs over in Welch, and the meat down in Mudhole and Snakeroot. But he'd heard rumors about a fox over on Sis's Mountain, so he set a special trap out for it. He did it for me."

Mom raised her eyes.

"I'd spread it around the mine as how I wanted a foxtail for my car antenna and would pay good money for it.

Foxtails were all the rage in the late forties, you may recall. Nate didn't know it was your fox. He hadn't heard that you had one. When he brought the tail to me, I recognized it by the silver on it, and called Homer. Homer got a shovel at the mine and headed up on Sis's Mountain to find your fox's body and bury it before you found out. Nate said the fox had chewed itself up something terrible, even eaten at its own guts. Homer never wanted you to find that out. He wanted you to think your fox was running free."

Mom put a hand on her cheek. Her frown softened. Her eyes turned into liquid blots.

"Nate felt terrible about it, vowed to make it up to you. When you asked for help, I think that's why he gave it."

Neither Mom or Dad moved. I didn't, either. I just kept thinking of Mom's story, how she loved to say at the end that at least she had hope Parky was running free, and how Dad had allowed her to have that hope over all those years while he and any dreams he might ever have had were locked forever into the Coalwood proposition.

> To me the emptys seem
> like dreams I sometimes dream . . .

"Well, I feel better," the Captain said, sighing. He looked toward the parlor doors. "Floretta, you out there?" he called softly.

Tag threw the doors open immediately. Floretta nearly stumbled inside the parlor. I guess she'd been leaning against the door pretty hard.

The Captain said, "Homer, I'd say you've got a job to do, like taking that pretty girl inside the mine. Me, I'm going to eat some pie!"

Floretta said, "Come on in the dining room, Captain, and set yourself down."

"Make me up a room, too, if you please, Floretta. I'd like to spend one more night breathing in Coalwood's sweet air."

"I'll get that fixed for you right away, sir." She looked at me. "Sonny, you come on. Right now, you hear?"

I did as I was told. Tag shut the doors behind us, but I turned and drew the curtain aside. Before Floretta slapped my hand away, I caught just a glimpse of my parents. Dad had gone down on one knee before my mom and was reaching up to touch her cheek.

41

JOHNNY'S LAST LESSON

CAPTAIN LAIRD had his blackberry pie and a last night's rest in Coalwood's mountain air and then, having patched up Coalwood business, at least to his satisfaction, left early the next morning. With his departure, it occurred to me that Coalwood was pretty much back the way it was before Tuck Dillon's accident, and the town's proposition, though eroded, was still in place. The biggest change, when I got down to it, was personal. My parents finally shared the truth about Mom's fox, and Elsie Hickam was back in town, if not to stay, at least not to leave—not yet, anyway. The beach house was still going to be there, her safety valve.

Over pie in the Club House dining room the night of the third testimony, Mom let me know that she was resuming her responsibility not only for her job as the mine superintendent's wife but for me as well. "I want you to move back to the house, Sonny," she said, tipping her fork in my direction. "And—"

"But I've got all my stuff here," I interrupted. "And Floretta's a great cook, too."

Her eyes narrowed, and then she shook her fork at me again. "*And* I want you to quit the mine."

"But I can't leave Bobby and Johnny in the lurch," I protested. "I mean, there's the bet for one thing, and for another—"

"You have an answer for everything, don't you?"

"No, ma'am," I said in the practiced deferential tone I used with her, especially when we were face-to-face. "But, you know, I've got to pay for my college tuition."

"In case you never noticed," Mom retorted, "your dad's not the one who signs your tuition checks. He probably doesn't even know where the checkbook is. I give him the cash money he needs to get around, not that he needs much. A haircut is about all he ever pays for out of his pocket. I gave him two hundred dollars when I went to the beach. I bet if I sneaked a look in his wallet, I'd find about a hundred and fifty of that left."

Upon reflection, I supposed that was why Dad needed me to give him the money to fix the Buick. But that no longer mattered. "I want to stay here, Mom," I told her. "I like my Club House room. And I have an obligation to finish my job at the mine." Then I thought to butter her up a bit. "I guess I'm like you. I start something, I have to finish it."

She wasn't much buttered. "I've started plenty of things I never finished. And you know why? Because I realized I was going the wrong direction." She shook her head. "Maybe it's a Hickam thing or maybe it's a man thing, I don't know. You're not much like your dad except in a couple of ways, and this is one of them. I swan he'll drive fifty miles the wrong way before he'll ask somebody for directions, and even then he won't follow them. One time I threatened to pee in his Buick if he didn't at least find me a gas station."

I rolled my eyes.

"Oh, look at you. Too grown-up to hear one of my stories!" She laughed. "If you were smaller, I'd get a switch, but you're nearly as big as your brother. I should have made you work more when you were a kid, I suppose, and maybe you'd have grown up quicker. I always left you to lay around with a book while I shoveled coal in the furnace to keep you warm. I rue the day."

"I'm sorry for my whole life," I said, deciding to go ahead and get it all covered.

"Well, you should be," she said, and for the first time since we'd begun our conversation, she looked pleased.

I took it as an opening to ask some questions. I knew, considering my mom's tendency to keep things to herself, that I'd never have a better opportunity to actually get some answers. "How'd you get involved in this?" I asked.

She sighed, pondered my innocent expression for a moment, then relented. "Your Jake Mosby, that's how. You got him all fired up, what with your theories on Nate Dooley and what happened that night. He called, wanting to know what I knew. I told him to ask Floretta or Tag or just about anybody along the fence in Coalwood. It all had to do with Nate, of course. Only somebody as dense as Jake Mosby or you wouldn't have seen that from the start."

"So you knew, even when you called to tell me to go home?"

She gave me a sour look. "I knew, at least most of it. I figured your dad was in for a hard time and that's why I sent you back here, to be with him while he went through it. I figured maybe this was what it would take for you two to finally get to know each other, having your dad in trouble and you around to worry with him. What I didn't figure was that you'd make such a hash of it, taking a job in the mine and all that. I could jerk a knot in John Dubonnet's tail about that even now." She looked me over. "But, gaw, I have to say it sure made you grow up. You're about as big as Jim!"

"What about Rita?" I asked. "She said you came up with the idea on how to get her in the mine."

"That girl just showed up on my doorstep," she answered. "Stayed with me three whole days. She knows everything, Sonny, how to drywall, best lumber to use for decking. I had her supervising those old Carolina boys one morning, she had them change out about half of what they were doing. Best engineer I ever saw."

"Rita came to visit you in Myrtle Beach? Why?"

Mom cocked her head. "Well, why do you think? She said talking to you gave her the idea that I was about the smartest woman who ever drew breath in Coalwood and that maybe I'd know what it would take to get her inside the mine. About then your Jake called and I gave up on my proposal and decided to just fix things back, at least for now."

I was lost. "Your proposal?"

She looked at me as if I were the most ignorant person on the planet. "To your dad. During miners' vacation, I proposed to your dad that if he'd quit and come live in Myrtle Beach, I'd agree to let him consult, spend a good part of his time up here in these godforsaken mountains telling other companies how to mine coal. I told him that way Nate's secret would stay a secret, he'd still get to worry about coal mining, and I'd get him at least part-time at the beach. I just about had him agreeing, but when Jake called, and I could see Nate's story was going to come out—*thank you so very much, young man*—I told him to go talk to the Captain. If there was anybody who could sort it all out, it was Captain Laird, who knows where all the skeletons in Coalwood are buried. I guess I was right, although I sure didn't know about that handshake agreement—or Parkyacarcass. That was a surprise."

"And Rita?"

"Thought I'd just go ahead and get that girl squared away while I was at it. I've known Saul Walicki for a coon's age, told the Captain if he wanted leverage over Ohio, Saul was the man who would do it, at least for the price I had in mind."

"Amazing," I said, shaking my head. "Do you write all these schemes down or do you just keep them in your head?"

"Be careful," she said, her eyes narrowing. "I'll get that switch."

I knew she just might, so I thought it best to change the subject, at least a little. "So how long are you going to stay in Coalwood?"

"The rest of the summer," she said. "My work crews have all gone off to build a hotel. When they finish, I'll go back to the beach and whip them hard until they get the place ready. Then I'll rent it out and come home and keep your dad company, at least until I can figure out some other way to get him to quit."

"Do you think he ever will?"

Mom poked at her pie. "Sonny, your father is my problem. You just worry about yourself. Now, as to this fool idea of yours of staying in the Club House, all right, I'll agree to it. If the food's so good, maybe I'll start taking my meals down here myself. Don't you think I don't know you prefer Floretta's cooking to mine!" She waved off my objection before I could get my mouth half opened. "And you can keep working in that filthy pit, at least until you get your track laid. But don't get killed. That's all I ask. Don't make me go to your funeral. A mother shouldn't have to go to a son's funeral."

"I'll do my best, Mom."

She shook her fork at me again. "You'd better, young man, or when I catch you in heaven, I'll tan your hide, don't think I won't."

"It's a comfort to know you're always going to keep me on the straight and narrow, Mom, even when I'm dead."

She eyed me for a long second, perhaps wondering if I was serious. Then, apparently satisfied that I was, she said, "It's the least a mother can do."

THE FOLLOWING Monday, on the man-trip ride in, Johnny and Bobby listened as I told them what had transpired the night of the third testimony. I figured to give them inside information that no one else could possibly know, including what my mom had told me, but it turned into a most frustrating exercise. Every time I told them something, they told me they'd already heard it. Apparently the fence-line had nearly burned up over the weekend with all the news. "Anyway, it's good to have it over," I said.

Bobby said, "Now maybe you can stay focused for more than ten minutes on your job."

"Just try to keep up with me," I said. I was in great spirits and felt filled to the brim with energy.

"We're still behind," Johnny said.

"Not for long," Bobby said. "We're going to catch up and we're going to win."

I marveled at his confidence, and then I admired it, too. "I think you're right," I said.

Johnny was a bit taken aback. "You two agree on something?"

We looked at each other. "Yeah!" we said.

Johnny shrugged. "Then let's lay some track."

THROUGH THE rest of July and on into the first weeks of August, we laid track. As the two teams battled ever closer, the chalkboard at the man-lift became the center of attention for the whole town. Even Reverend Richard turned up to give us a short Bible verse to consider:

> *In all toil there is profit, but mere talk leads only to want.*

"So let's stop talking and get these boys down in the mine to beat the socks off those Caretta boys!" he cried, clapping his Bible shut. It occurred to me that maybe the Reverend had laid some coin on our endeavors himself.

At the Big Store, the women admired my biceps while the men bought me soda pop and wanted to hear the latest, what new scheme we might have to lay our track faster. I was always happy to talk about it, but the truth was we were going about as fast as we could go. We and the Caretta boys were accelerating toward one another like locomotives on a downhill grade.

Only once did I slow down on a shift, and that was when I looked up and found Dad and Rita standing in the gob watching us work. I couldn't hear anything they were saying over the din of our pounding spikes and uprooting ties, but Rita was in Dad's ear about something. Now that she had been allowed to go down into the mine, I'd heard she had already accomplished some remarkable engineering, including the installation of a new kind of ventilation fan that used variable dampers, whatever they were. By the look on Dad's face as he listened to her, it occurred to me that Rita was the son he'd always wanted. I allowed myself a long sigh and got back to work. Rita had always been after a Hickam's heart. It just wasn't mine.

It was the third day of the third week in August when we saw the lights of the Caretta boys up ahead. "Two more days," Johnny said, "and we'll meet." He didn't say what Bobby and I were thinking. Would we meet in front or behind the lime-marked post? It was going to be close. We had twenty rails to go. They had sixteen.

It had become apparent during August that there was a very real chance that the two teams might reach the limed post at the same time. Fearing that we might start a fight over the last rail, the Main Line Track-Laying Bet Rules Committee (the MLTLBRC), an ad hoc organization formed by the bettors and John Eye, went to Mr. Bundini for an idea in the case of a tie. Mr. Bundini's solution was to paint red the two sections of track that overlapped the limed post. If one team reached those rails before the other one, a clean win would be declared. But if the two teams reached the two red-painted tracks at the same time, then a sudden-death play-off would be declared. Each team would then start at the same time with one red rail each to change out. Whoever drove the last spike in their rail would win the whole bet. This was such a satisfactory solution it started a whole new series of side bets, on whether there'd be a tie or not. Pretty soon, John Eye had collected so much town money that Tag was assigned to keep an eye on him, lest he leave with his fortune. I didn't think there was cause for concern. John Eye was a businessman and he was going to make money, no matter what happened.

As we put down track during the last days before we reached the red rails, I noticed that Johnny kept getting quieter and quieter. He'd cry out an occasional "Praise God!" at a well-driven spike, but otherwise he didn't always seem to have his heart in his work. Bobby and I, however, were finding more and more things to talk about, more or less constantly. Maybe it was our chatter that drove Johnny to silence. I had pretty well concluded, in fact, that Bobby Likens was about as smart a fellow as I'd ever been privileged to know, although I did have to point out once that I thought he was maybe a tad more arrogant and conceited than what was healthy for a young man. Bobby responded that he couldn't help it and that was that. I was astonished at the simple notion of accepting what couldn't be changed about yourself. It opened my mind to a wealth of possibilities.

One day, as we were carrying a tie on the run, I said, "You know, Bobby, you're like the brother I never had."

"But you have a brother," he pointed out, ducking under a protruding roof bolt.

"True enough," I replied, simultaneously jumping a rail and ducking a high-voltage tram cable, "but Jim never gave me the first advice about life and love."

"But you hardly ever listen to what I say, anyway," he said, throwing down his end of the tie the same time I did mine.

"That's true," I replied. I jumped down in the ditchline to roll a rail into position. "But I appreciate you trying, all the same."

Bobby laughed as he raced for the hammer. I went after the spikes. I dropped them along the rail as he started pounding. "I like you, Sonny Hickam," he said suddenly.

"I like you, too, Bobby Likens," I replied, and then we stopped talking for about an hour. In Coalwood, you were allowed to like a man who wasn't your relative, but it was best if you kept it to yourself.

The last day came. Eighteen tracks lay between the two teams. We weren't allowed to tear up our ten sets of rails and work backward as usual. According to the rules as formulated by the MLTLBRC, the last day was to be a straightforward tear to reach the final two rails. At the nods of our foremen, we started. "Full-court press!" Bobby yelled, and off we went on the run.

As the day wore on, more and more men showed up to watch, off-shift men who'd been allowed to come witness the final push. Every so often, I'd look up and see the helmet lights flashing from the Caretta team. They were running, too. Then, all of a sudden, we were just yards apart. I could even hear them breathing as they fell like crazed animals on their track. We threw down our last rail before the red ones and started hammering spikes. I kept looking over at the other team. "Don't look at them!" Bobby yelled. "It doesn't matter what they do!"

Bobby was right. We needed to keep our heads down and go at it. I didn't look up until Johnny drove in the last spike. Then we ran to the next rail, a red one. Then somebody yelled, *"Hold it!"* and we froze in place. I looked up. Garrett, Delmar, and Chinky were standing at their red rail, too. That meant we had either lost or . . .

Mr. Strong came up and shined his light in our eyes, one by one by one. He had a big chaw and spat over into the gob, then laughed mirthlessly. "It's a tie," he said. "Sudden-death play-off."

BOTH TEAMS were allowed ten minutes to gather themselves and plot out strategy. When Johnny didn't have much to say, Bobby took over. "All right, we play to our strengths. Johnny, you pull the spikes, roll the rails off, and shovel gob while Sonny and I hump the new ties and the new spikes into position. Then—Sonny, you rip out the old ties while Johnny and I put in the new ones and level them behind you. Then we'll all three push the rails up and start spiking. I'll spike one side, Johnny, you the other. Sonny, you be prepared with fresh spikes if either Johnny or I bend one. Got it?"

"Got it," I said.

Johnny didn't say anything. Our lights flashed into his face. "How about it, Johnny?" Bobby demanded.

Johnny nodded. "I understand." He was down in the mouth about something, but there was no time to ask what it was.

Mr. Strong came up. "Let's go, boys. Now or never. It's going to be Coalwood's day or Caretta's. It's all up to you."

I stood up, dusted myself off. "It's going to be Coalwood's day," I said. I'd never been so certain of anything in my life.

"Let's show them who the real track-laying men are," Bobby said, and led the way.

"START!" MR. STRONG cried, and Bobby and I went off on a run to our stack of ties and barrels of spikes. Behind us, we could hear the ratcheting sounds of Johnny jerking out the old spikes. I kept my head down, watching my boots. It was no time to hit the roof with my head or trip over the track we'd just put down. Bobby and I didn't have to talk. Our movements were practice perfect, like ballet dancers. We grabbed ties and ran back and forth, our pockets filled with spikes. We flung them down and kept going. I got a momentary glance at Johnny. He was a flurry of action. Spikes flew into the air. As we got back with the last tie, he rolled the second rail off. I pounced on the old ties, swinging my pick.

Sweat streamed into my eyes, but I ignored it. I was on my hands and knees throwing old pieces of rotted tie over my shoulder. Behind me, Bobby and Johnny grunted as they wedged in a new tie. Johnny leveled and we worked on.

Johnny was fussing with the level of the last tie when Bobby and I jumped down in the ditch and grabbed the first rail to push it up. "Level!" Johnny yelled, and Bobby and I heaved with all our might. With a heavy metallic thud, the rail landed on the fresh ties. We crabbed across it to get to the other rail. Johnny began to lever the first one into position with his pry bar.

"Push, Sonny!" Bobby yelled, and I pushed. The second rail was flung up into position. All we had to do was spike the rails in and we were done.

I glanced toward the Caretta boys. Both of their red rails were up on fresh ties, too, and Delmar and Garrett were going after their hammers. I raced to our hammers, tossed one each to Bobby and Johnny. Then I ran along the rails, laying the spikes where they were needed. Then I stopped. I had worked myself out of a job. Now it was all up to Bobby and Johnny to drive in the spikes.

I looked again at the Caretta team. A helmet light flashed back at me. It was Chinky. He was doing the same as me, ready to jump in if needed but on the sidelines now while Garrett and Delmar did the spiking.

My ears throbbed with the noise of hammers on steel. Men crowded in closer. They were yelling, urging their teams on. In the tight space of the main line, it was a rumble like thunder. A spike went flying. I saw its flash out of the corner of my eye. Bobby had missed one. I saw his lips move as he cursed, but he drew another spike from his pocket and started pounding again. Once, twice, three times, and the spike was driven home. He scrambled to the next one. I looked at Johnny. His mouth was open in a scream I couldn't hear as he pounded his spikes into the hard wood of the ties. Two powerful blows of his hammer and the spikes were in. It was an awesome thing to see.

Then we were done, or nearly so. One spike to go. Johnny had it. We were in a flood of lights from the other men. I looked and saw Garrett and Delmar were still working. We were two spikes ahead!

Bobby pounded my back, yelling something I couldn't hear. Johnny was down on his knees, placing the spike, raising his hammer. It fell, once—and struck a glancing blow. I couldn't believe it. All summer, Johnny had never missed a spike!

On the Caretta side, Delmar threw his hammer down. He was done. Garrett scrambled to put down his last spike.

Bobby was past me, grabbing Johnny by his shoulders. Johnny was shaking his head. I heard him yell, *"It's bent!"* and saw him pointing at the spike. I grabbed a spike puller and flipped the spike out and stuck another in the hole.

"Go, go, *go*!" Bobby screamed. Other men screamed their encouragement, their roar like a sonic waterfall.

Johnny struck another blow and sparks flew. *Missed again!* I flung myself at the rail, pulling the bent spike out with my bare hands and jamming the new spike in place. I rolled out of the way. Johnny swung again, this time a solid blow. Then he raised his hammer again.

"Hit it, Johnny!" Bobby cried.

I heard a roar go up from the Caretta side just as Johnny let his hammer drop. I'd never seen him hit a spike so hard. *"Done!"*

Bobby and I looked at each other, and then at Johnny. Johnny was still kneeling before the last spike on the last rail, just staring at it. Then he threw down his hammer.

BOBBY AND I sat leaning against a crib. Men's faces seemed to be swirling around me, their lips moving, but what they were saying, I couldn't tell. Johnny was by himself, sitting on the last rail, his head bowed. I crawled over to him. I couldn't help it. I had to know the answer. We hadn't been beaten. Johnny had let the other team win. Maybe nobody else understood that, but I did. "Why?" I asked him.

Johnny raised his head. He'd taken his helmet off. Sweat had made rivulets through the crust of gob on his face. There were also fresh tracks from the corners of his eyes where tears still leaked. "Because you cheated," he said.

I went numb. "When did you find out?" I asked, not that it mattered.

"Just now," he replied. "For certain."

I crawled up on the rail beside him, took off my helmet, and gave my head a good scratch. "When did you suspect?"

"Maybe a week ago. I ran across a Caretta man who works on the hoot-owl shift. He told me how the engineering work orders covering Garrett's team were so screwed up right after the bet. You and that enginette— Rita. You were really friends back then. I remember how much you talked about her to Bobby. I put two and two together. But I wasn't sure until now."

"I didn't ask her to do it, Johnny. I swear I didn't. When I found out about it, I made her stop."

"Cheating is cheating, don't matter when you start or when you stop."

"But you cheated, too! All those men who bet on us—"

"I didn't do anything but miss those spikes!" Johnny hissed. "I didn't know what to do so I prayed to God, begged Him to take charge. *He* made me miss!"

I held my head in my hands. Bobby clambered over the rails and squatted in front of us. "What?" he demanded, and Johnny dully told him the whole thing.

Bobby sat on the rail beside me. I felt his hand on my back. All I could say was "I'm sorry," and I did.

"Never forget how you feel right now, Sonny," Bobby said. "And it won't be for nothing."

I don't know how long Johnny, Bobby, and I sat on that rail together, just being quiet. After a while, we noticed we were alone and got up and walked back down the main line, toward Coalwood. Man-trips passed us by, but we waved them on. We didn't say much. We just walked, admiring our handiwork. When we reached the man-lift and stepped aboard, Bobby said, "Well, we laid some good track this summer. They can't take that away from us."

I nodded, not trusting myself to speak.

Johnny kept to himself all the way up the shaft. At the surface, the attendant swung open the gate and we stepped out. "Take it easy, Johnny," Bobby said.

"See you, Johnny," I said. There was no use apologizing anymore.

Johnny stopped. "Come here," he said. His expression was fierce.

Bobby and I gathered in front of him.

"There's only one thing I got to say to you two," he said. He looked at Bobby and then at me. "I have worked in the coal mines all my life." He spat in the gob. "But I have *never* been in the company of better men!"

He stuck out his hand and we grasped it, one on top of the other. *Johnny's team.*

42

COALWOOD FOREVER

WITH THE track finished on the main line, Bobby and I were sent to toil with a variety of crews. We worked split shifts, sometimes in the evening, a few times even on the hoot-owl shift. I learned how to rockdust, put in a roof bolt, and even took a turn operating a shuttle car. I apologized when I clipped a pillar, sending all the miners in the section more or less running for their lives. Jake came by when Bobby and I were building a crib. "How about taking a turn through the mine?" he asked. "I want to show you something."

Bobby said he could finish the crib by himself, so Jake and I took off on an electric tram. On the main line, the ride was as smooth as grease. "You boys did a good job," Jake said.

"We sure did."

"I've studied the job Rita did," he went on. "She's really a remarkable engineer. The new main line is going to up production considerably."

I didn't much want to talk about Rita, and I think Jake

sensed that. We rode on in silence until he turned at a sign that was marked 10 WEST, Tuck's old section. New posts had been put in, new headers and cribs, too. There was no sign that there had ever been an explosion. We walked to the face in the bent-over, head-up posture that now seemed completely normal. A continuous miner crew was tearing away at the coal, a foreman in his white helmet watching over them. The shuttle cars moved in and out, scraping up the coal. It was the choreography of the face. "What is it you wanted me to see?" I asked over the din.

Jake pointed. "I wanted you to see your father's mine. All that sound and fury in the investigation, and now it's back to work as usual, digging the coal, shipping it to Ohio and Pennsylvania to make the steel."

"Thanks to you," I said.

He shook his head, his light flashing across the work crew. "No, not really." His light fell on the foreman, who turned briefly and waved. "Sonny, I don't think the steel company would have sold Coalwood, anyway. Some of the big boys up there thought it would be best but, in the cold light of the new day, I think they would have reconsidered. Kennedy's tax cut is kicking in. A lot of cars are going to be bought next year and Detroit's going to need steel and a bunch of it. The steel mill that has a ready supply of inexpensive coal is the one that's going to get the contract— and nobody delivers coal any faster or cheaper than a mine supervised by Homer Hickam."

"So nothing mattered, not what you did or Mom did or anybody else?"

Jake shrugged. "I don't think so."

"Amazing."

"That's the Coalwood way."

We laughed together. It certainly was.

"What's next for you, Jake?" I asked. "Back to Ohio?" He surprised me with his response. "I'm staying here." I peered at him. "And do what?"

"I'm going to work for your dad."

I guess I should have been surprised, but I wasn't. "Mom said a long time ago that someday this would happen."

"Your mom is a very smart woman, Sonny. You should always listen to her."

"Do I have a choice?"

We laughed together again, then fell silent and watched the ancient ore being torn from the earth. Then I said, "I'd be proud to have you visit VPI, Jake. You could come see a football game, watch Jim play, and then I'll show you around the engineering school."

"I just might do that," Jake replied. "So you're going to stay in engineering school?"

"I'm going to help men go into space, Jake. Then maybe I'll write about it."

"Seems to me you've got some military service in your future, too," he said worriedly. "Kennedy's not only planning on going to the moon. He's trying to push the Communists around and they don't like it. You be careful out there, old son. Could be a war coming."

"I will, Jake," I said, although I didn't much believe I had a thing in the world to worry about. "You be careful, too."

He put his hand out for me to shake. I took it. "I'm staying sober, if that's what you mean," he said.

It wasn't, but it would do.

THE COALWOOD Labor Day party was held in the Club House dining room. Ginger Dantzler finally made her appearance. "What a summer you must have had," I said after asking her for a waltz. She was stunning. She had always been a pretty girl, but a year had done a little extra with her figure. She wasn't a girl anymore. She was a young woman.

"I heard you've been busy, too," she said. "Boy, you've grown!"

I grinned. "You're looking at a track-laying man!"

"Well, I hope a track-laying man can dance all night, 'cause I'm ready to kick up my heels a bit."

"I'm here to serve," I said.

She gave me a sweet smile. "I still think we would have made a cute couple."

"I do, too."

Ginger looked into my eyes with her big baby browns. "But we're never going to be anything but friends, are we?"

"I guess not."

She studied me. "I'm glad, Sonny. Friends are the best things in life."

I could not have possibly agreed more. I held her close and we dipped, then kept dancing nearly every dance.

When I took a break for a glass of punch, I saw that Dad and Mr. Dubonnet had pulled off into a corner. They were arguing, that much I could tell, but about what I didn't know, nor did I suppose it mattered. I surveyed the room. Doc Lassiter and his wife were chatting with the Bundinis. They were joined by Doc Hale, who had brought a pretty lady friend back with him from Florida. Other groups cloistered—union men, foremen, C.O.W. ladies, teachers, preachers, and deacons. Congenial as it was, I could sense undercurrents in the room, maneuverings, subtle tensions. It was Coalwood going about its business, always half hidden.

I spotted Rita. She was surrounded by engineers. She wore a low-cut midnight-blue gown, but, as beautiful as she was in it, I liked her better in her junior engineer khakis. By the way she was moving her hands, I could tell she was telling her fellow engineers how to mine coal even better. What a mystery she was, at least to me.

Mr. Dubonnet walked into the center of the room and held up his drink. "A toast," he said.

Everybody gathered around. This was Labor Day, after all, and therefore the union's party.

I expected to hear some grand oration from Mr. Dubonnet, maybe about how great the United Mine Workers was, or something about the genius of John L. Lewis, or the triumph of the labor movement across the world. But he surprised me. Mr. Dubonnet raised his glass and said, "To Coalwood."

Everybody raised their glasses. *"To Coalwood!"*

BOBBY AND I worked one more week past Labor Day and then came out of the mine and shook hands. "Quite a summer we've had," I said.

"I hope you'll remember all that I've taught you," he said in his most aggravating, conceited way.

I said, "Maybe you should tell me again."

He laughed, shook his head, and started walking away. I called after him. "Bobby?"

He turned. "What now?"

"Be a good doctor."

He grinned, then pushed his glasses back up on his nose. "If you ever get sick, look me up."

"If you ever want to fly into space, look *me* up."

We would not speak again for forty years.

My last day in the mine was also my last day in the Club House. I'd promised Mom I would spend the weekend with her before I stuck my thumb out to go back to college. Floretta met me in the foyer on my way out. "Law, I'll miss you, Sonny boy."

"I couldn't have made it through this summer without you."

"Well, don't forget your old Club House mama."

"You don't have to worry about that. Wherever I go, I'll think of you."

I folded her in my arms. She began shaking, and I could feel my shoulder getting damp where her face was pressed. I just kept holding her until she pushed me away. "Get on with you, now." She headed for the kitchen, the handkerchief pressed to her eyes. I looked after her, then walked out onto the porch into the waning evening sun. It was still summer, the trees on the mountain a dense green, but I could almost smell the coming of autumn. In a few weeks, V-shaped patterns of geese would be flying overhead and the mountains would be ablaze with color. The fall was Coalwood's most glorious time, and I couldn't help but regret that I wouldn't be there to see it.

That evening, I stayed in my old bedroom, absorbing its sight, its smell, and its touch. I could never be in there without thinking about the boy I had been, that boy so filled with hopes and dreams, that rocket boy. I sat at my desk, running my fingertips over the dried glue left from a hundred model airplanes built on its surface. I slid open a side drawer in the desk and looked at the rocket drawings still stacked there. I drew out the sheath of papers, turned them over one by one, studying them. My first attempts to draw a working rocket were crude, but they'd grown more sophisticated with each attempt until the final, well-drawn engineering designs. For those, I'd used professional engineering drawing instruments, gifts from my dad on my last Christmas as a Coalwood boy.

I looked at my bed where once Daisy Mae, my sweet little calico cat, had watched me do my high school homework. I got up and looked out the window to her resting place beneath the little crab-apple tree, its leafy branches waving gently in the slight breeze. As I searched the darkness, my eyes raised toward Substation Mountain, where Lucifer probably slept for eternity. He had been a tough old cat, but somehow wise. And Dandy was up on Water Tank Mountain now. I thought of him as he had been as a pup, a blond ball of fluff with a furiously waving tail stub, his snout turned up into a licking grin. Now he was gone.

They were all gone except Chipper, who was quickly getting old, as squirrels do, and Poteet.

Then I thought of Mom's painting. She'd worked on it again. Beside her fox were her other angels: Dandy, Daisy Mae, Lucifer, Poteet, and Chipper. Maybe she'd let Dad, Jim, and me join her in time.

Nothing was the same, yet it was all the same. My room, the house, our pets, each other, and all the town had changed, yet we all still existed as we had once been somewhere, if only in our thoughts and dreams.

As I went to bed, I saw a wink of heat lightning off in the distance. Then another, without thunder. I couldn't help but think of something I'd read by Mark Twain: *Thunder is good, thunder is impressive; but it is lightning that does the work.*

I'm not certain even now how I knew that something was wrong. I rose in the night and went to the window that faced toward the tipple and saw the flickering of flames lighting the darkness. Water Tank Mountain was on fire.

I pulled on my clothes and went outside, and found Mom and Dad already in the front yard. The smell of woodsmoke burned my nostrils. People were coming from everywhere. There was an ugly orange scar on the mountain, and it was racing straight toward Tipple Row. "Go get some shovels, Sonny," Dad said, his voice even but commanding.

I rushed to the basement, picked up two shovels, and ran back, handing Dad one of them. Mom grabbed the other shovel from my hands. "Get one for yourself, too," she said.

I started to argue, saw the futility of it, and dashed back to the basement. By the time I'd returned, my parents were gone. I looked up and saw clusters of people climbing the mountain. I ran to join them.

Mine foremen were taking charge, each one directing groups of people fighting the fire. Mr. Strong spotted me. "Come on, Sonny," he called, and I followed him. We spread out and started digging firebreaks in the brush. If fire reached Tipple Row and the Captain's house burst into flames, it would ignite the Sharitzes' house, and so on down Main Street. The whole town was in danger.

All night we dug, and when a tongue of fire leapt one of our breaks, we beat it down with our shovels. When a thicket burst into flames, I caught sight of the faces of the other men. All were black, just as they were in the mine. Everybody was the same color in the battle against the fire, just Coalwood men—and women, too.

Jugs of water arrived. Mrs. Sharitz handed me a jug, and I gratefully took it and nearly drained the whole thing. "Leave some for me!" someone said in a voice charged with adrenaline.

It was Rita, reaching for the jug with a gloved hand. I handed it over, and she threw it up to her lips and finished it off. She wiped her mouth with the back of her arm. I took the empty jug from her and nodded my thanks to Mrs. Sharitz. "You be careful, you hear?" she warned, and headed back down the mountain.

Rita had her hair tucked up inside a ball cap, and her face was black with soot. There was an eager gleam in her eye. "We're going to kick this fire's butt!" she crowed. She gave me a look. It was almost as if she didn't recognize me until that moment. "Aren't we?"

"You bet we are," I said.

She looked around as a shout went up. The fire had found a small pine tree and grabbed it. People charged up after it. "I love this," she said suddenly. "I love the battle."

"I know." My voice was glum. I couldn't help it.

Her eyes flashed. "Stop it, Sonny."

"Stop what?"

"Feeling sorry for yourself. I know you had a crush on me. I liked you, too. But our lives are on entirely different trajectories."

Trajectories. It was a good engineering term. I'd used it often enough for my rockets. Some of them flew straight, others wobbled off at an angle, but they still got where they were going.

"I told you I'd get inside the mine," she said.

"Dad's already saying you're the best engineer he's ever had."

She laughed, and I saw her perfect teeth like pearls against her blackened face. "He's right." Then she threw herself in my arms and kissed me. Though she smelled of smoke, her lips were like velvet. "There!" she said, as if that cured everything for all time.

And then she was gone into the acrid clouds cascading across the mountain. I heard more yelling and charged off in that direction, my shovel at high port, ready for action.

Slowly, slowly, as the night went on, we began to win. Whooping victoriously, we closed in on the last line of fire until it came apart and separated into frustrated whorls of hot flame. We beat at them with the flats of our shovels until they flickered out, and then we came down the mountain in triumph.

I watched as Coalwood people surged together, their faces lined with soot and sweat, their raw-throated voices raised with spirited tales, some of them even true, of what they'd just done. Then food arrived, lots of it. From the trunks of cars came fried chicken and smoked wild turkey and corrugated aluminum kegs filled sloshing to the brim with gallons of iced tea. An impromptu banquet began at the gas station. Ravenous as only the victorious can be, we ate and drank until again there was lightning in the sky, not heat lightning this time, but a broken streak that cracked across the valley from one end to the other and brought with it a sudden rush of cool air that cascaded down the mountains and into our faces. *Rain!* It started in a patter, and behind it came big drops. The sky, tight against us for months, relaxed and gave us all it had. Some people got under the narrow roof ledge of the gas station, but most of them, including me, stood in the sink of cooling air and just let the rain pelt down on us, our faces raised to the miracle it had come to be.

I knew then, as I faced the sky, that Coalwood would go on. Its buildings might be torn down, its mine closed, its people might even die, but Coalwood would persevere. There was something about this place that maybe, as the Reverend Richard maintained, God just *liked*. Coalwood had nothing to fear and I guessed I didn't, either. When I needed it, the old place of my boyhood would yet be there waiting for me with all its wisdom and purpose, if not in stone and wood and iron, then still in my memory and my heart. I closed my eyes and felt the rain against my face, and smelled the smoke of the defeated fire, and thought of Coalwood. Coalwood, as it was, and shall be. Coalwood my home. Coalwood forever.

EPILOGUE

I RETURNED to VPI in the fall of 1961 and discovered I needed all new uniforms. I had not only gained twenty pounds of muscle but had grown nearly two inches in height. My mother's plan to get me closer to my father had instead resulted in a profound change in my body. For the first time in my life, I was physically powerful. Without breathing very hard, I could easily do a hundred push-ups and run for miles. My fellow cadets scarcely recognized me. I became quite the bruiser on the intramural football team.

My studies at VPI's engineering school continued. I persevered in all my classes, sometimes against my mental grain, and wrote for the college newspaper. During my tenure in the cadet corps, I joined a group of classmates who soon came to be known as the "cannon boys." With virtually no support from the school administration, we constructed a Civil War–style brass cannon to be used at parades and football games. We had many adventures, including an incident where I was nearly kicked out of school for flagrant disregard of cadet regulations. When we fired our cannon for the first time in public at the 1963 Thanksgiving game against the Virginia Military Institute, its shock wave bowled over football players, rocked back startled fans in the opposing bleachers, and blew out the windows in the press box. The state police came running, and, as I'd practiced to perfection in my days as a rocket boy, I had to confess that I perhaps didn't know exactly what I was doing. Our cannon was named "Skipper," after President John F. Kennedy, who had been a PT boat skipper during World War II. My father, perhaps recalling one of his favorite maxims—"'Tis better to give than have it stolen"—provided much of the brass for the Skipper from coal mine scrap.

Every summer for the remainder of my college career, I returned to Coalwood to work in the mine. I became sort of an honorary junior engineer. My father put me through his boot camp, and Jake Mosby taught me much about mining, too. A young engineer by the name of Tom Musick especially took me under his wing. I learned more practical engineering under their tutelage than a thousand classrooms could ever hope to provide. I graduated from VPI (now known as Virginia Tech) with a degree in industrial engineering.

Jake had been correct in his assessment of my immediate future. There was no glory in store for me on the moon-landing program. Instead, with the war in Vietnam heating up, I entered the United States Army in 1965, and, after Combat Engineer Officer Candidate School, was commissioned as an officer in the Ordnance Corps. In October 1967, I joined the 4th Infantry Division in the Vietnamese central highlands, my assignment to take a team of mechanics and technicians into the bush, link up with armored units, and keep their tanks and armored personnel carriers operating in the harsh jungle conditions. My people, traversing the hills and hollows, got shot at by all sides. I was present for the Battle of Dak To, where I saw a line of

American infantrymen bravely claw up a mountain against the murderous onslaught of an entrenched main-force North Vietnamese Army regiment. After victory, I watched those same grunts march back down again. Within days, the North Vietnamese moved back into their positions on the mountain. A few months later, I was at the Oasis, a tiny, exposed firebase near the Cambodian border, when the Tet Offensive was launched. I fought the first day's battle with my boots on the wrong feet, don't ask me why, and was rescued by F-100 Super Sabre jet bombers flown in, via Thailand, from Myrtle Beach Air Force Base. I figured my mom had sent them. A few days later, I found myself inside the ravaged city of Pleiku, looking for some of my men who'd been trapped by the invading Vietcong and North Vietnamese forces. Just as American units began to batter their way back inside the city, I found my people asleep in the Pleiku jail. We sneaked out, and away. During the months that followed, my team and I rejoined an army being torn apart, not by the enemy, but by itself. Very tired, I returned to the United States in October 1968, where many Americans, mostly my own age, went out of their way to insult me. Before I learned not to wear my uniform in public, I was threatened and spat upon. I have forgiven them, but it wasn't easy.

My parents seemed much as they'd always been when I visited Coalwood after I returned from Vietnam. My father continued his work, as did my mother. While I was gone, she had purchased another house in Myrtle Beach and was beginning to divide her time between it and the Captain's house. My parents seemed to be satisfied with the arrangement. I went to work for the Thiokol company in Utah. Thiokol made solid-propellant rocket motors, and I worked on the Minuteman and the Poseidon programs. I wrote a novel about my experiences in the war and then discarded it. Perhaps I will someday resurrect it, but in 1969, it was too raw and too close. Still searching for what

I should do with the rest of my life, I rejoined the army and was sent to Puerto Rico. There, at the Roosevelt Roads navy base, two drunken ensigns showed me how to scuba dive. Although nearly everything they told me was wrong, and I came near to drowning, I survived their instruction, and my life began to take on new meaning. A long romance with the sea began.

I resigned my army commission and hired on as a civilian with the Army Missile Command in Huntsville, Alabama. Also in Huntsville was NASA's Marshall Space Flight Center (MSFC), the place built by Dr. Wernher von Braun and his team of rocket scientists. I had been wrong all those years when I'd been a rocket boy, thinking Dr. von Braun was at Cape Canaveral. In fact, he and his team were in Huntsville, Rocket City, U.S.A. I tried to hire on at MSFC, without success. NASA was letting engineers go at the time, not taking on new ones. In an attempt to revitalize the space program, Dr. von Braun left Huntsville to take a new assignment in Washington, D.C. He died soon of stomach cancer. Sadly, I never got to meet him. I am told his presence in a room was like electricity. I can only imagine what it must have been like when President Kennedy and Dr. von Braun were together. I suspect there would have been enough energy to light up the night sky.

Bobby Likens, my track-laying buddy, became a doctor, according to his plan. He graduated from West Virginia University's medical school and then became an air force flight surgeon. He also served in Vietnam. From there, he moved to Florida to be near his parents. In a small town near Orlando, he set up private practice and devoted much of his free time to assisting local youth programs. He has two children, and is now a grandfather. He continues to be an avid fisherman. When I started to write this book, I tracked him down and we shared memories of our summer with Johnny Basso. It was good to talk to him. He claimed I hadn't changed, and I claimed he hadn't, either. If placed inside the mine with all our tools, I believe we could still pick them up without a thought and lay track. Unfortunately, we would have to do it without Johnny. One of the best miners who ever thumped a roof, Johnny Basso died in Coalwood in 1994, a victim of black lung disease, the same affliction that killed my father in 1989.

In 1973, I became a scuba instructor, trained by Cliff McClure, who had been one of the Man High Project proto-astronauts, a group of true daredevils who flew to the edge of space in balloons. Cliff owned a dive shop in Huntsville called Aquaspace, and I began to work for him on a part-time basis as an instructor. About the same time, I also began to write again and was soon selling my work, mostly to scuba-oriented magazines. In 1975, I was called by an excited team of North Carolina divers who'd chanced upon the wreck of a U-boat off Cape Hatteras. They asked me if I'd be willing to dive on it and perhaps write about it. An extraordinary series of adventures began for me and other Huntsville and North Carolina divers, as we dived and researched the great wrecks of the Graveyard of the Atlantic. I wrote articles on our discoveries for many magazines, including *American History Illustrated*. I decided to take a job in Germany so that I could do more research on the U-boats. After three years of living in the wonderful little Bavarian town of Grafenwöhr, my old dream of working for NASA was refreshed when the first space shuttle, glorious *Columbia*, was successfully launched. Since I was thirty-eight years old, I doubted that NASA would be interested in hiring me, but, remembering my debt to Miss Riley and her belief that we must always keep persevering for our dreams, I gave it another try. To my utter amazement, I was offered a job at MSFC as an engineer on the Spacelab Program, a project that was building a canister-laboratory to fit in the space shuttle's cargo bay. I returned to Huntsville and got busy learning how to design spacecraft. I also began to dive and instruct in MSFC's Neutral Buoyancy Simulator (NBS), a huge forty-foot-deep water tank where the astronauts were trained to work in space suits in weightless conditions. I must have been considered at least adequate in my work. Soon, I was also wearing the space suits in the NBS and helping to develop the procedures necessary to deploy the Hubble Space Telescope, NASA's giant eye on the universe.

I also learned to fly. In the summer of 1985, I was piloting a Cessna-150 around Huntsville when I spotted a black wall of clouds advancing from the west. Since I had a plan to do some waterskiing on the Tennessee River, I raced ahead of the clouds, landed, and drove to the river, hoping the weather would clear. Instead, as soon as I got there, the storm struck, a massive onslaught of wind and rain. A cry went up that a big paddleboat hired for a company family party had overturned. I caught a ride on a boat and went out to the scene. Over the next hour, while wearing borrowed scuba gear, I searched through the submerged upside-down wreck. I found twelve people and brought them out. All were drowned. I had missed saving their lives by only minutes. I still think about them and wonder why I was allowed to come so close to saving them, but didn't. All that I can conclude is God has His ways, and they're not ours.

In January 1986, the crew of the space shuttle *Challenger* died in an explosion over the Atlantic Ocean. I had met all of the *Challenger* astronauts but counted Ellison Onizuka as a friend. I was in Japan at the time, negotiating with the Japanese on cooperating with them in future space activities. My work was put on hold, and I was sent back to Huntsville. I assisted briefly on the shuttle's solid-rocket motor redesign, then requested permission to help the United States Space Camp and Academy in their plan to build a smaller version of the Neutral Buoyancy Simulator. NASA gave me permission to form a small company, which I called Deep Space. Deep Space designed the Underwater Astronaut Trainer and pioneered some unique underwater space simulations. One of them, involving a French-made bubble helmet, led me to New York City to teach David Letterman, the talk-show host, how to scuba dive. In 1989, NASA assigned me the position of training manager of Spacelab-J, the first joint Japanese-American human spaceflight program. After being thoroughly redesigned, the space shuttle started flying again. NASA was back in business.

Even while I worked for NASA and managed Deep Space, my freelance writing continued. In 1989, my first book, *Torpedo Junction,* a military history of the battle against the U-boats along the American East Coast during World War II, was published by the Naval Institute Press. It became a national bestseller and I proudly placed it in the hands of my father, who had been forced to retire from the mine and move permanently with my mom to Myrtle Beach. He read my book carefully, and critically, and pronounced it "well researched." Since my father was an avid and meticulous reader all his life, I took his comment as high praise. He died that fall, just before I began training the first Japanese astronauts. I had little time to mourn my father, which was the way he would have wanted it. I spent much of the next several years in Japan, where I met many wonderful people and fell in love with the country. In 1992, Spacelab-J flew and I was privileged to talk the astronauts through their science duties. One of the American astronauts I trained and talked to in orbit was Dr. Mae Jemison, the first American woman of color in space. I could only imagine how proud Reverend Richard and Floretta and Big Jeb would have been. Sadly, they did not live long enough to see it happen.

Although I'm certain he would have enjoyed hearing about my professional successes, I don't believe the Reverend Richard would have been particularly proud of my personal life. I married and was divorced. The fault was mine. I think, however, the Reverend would have liked what happened next. I met Linda Terry, the daughter of an old Huntsville family. She was a diver, too, just returned to her hometown from a stint as a divemaster in the Caribbean. We soon began one of the longest engagements in the history of mankind. We were married thirteen years after we met. I wonder to this day why I waited so long. Linda is my helpmate, my assistant, my first editor, and the mother to our cats, all of whom we love dearly. When I suffered a serious bout of decompression sickness on the island of Guanaja in the Republic of Honduras, she personally went out on a limb for fifteen thousand more dollars than she had to get me home. NASA put me into their decompression chamber and I emerged, somewhat physically damaged but determined to return to diving. I did, in short order. I also realized I loved Linda and that we were meant to be together. Sometimes God has to reach out and give us a good shake, just to get our attention.

When the Hubble Space Telescope was launched with blurred optics, I joined the team that worked in the NBS to train the astronauts going up to repair it. It was pure hands-on, practical engineering work. Johnny Basso, Jake Mosby, Tom Musick, and my father would have admired it. We worked so hard and so long that often divers would fall asleep underwater. Once, I nodded off and fell from my perch on a mock-up of the Hubble, waking only when I hit the bottom of the tank. NASA's finest post-*Apollo* moment came when Story Musgrave and his crew fixed the space telescope and opened its eye to time and the universe. The Hubble has changed the very way we understand who we, as citizens of Planet Earth, are, and of what we're made, and where we are going. I am proud to have been one of thousands of dedicated engineers and scientists who designed, built, and then fixed this magnificent observatory.

When the Olympics were held in Atlanta, I was selected

to run the Olympic torch through a portion of Huntsville. I had two goals: to not drop the torch or set my hair on fire. I succeeded in avoiding both disasters. A little later, I became the payload training manager for the International Space Station, and traveled to Europe and Russia to negotiate with the space agencies there on how we would train future astronauts and cosmonauts. Life was good. My writing was also going well, and I could see retirement approaching. After that, I figured to start writing full-time. But my future didn't wait around for me to hit all my little milestones. Jeremiah's wheel, which Reverend Richard loved to contemplate, was turning in the direction of a miracle.

In December 1994, the editor of *Air & Space/ Smithsonian* magazine called me with an urgent request for a short article for the next issue. I had the reputation of being a fast writer with aerospace lore at my fingertips. Could I please provide something overnight? Unfortunately, I had nothing prepared, but then I glanced at a small cylindrical object I was using as a paperweight. It was a sophisticated but tiny rocket nozzle. Its story was only a hazy memory. As I talked to the editor, pieces of it started to come back. "You know," I told her, "when I was a kid— growing up in a place called Coalwood, West Virginia— would you believe it? We—some boys and I—we were miners' kids—we built rockets. We won a medal—at a science fair . . . wait, it was the *National* Science Fair." The editor was silent for a moment and then said, with a noticeable lack of enthusiasm, "Okay, if that's all you've got. Write it and fax it to me and we'll see." I wrote the article in three hours, the memories tumbling out of places I had not looked at for decades. I didn't remember everything, but enough for the two thousand words required. I sent in the fax and forgot about it. The next day the editor called. She loved it. Would I send pictures? The medal?

Anything I had? The magazine was going with the story as an expanded feature.

I was surprised at her reaction, but I was to be absolutely astonished when the article came out. Letters and phone calls poured in from parents and students all over the country. The article had touched and inspired them, they said. My agent suggested there might be a market for a book about my days as a rocket boy in Coalwood. I agreed and began to work on it.

Since I was a full-time employee for NASA at the time, I had to write during late evenings, early mornings, and on weekends. I even wrote after-hours during travel. One chapter was written entirely in Moscow. But I kept writing, and as I wrote, Coalwood came alive again. The miners trudged up the old path to the mine, their lunch pails clunking against their legs, their helmets perched on their heads. Dad was there among them, wearing his old snap-brim hat and his cowhide coat, encouraging them. The people of the town bustled in and out of the company store and gathered on the church steps after Sunday services to gossip. My mother was in her kitchen, in her refuge in front of the big painted picture of the beach and the ocean. Chipper was there, giggling because he'd just eaten the family Bible. Dandy and Poteet waited in my basement laboratory, their tails wagging at the sight of me as I picked up and inspected the implements of my chosen trade, the high school rocket builder—the potassium nitrate and sugar, the zinc dust and sulfur, the moonshine we used as a propellant binder. In my room, there was my old desk and the book our Miss Riley had given the rocket boys, the one with all the answers written in a mathematical script no one believed we could learn but we had, against all odds. The church bell was ringing as once more we boys stood on the roof of the old Club House and peered through the telescope Jake Mosby had loaned us, to see once more the bands of Jupiter, the rings of Saturn, the craters of the moon. The old high school was there, the halls ringing with the excitement of youth, the classrooms echoing with our lessons, the awareness slowly dawning on us that we were the designated refugees of our town and our school, that we were being prepared to leave and never return.

To re-create the days of the rocket boys of the Big Creek Missile Agency turned out to be one of the most difficult things I had ever done. I reached as deeply as ever I could into my soul to bring them all back, all the miners and miners' wives, the teachers and the preachers, the boys, and, of course, my parents, the most interesting people I would ever know.

Rocket Boys, the book that resulted, was published in the fall of 1998 to national and international acclaim. The following February, *October Sky,* the movie based on the book while it was still in its manuscript form, was released. My life took on profound change. All of a sudden, I was in demand for speeches all around the country. I was given many awards. Dan Goldin, the NASA administrator, hugged me. Astronauts who had walked on the moon met me with tears in their eyes and asked for my autograph. General Chuck Yeager, another West Virginia boy, took me flying. Hundreds of fans wrote me and told me how much they loved the book and the film. After I retired from NASA, I wrote another book, *Back to the Moon,* a scientific thriller novel, and it was snapped up almost immediately by Hollywood. My publisher also asked me to consider writing a sequel to *Rocket Boys,* and I agreed. The result was *The Coalwood Way,* a memoir of the last Christmas I would know as a Coalwood boy, and this book.

Because of the popularity of my books and the movie, I am often invited back to West Virginia. When I first returned after many years' absence, I was shocked by what I found. Although I knew the Coalwood mine had been closed in 1985, I had no idea that the town had suffered so horribly. Houses were abandoned, the Big Store and the Club House boarded up, the Coalwood School burned down by vandals, and there was no evidence that a coal mine had ever been there. During the intervening years, the federal government had come in and dismantled the tipple grounds and scrubbed the area clean. In the process, it destroyed much of my heritage, and that of the people of Coalwood. As I looked around, I realized what had happened in Coalwood had occurred throughout the coalfields of southern West Virginia. Entire towns had ceased to exist, been bulldozed, and buried. The population of McDowell County had decreased by two thirds. While the rest of the United States enjoyed an economic boom, southern West Virginia had endured an economic cleansing that made refugees of its people as bad or worse than in places such as Kosovo.

Today, however, there are a few glimmers of hope. Across from the Captain's house there stands a small museum, celebrating not only the rocket boys but, more importantly, Coalwood's mining heritage. A group of Coalwood citizens have also banded together to form the Cape Coalwood Restoration Association. Their first project was to rebuild our old rocket launch range. Amateur rocketry groups go there now to launch their rockets on what is considered nearly a holy site for rocketeers. Forty years after he was the governor during the rocket boys' first career, Cecil Underwood was reelected and, partly because of the book and film, began to pay attention to McDowell County. Soon there was not a pothole to be found anywhere in the county, and signs saying WELCOME TO THE HOME OF THE ROCKET BOYS began to blossom like flowering rhododendron. Tourists began to arrive from all around the United States and the world to see and touch Coalwood. The guest book in the museum attests to the hospitality they have received. Red Carroll, the only surviving rocket boys father, acts as the unofficial tour guide for the town. In 1999, the first annual Rocket Boys Day in Coalwood was proclaimed by the governor, followed soon after by the first annual October Sky Festival. Coalwood endures, as it always has, but with a new vigor and a new pride. A place where the old ways are still sacred, it still has much to teach us. Perhaps that is why I was allowed to bring it alive again.

As for me, I hope to continue writing and entertaining my readers, and maybe even providing some occasional illumination on life as it was, is, or shall be. I am a lucky man and I know it. The Engineer of the Universe has looked after this Coalwood boy, don't ask me why. The wheel of Jeremiah continues to turn with those great hands on it, shaping me, shaping us all. There are miracles everywhere, although sometimes they are concealed, not by God, but by our own eyes. All we need to do is look, and they will be seen.

ABOUT THE AUTHOR

HOMER HICKAM is the author of the #1 *New York Times* bestseller *October Sky* as well as the acclaimed follow-up to *October Sky*, *The Coalwood Way*. He is also the author of *Back to the Moon* and *Torpedo Junction*, as well as numerous articles for such publications as *Smithsonian Air & Space* and *American History Illustrated*. He lives with his wife in Huntsville, Alabama—Rocket City, USA.